THE THREE OF U.S.

A New Life in New York

THE THREE OF U.S.

A New Life in New York

JOANNA COLES
&
PETER GODWIN

HarperCollins*Publishers*

HarperCollins*Publishers*
77–85 Fulham Palace Road,
Hammersmith, London W6 8JB

The HarperCollins website address is:
www.**fire**and**water**.com

Published by HarperCollins*Publishers* 1999
1 3 5 7 9 8 6 4 2

The authors and publisher are grateful to
Dorling Kindersley and Dr Miriam Stoppard
for permission to quote from
Conception, Pregnancy and Birth by
Dr Miriam Stoppard (Dorling Kindersley, 1993).
The Complete Book of Pregnancy and Childbirth
by Sheila Kitzinger (Penguin Books, 1997)
is reproduced by permission of Penguin Books Ltd.
Oh, the Places You'll Go! by Dr. Seuss
© Dr. Seuss Enterprises, L.P. 1990.
All rights reserved. Used by permission.

A catalogue record for this book
is available from the British Library

ISBN 0 00 257102 1

Set in Linotype PostScript Sabon and Frutiger by
Rowland Phototypesetting Ltd, Bury St Edmunds, Suffolk

Printed and bound in Great Britain by
Caledonian International Book Manufacturing Ltd, Glasgow

CONTENTS

For TAG, whose pram is in the hall

PREFACE

At the risk of degenerating into Oscar speak, we would like to thank the following: our agent, Gil Coleridge and our editors, Val Hudson and Andrea Henry, for doing their respective jobs with such elan; Jane Thynne and Andrew Solomon for allowing us to quote from their emails; and our New York friends (especially Dani Shapiro, Michael Maren, Suzanna Andrews, Dana and John Tierney, Andre and Leina Schiffrin, Ron Gallen, Betsy Fagan, Sheenah Hankin and Tom Masland) for their patience and humour in dealing with our incessant questions; Sheila Kitzinger and Dr Miriam Stoppard for letting us quote from their work. We are also grateful to be able to quote from Dr Seuss and from the websites of BabySoon.com and BabyCenter.com.

Joanna would like to thank Alan Rusbridger and Roger Alton at the *Guardian*, for posting her to New York. And Peter Stothard and Sandra Parsons at *The Times*, for continuing to accommodate her dispatches.

The Three of U.S. is not a forensic record – occasionally we have changed names, dates and other identifying details, largely to prevent intrusion. But this principle is defined in the exception. Our labour coach, for example, is so instantly identifiable to any of the scores of New Yorkers who have passed through her ante-natal academy, that to change her name would be pointless.

Joanna Coles
Peter Godwin
Manhattan 1999

THE THREE OF U.S.

A New Life in New York

MAY

MANHATTAN

Friday, 1 May
Joanna

The test is negative. There is no pink line in the second box on the tester stick, but I'm sure I am pregnant. I haven't done it wrong either. Over the years I've done enough of these tests to know exactly how to use them; how to pee in a squatting position without splashing all over the tester stick and precisely how long to wait before looking for the tell-tale sign. Sometimes they use a red tick to indicate you're pregnant; sometimes it's a blue cross. With this one, the Answer Test, a positive answer is indicated by two pink lines. But there is only one. The other box, the important box, remains clear, white and unambiguous. I am not pregnant.

Friday, 1 May
Peter

I have just returned from the doctor, who has managed to convince me that I am dying. The cause of my premature death will be the polyp that has developed under the skin of my left elbow. I became aware of it a few days ago as I walked along Hudson Street from the Printing House gym, favoured exercise yard of the West Village literati, back to our loft on Horatio Street. My polyp is hard to the touch, like a walnut, and curiously mobile. I fiddle with it constantly, my own internal worry bead.

3

At first I thought I had overdone it with the free weights. Although in denial about my own competitiveness, I am loath to lessen the weights when alternating on a machine with someone else of comparable size. Over the years I have sustained various injuries to ligaments and muscles due to such hubris, and this elbow polyp, I figured, was simply the latest. But there were worrying differences: the suddenness of my polyp's first appearance. One minute nothing, the next a subcutaneous walnut. The lack of surrounding swelling. And the fact that it didn't actually hurt. Finally, when the walnut refused to diminish on its own, I went to the doctor.

Under the American health insurance system my family doctor is, as far as I can deduce, a gatekeeper. He is there to prevent me from having access to specialists. The more often he can stymie my attempts to reach the doctors who really know what they're doing, the expensive doctors, the more lavishly he is rewarded by our insurers.

Dr Epstein has a practice on 14th Street, between 8th and 9th Avenue. It is one of the most depressing streets downtown – not quite Chelsea, not yet Greenwich Village – strewn with tacky shops selling cheap plastic luggage and knock-off trainers, polyester clothes and tinny boom boxes. Many of the shops urgently proclaim that they are in the throes of closing-down sales. EVERYTHING MUST GO, their banners read. Several announce that they are going bankrupt and in POSITIVELY OUR VERY LAST WEEK. But in all the months I have traversed the street, none of these shops has actually closed.

The other patients waiting in Dr Epstein's reception are all longshoremen – wide men in steel-toed boots, checked flannel shirts and jeans. For Dr Epstein's practice is above the Longshoremen's Union headquarters. My appointment comes and goes, but my name remains uncalled. Perhaps, among these giants, I am not big enough for my physical presence even to register.

'Mr Gobwun?'

'Godwin. It's Godwin, actually.'

'Whatever. Dr Epstein will see you now.'

Dr Epstein is small and hairy and rotund. He is evidently suffering from a terrible cold and his voice is clogged with catarrh. After taking a brief medical history, he places two stubby fingers on my polyp and chases it around my elbow. 'Hmm,' he muses. 'Odd.'

Odd? I am a doctor's son and I know that 'odd' is not good.

'Does it hurt?' he asks.

'Not really.'

'Is it growing?'

'No, it was that size when it arrived.'

Dr Epstein rapidly fills out a large form. It is latticed with boxes, most of which he is ticking.

'Tests,' he explains. 'You need tests, a lot of 'em.'

I feel like I'm in an opening sequence of *ER*, with the first plot line being wheeled in on the gurney while Dr Ross or Dr Green rattles off a battery of acronyms.

'What seems to be the problem?' I ask, realizing this should be his line.

'Let's just wait until the test results come in, shall we?'

'But what kind of thing might it be?' I insist.

'Well, I'm really not sure, but . . .' He trails off.

'But what?' I prompt.

'It might be a lymphoma.'

Lymphoma, I know from *ER*, is American doctor-speak for cancer, and I return to our apartment in the West Village convinced that my future is mostly behind me.

Saturday, 2 May
Joanna

I am more than a week late now. On the back of the packet it proclaims the Answer Test is so sensitive it can detect pregnancy within twenty-four hours of an overdue period. On the front it claims to be '99 per cent accurate!' so I think perhaps the test is past its sell-by date. I didn't much trust the pharmacist who sold it to me. He looked shifty and I had to wait for ages while a tall, balding man was interrogating him about Viagra, Pfizer's wonder drug to overcome 'erectile dysfunction'.

'How much is it?' he asked in a heavy Hispanic whisper.

'It's about ten bucks a shot, but you can only get it on prescription,' said the pharmacist.

'Ten bucks? Each tablet is ten bucks?' demanded the man, louder and alarmed.

'Yes, but it's only available on prescription,' the pharmacist repeated, tidying the breath mints by the till. 'I can't just sell it over the counter, you need a doctor's recommendation.'

'Oh it's not for me,' said the customer hastily. 'It's for my friend.'

'Then you tell your friend he has to see a doctor before he can get some.'

'But this is not possible,' the customer replied. 'My friend, he is in Brazil. He is desperate . . .'

'Tell you what,' said the pharmacist, lowering his voice, 'come back around seven p.m. when things are a little quieter round here, and I'll see what I can do for you, OK?'

'Seven p.m. today? I'll be here, seven p.m. Thank you, thank you.'

'But you better tell your friend how much this stuff is gonna cost him, OK?' said the pharmacist.

'I tell him, I tell him exactly,' said the customer, giving him a discreet thumbs up and hurrying out of the store.

Sunday, 3 May
Peter

I am preoccupied with the wait for my test results and I cannot possibly concentrate on my novel. Despite a recent spurt, my book is going terribly anyway. Dog metaphors besiege me when I try to describe its progress. Sometimes I feel like a dog that circles interminably around something unknown, something it hasn't quite got the confidence to confront. Sometimes when I approach passages which cry out for major rewriting, I feel a nauseating *déjà vu*, like a dog returning to its own vomit.

The truth is I have had writer's block for months, but I cannot bear to admit it. It seems I need the Zimmer frame of non-fiction on which to rest the body of my imagination; I am crippled without the firm aluminium stroller of fact. Scared by the multitude of options out there, I have to impose a false horizon, a fake polystyrene ceiling, on my literary ambitions.

It's like loft living. We thought that this loft we now inhabit, with its vast, high ceilings, would be the most aesthetic living machine possible; a white-walled, parquet-floored, 2,000-square-foot playground for adults. But soon a strange attitude developed. We found ourselves delineating areas. At first it was just in our minds, as defined by clusters of furniture, the dining-room table, my study desk, the TV. But then we began, little by little, to cordon off areas with bookshelves and sofas and filing cabinets, trying to create a conventional apartment out of our soaring, unfettered space. Such, I have begun to fear, is the story of my literary imagination too.

I have printed out a sign which says: THIS IS YOUR JOB. It is supposed to urge me to take writing more seriously and to remind me that the novel is now my main source of income – because I have virtually no other source. I have blown up the message in 29-point Times New Roman bold type and affixed it to the pillar opposite my desk with a blob of chewing gum. I know I am far too old for gum, but it seems to alleviate the headaches that have been plaguing me.

Sunday, 3 May
Joanna

Wandering over to Peter's desk, I stretch my right leg out on the window sill as I imagine the dancer Sylvie Guillaume might do to stretch her astonishingly long hamstrings, and announce, 'I'm not pregnant.'

'What do you mean?' he says, hunched over his Powerbook without looking up.

'I mean I've done a test and I'm not pregnant.'

'That's good,' he says, tapping the space bar and still not looking up. 'Did you think you might be?'

'Well, it's very odd because I'm late and I'm never usually late. But the test is negative, so I can't be pregnant.'

There is a short pause. 'Good oh,' he says cheerfully.

Sunday, 3 May
Peter

Joanna is behaving very oddly. Suddenly she announces that she's not pregnant. I hadn't even realized that she might be. I assume that being unpregnant is the standard template, one that doesn't require confirmation by way of regular bulletins. In any case I am relieved by the all clear.

Later, on my way to buy groceries at D'Agostino's on Washington Street, I pass a man unloading boxes from a truck into the twenty-four-hour City Deli at the corner of our building. On the side of the truck is painted the name of the company: 'Lo Boy Foods'. Underneath it advertises 'Individual portions of meats and fish'. An entire company devoted to the catering needs of solitary diners? Maybe that is my fate, sitting alone in middle age, eating individual portions of meat and fish from 'Lo Boy Foods'.

The prospect of Joanna being pregnant suddenly doesn't seem so unpalatable, well, no less palatable than a future fuelled by 'Lo Boy Foods'.

On my return from shopping, on the corner of Bank and Hudson, the old folks are sitting in their wheelchairs on the pavement in front of the Village Nursing Home, rolled there by the white-uniformed nursing aides for some 'fresh air'. Their the worn-out bodies will slowly toast the morning away in their wheelchairs, empty eyes staring out at the traffic.

And I notice, yet again, the smartly dressed middle-aged man sitting on a bench to one side, with his mother. He reads the *New York Times* intently, while she sits twitching next to him, one leg crossed tightly over the other, bony knuckles clenched over the armrests of her wheelchair. She is unable to talk or even to listen, it seems. I'm sure she wouldn't notice whether he's there or not, but that doesn't dissuade this conscientious son from his daily vigil. His dedication to his uncomprehending mother makes me feel ashamed of myself.

And again a baser thought worms its way into my mind. Maybe it's just as well to have kids around in case I happen to survive into my own dotage.

Friday, 8 May
Joanna

My period is now two weeks late, though every day it feels as if it's about to start. I can't face the uncertainty of another home test, so I am sitting in the offices of my Murray Hill gynaecologist. I am thirty-six and this is the first time I have ever visited a gynaecologist. At home, in England, I relied on the GP for everything, but in New York everyone has a different doctor for every part of the body. Americans recommend them to each other as a sign of trust and friendship, like hot stock-market tips. I remember asking Kelly, shortly after we'd met and we were sitting in Bar Pitti on Sixth Avenue, if she could suggest a good doctor.

'What sort?'

'Well, you know, a good family doctor, a generalist.'

'You know, that's kinda hard and I really wouldn't recommend mine,' she said, pushing a manicured index finger around the salt-fringed rim of her margarita so it made a dry, squeaking noise. 'I really don't think he's very good. He won't diagnose over the phone, so you have to go to his office every time you need him. But I do have a very good dermatologist, my gynaecologist is excellent and I have a truly excellent podiatrist. But he may be full, I was lucky, he was mentioned in *New York* magazine's top ten doctors, and now he's got a waiting list longer than the Coney Island boardwalk . . .'

'Honey, you should tell her about our neurologist too,' interrupted Jeff, her husband. 'And somewhere', he added, fishing out his Palm Pilot and whipping the stylus over the screen, 'I have the number of a very good orthopediologist. How much do you pay for insurance?'

'Three hundred and eighty-nine dollars a month. Each.'

'What? Are you nuts? Three eighty nine! We only pay two hundred and fifty each.'

'It was the cheapest I could find that would take us on,' I protested.

'Health care in this country is screwed,' said Jeff, tapping his margarita glass and mouthing 'Three more, please' to the bartender. 'Hey, is that Madonna over there?' Outside the bar a white stretch limo had pulled up and the singer, accompanied by another woman, got out and disappeared into the bar next door.

'Well screw her,' said Jeff, who, I have noticed recently, can get pretty angry over nothing much at all. 'Screw her and her slutty friends. We don't want them in here anyway.'

'Doctors?' I murmured trying to bring the subject back.

He shook his head. 'You want a general doctor, right?'

'Yes,' I said, thinking back to Dr O'Reilly in Notting Hill, whom I had chosen because, like every other GP I have ever been to in my life, she was the nearest.

'Well, it all depends. Do you self-medicate?' he demanded.

'Self what?'

'Self-medicate. You know, self-diagnose, call your doctor and self-prescribe?'

I confessed this was not a common practice in Britain.

'Oh it should be, it saves them time and you can just pick up the prescription . . . I mean three years ago I was going through a bad time – before I met you, honey,' he grinned at Kelly. 'And I knew I was having a depression. So I phoned up and self-prescribed Prozac.'

'Really?' I exclaimed, imagining how Dr O'Reilly – a taciturn Irish woman whose sole driving force appeared to come from resisting local pressure to become a GP

11

fundholder – would have reacted if I had phoned and casually self-prescribed Prozac.

'Yeah, well, as it turned out I didn't suit Prozac at all, in fact it made me a little paranoid. But then I did go to see my doctor and she switched me to Zoloft, which has been great. It's a much better drug for me in fact. Still is.

'Whatever, you'll love my doctor,' he added, retrieving a pen from his wife's Prada Kelly bag. 'Give her a call and say I recommended you. Leah Falzone, she's over on Union Square.'

Friday, 8 May
Peter

It is nearly midnight and I'm in my customary position, slumped at my desk staring out of the window. The meat trucks have just started their deliveries outside, so instead of going to bed and lying awake, fretting about my test results, I am trying to work. Our apartment block is in a supposedly 'happening' area called the Meat Packing District, and we are surrounded by giant meat warehouses that supply New York's restaurants and hotels. Unbeknown to us when we moved in, the Meat Packing District is deserted during the day, beginning its work each night at about midnight, when convoys of huge refrigerated trucks arrive from the Mid-West to unload chilled carcasses of cows, sheep and pigs. These trucks back up into the warehouses emitting a continuous screech of warning beeps, a sound specifically designed to penetrate. And penetrate it does, right through our storm windows and over the roar of the air-conditioner.

So I sit at my desk, trying to work and looking out at the view. It is an interesting view, more interesting than the stale words of my novel. To the north it takes in the illuminated ribbons of traffic of the West Side Highway, busy at any hour; a vast floodlit billboard of the Marlboro cowboy lighting up against a bucolic Montana backdrop; and a large black 'V' sign on an orange background, which marks the entrance to the Vault, which bills itself as New York's favourite S&M club.

Across to the west is the chimneyed husk of the decommissioned Chelsea branch of the New York Sanitation Department, now used as a parking lot for city garbage trucks; a broad band of the Hudson River and the twinkling lights of the condo towers that have recently risen from the New Jersey shoreline. In the strip of wall mirror at right angles to the window, I can see the reflection of the massive mausoleum of the Port Authority Terminal and across to the Empire State Building.

Six floors below me are the uneven Belgian cobbles of Gansevoort Street, which, the real estate agent forgot to mention, is a main night-time drag for transvestite prostitutes. They patrol up and down among the warehouses, conforming precisely to the meat-market metaphor.

All of them are black and tall, even taller as they totter on their high heels up and down the broken sidewalk, sashaying for the headlights of potential customers who drive by, often twice or three times, checking out the goods before pulling over. The deed is usually done right there, behind a skip of offal, under a fire escape or between parked meat-delivery vans. This might obscure them from casual passers-by (there are none), but it leaves them totally exposed to my gaze. Curiosity about the details of who does what to whom has overcome my initial distaste at the scene below and I remain in position, a voyeur from our own home.

It is a strange business. Oral sex plays a prominent role,

but so do masturbation and other variations which remain irritatingly just out of sight, behind jiggling bodies. What occurs to me is how brief it is, spectacularly so. I suppose this is because of the furtive nature of the transaction.

Surprisingly soon it has lost its capacity to shock us, it has become mundane, just part of the local scene. We now recognize the different 'girls'. Tonight I have spotted Ru. We have nicknamed her Ru, partly because she is the most diligent streetwalker, and partly after the black transvestite celebrity Ru Paul, who now has her own television talk show.

We find that we have started to worry about the girls' safety, fearing that one may be beaten up or killed. We have become invisible guardians, ready to dial 911 at the first sign of trouble. But all goes smoothly; there is a well-worn ritual to the transaction. Even the price appears to be pre-set, with a quick transfer of notes before business is initiated.

Joanna emerges sleepily from the bedroom.

'What you doing?' she slurs.

'Being a peeping Tom,' I reply dryly.

Just then a yellow cab stops beneath us, and its Sikh driver gets out and walks round to check one of his tyres. He kicks it a couple of times and then has a leisurely piss against the wall. As he is waggling to a finish, Ru strolls nonchalantly past him. We can see them having a conversation, but we cannot hear it. It is very brief, he utters four or five words, and she gives a similarly terse reply.

Then the Sikh reaches out and very deliberately squeezes Ru's left breast, like a farmer at a livestock market checking the consistency of a dairy cow he's considering purchasing. He climbs back in his cab and drives away, and Ru continues her lonely patrol. Whatever has occurred was clearly consensual.

'What do you think they said to each other?' asks Joanna.

I imagine he asked her, 'What are they made of?' or even, 'Are they real?'

And Ru replied, 'Check 'em out for yourself, darling. On the house.'

Monday, 11 May
Joanna

The gynaecologist's office recommended by Dr Falzone is far smarter than anything I have encountered in the British Health Service. With black-leather seating and the latest editions of *Vogue*, *Harper's Bazaar*, *Elle*, *National Geographic*, the *New Yorker* and *Time*, the reception is more like a discreet hotel lobby. The walls are quietly green, decorated with soothing scenes from Yosemite, each framed in black; thundering waterfalls and proud snow-capped mountains. Each one is accompanied by a motivational slogan: 'The bend in the road is not the end of the road – unless you fail to make the turn'; 'Some people dream of success – others wake up and work at it.'

Indeed, there is nothing in our surroundings to suggest we are in a doctor's waiting room at all, until I notice a discreet plastic box of leaflets dispensing advice on how to avoid genital herpes: 'Genital herpes. One in four American adults suffers. There is no cure!'

'Ms Coles?' one of a troika of receptionists calls, beckoning with a silver-polished nail so long it has curled round on itself like a miniature dough hook.

'Your insurance card?' I hand over the blue plastic card which I have learned to keep alongside my credit and social security cards at all times in case of emergency. 'Please fill these forms out and give them back to me before you see the doctor.'

There are four pages of intricate forms demanding my entire medical history, that of my immediate family, and then another sheet demanding my signature to take full responsibility for payment should there prove to be a problem with my insurance.

'Ms Coles,' a bouncy-haired woman in a white coat with a badge on indicating she is Beth, and whom I assume to be a doctor, waves a clipboard at me and I follow her into a large wooden-panelled office, where several impressively framed certificates compete for wall space with more motivational photos of Yosemite.

'So, Joanna, I'm Beth. This is the first time you've been to us?'

'Yes.'

'And you've filled in all the forms and we've seen your insurance card, right?'

I nod.

'Great. So, what can I do you for today?'

'Well, I'm ten days late and I'm never normally late. So I did a home pregnancy test, but that was negative. But I think I'm pregnant anyway.'

'Why do you think that, Joanna?'

'Well, I just sort of feel it. You know, painful breasts, prolonged period pain . . .'

'You know what, I'm gonna give you a blood test, but it doesn't sound to me as if you're pregnant. Those shop tests are pretty accurate. How old are you?' She glances down at one of the sheets I've filled in.

'Thirty-six.'

She pulls a face, then shrugs. 'Thirty-six? The female body starts winding down, hun. Tell you what I'm gonna do . . .' And she takes a deep breath. 'I'm gonna prescribe you Provera which you gotta take for seven full days, that'll bring your period on, but don't take it until we have the results of the blood test, just to be sure, OK? Go down the corridor and ask for Donna, the lab technician, she'll take your blood and then call me on Thursday between 12.30 p.m. and 1.30 p.m., and we'll give you the results, OK, oh and leave a urine sample too, if it's negative, your system's probably adjusting itself to being thirty-six; sorry but that's the way the cookie crumbles, and you take the Provera.' Another breath: 'If it's positive, well, you make another appointment to see an obstetrician.'

Down the corridor, Donna, the technician, snaps on skintight cream rubber gloves, ties a rubber tube round my left arm and flicks at my veins like I've seen junkies do in movies. 'You do look a little peaky,' she observes, withdrawing the needle with one hand and skilfully unpeeling a Band-Aid with the other. 'Could be a sign. I'll keep my fingers crossed for ya.'

Tuesday, 12 May
Peter

Our curiosity piqued by the outsize V sign in our view, Joanna has asked me to phone the Vault, which, she suggests, we should visit. I refuse. S&M is not really my scene. I am a coward. I treat pain as an enemy and go to great lengths to avoid humiliation.

'But it'll make a great story,' she wheedles. She is always desperate for column ideas.

Later in the day, running short of work-displacement activities to divert myself from my book, I pick up the phone and dial the Vault.

'Welcome to the Vault,' says the earnestly perky male voice on the answering machine. 'America's most popular S&M club. Please listen to our upcoming attractions:

17

Friday is our bare buns contest;
Saturday is our foot fetish night;
Sunday is the finals of our bald beaver competition;
Monday is our popular schoolgirl evening;
Tuesday features hot-wax branding;
on Wednesday our weekly slave auction takes place;
join us Thursday for Shiatsu bondage;
and next Friday is our speciality dental 'n' head restraint.

We supper at the garage-like Café Braque, voted New York's coolest summer hangout, full of slender models nibbling tiny organic mesclun leaves, and I tell Joanna of the varied fare offered by our neighbourhood club. 'What do you fancy being entered for,' I enquire. 'Bare buns? Perhaps a little hot-wax branding?'

'What really intrigues me,' she confides, 'is the speciality dental 'n' head restraint. What on earth could that be?'

Thursday, 14 May
Joanna

Though my period has still not arrived, all other symptoms have disappeared. I don't feel sick and I've lost two lbs, but I spend the weekend imagining I may be pregnant. And, as my friends constantly remind me, I am thirty-six and it's about time.

At exactly 12.35 p.m., as instructed, I phone Dr Beth's number and am immediately plunged into another curse of contemporary America: voicemail hell.

'Please listen to the following information BEFORE pressing your relevant number.

'If you are an existing patient press one to hear a series of options.

18

'If you are a new patient wishing to register with us, please have your insurance number ready to enter via your keypad.'

I press one.

'If you need help with our fax number, website or e-mail address, press one followed by the pound sign.

'If you would like to book an urgent appointment press two.

'If you would like to make a routine appointment press three.

'To cancel an appointment press four.

'For all queries about billing or to review your account press five.

'For all other enquiries press six.'

I press six.

'To book a pap-smear test press one.

'To receive results of a recent pap-smear test only, press two; do not press this number if you require results from any other test.

'To book a hospital appointment needing your doctor's consent press three.

'To change the date or time of a hospital appointment press four.

'To request a repeat prescription press five.

'To request a new prescription press six.

'To request information for legal reasons which may be confidential from your personal file, press seven.

'All those needing to speak with an operator press eight and stay on the line.'

I press eight to be greeted by a short burst of Barbra Streisand singing 'Evergreen', quickly interrupted by another message.

'Thank you for calling. All our operators are busy.

Please call back later. Our office hours are from 9.30 a.m. until 5 p.m.'

I phone back again. And again, swearing as I hit the redial button. Would it be quicker to walk there? At 1.28 p.m. I finally get through and ask for Donna, the technician.

'Hello, Jo-wanna,' she says, uncertainly. 'How you doin' today?'

'Oh fine. I was just calling to get my results from the blood tests on Friday.'

'Right, just hang on, Joanna, I'm gonna get Dr Beth to explain them to ya. Stay right where y'are.' And before I can say anything I hear her pick up another receiver. 'Dr Beth? Ya gotta minute? I got Joanna Coles on the line, you said to call you when she got through?'

'Hi, Joanna,' says Dr Beth. 'It's not good news I'm afraid.'

I feel my insides deflate.

'To be honest with you, hun, I don't know exactly what's going on, you're certainly something – but it's not pregnant. We need you to come back and have another blood test. Can you come in soon, like this afternoon?'

'How do you mean it's certainly something?' I ask, feeling weak.

'Are you OK, hun?' asks Dr Beth.

'Um, yes, just a bit disappointed,' I mumble. 'I could be there in about ten minutes? Do you think it's something serious?'

'Nah, probably not, but we need to make sure, OK? I'll tell Donna to expect you,' she says, before adding gently, 'I'll speak to you tomorrow, when we've got the new results in. And take care, OK?'

I call Peter, but he's out so I leave a message. 'I've got

to go back for more blood tests,' I say melodramatically. 'But apparently I'm still not pregnant.'

Ovarian cysts, cancer, fibroids, early menopause . . . I run through the list in the cab as we hurtle down Fifth, past New York's glorious Public Library, which my mother once compared unfavourably to Leeds Town Hall, and swing onto 30th Street in front of the surgery.

After taking a photocopy of my insurance card, the receptionist sends me straight through to Donna. 'Did you wanna be pregnant?' she asks sympathetically.

I nod, suddenly realizing that after years of denying it, I really do.

'What do you think is wrong?' I manage.

'Well, a reading of under five is definitely negative. Your score was eleven, which is too low to be positive but too high to be negative, so that's why we're doing you another test. Do you feel pregnant?'

I shrug, suddenly exhausted, as she snaps on her gloves again and taps my arm. 'This time call me on my direct line and I'll give you the results myself,' she whispers, handing me her card.

Friday, 15 May
Peter

I am determined not to allow the wait for my test results to paralyse me into a state of limbo. I must keep active. Physically active. Today I decide to go rollerblading along Riverside Walk. This stretch of sidewalk from Chelsea Piers down to Battery Park must be one of the most congenial rollerblading courses in the world. It is a safe, level, cement strip with views on one side across the Hudson River and on the other over to Greenwich Village then TriBeCa, City Hall and the World Trade Towers.

I am a reasonable blader, about intermediate level, I think. I very seldom fall, but I take no chances, strapping myself into my matte black safety gear: helmet, elbow pads, wrist protectors with Velcro fasteners and plastic re-inforcers, mittens, and knee pads with black plastic cups over the joints themselves. Thus attired, I can blade for about fifteen minutes before I need to rest, or else I risk cramping up. I think there is something wrong with my blading posture. I have even been to blading school at Chelsea Piers, once. I went to the intermediate class, where I found myself surrounded by large middle-aged women and small children. I was the only adult male. Since then I have tried to self-tutor by watching other, more advanced bladers and attempting to ape them, straightening my back and assuming a more open, balletic posture. Invariably I soon revert to my clenched, bent stance.

There is one physical barrier that seriously blights my blading enjoyment. It is the West Side Highway, the eight-lane stream of traffic that I am forced to cross to get to the river walk. Although there is a pedestrian crossing, the flashing green man has been wrongly adjusted by the Traffic Department. For intermediate bladers like myself, he provides an inadequately fleeting window of opportunity in which to blade across, and the impatient traffic sits on the line revving up for their green, like racing cars waiting for a chequered starting-flag to fall. Nor is it unknown for them to jump the lights. I find that under the close scrutiny of eight rows of New York drivers, my blading deteriorates significantly. I wobble nervously and falter like a beginner. Once I reach the other side I feel triumphant, liberated. Until the time approaches to cross again, as it always does.

But today, today is my last crossing of the West Side Highway. Today I have almost reached the other side when,

22

unaccountably, my left skate jams and I fall heavily – just as the lights turn in favour of a grid of trucks. The Mack truck nearest me releases its brakes with a menacing pneumatic wheeze, kicks into gear and advances. I look up desperately, but my perspective is too low to allow me to see the driver, too low to fix him with pleading eyes. The truck looms dangerously and then emits a vast, throaty, customized hoot. My whole body resonates, right to the fillings in my molars. I scuttle desperately to the kerb, a spidery, Gothic figure in my matte black safety outfit and the goat's hooves of my black skates. I felt that I must look like one of those Calcutta pavement cripples, cosmetically enhanced by callous relatives for more proficient begging. I haul myself up over the concrete lip to safety, where I sit, feeling the laughter of the driver wash over me. Fast, proficient skaters, the ones I have been trying to emulate, blade gracefully past me.

'Bad blades, man. You OK?' yells one cheerily, as he whisks past shirtless, and without any safety gear, casually ramping some substantial obstacle. He is well out of earshot before I can reply.

I bend down to examine my recalcitrant skate, expecting to find a shard of gravel from the nearby roadworks, wedged in my axle. Instead I find a used condom has wrapped itself around a wheel with the aid of a puce blob of chewing gum. I gingerly peel off the condom and its attendant gluey tendrils of gum, remove my skates and hobble home in my socks.

I check for phone messages, but my test results still aren't in.

Monday, 18 May
Joanna

Though part of me wants to sit and obsess until the next set of results comes through, Peter persuades me that I would be better kept busy and so, at 7 p.m., we set off for the Royal Shakespeare Company's summer fund-raiser organized by Tina Brown, the editor of the *New Yorker*. It takes place at the Manhattan Center, a vast indoor stadium in midtown. As we arrive, a motorcade of stretch limos is disgorging its passengers.

'Oh God, I don't know if I can face this,' I grumble.

'Well, we can go if you like,' says Peter reasonably. We are about to leave when I hear a low mellifluous rumble of a voice behind me. Could it possibly be? . . . Is it really? . . . I turn around. It is. Alan Rickman is standing fewer than ten feet away.

'Oh well, I suppose we're here now,' I say. 'Let's just see how it goes.'

Originally, the RSC had earnestly planned to perform a play in its entirety, but Tina Brown, conversant with New Yorkers' bantam attention span, has cleverly persuaded them to offer us a medley of the Bard's Greatest Hits instead.

The audience is huge, there are at least 1,000 of us, with many having paid $20,000 a table. As usual, however, we have slipped in on a press freebie. To my right sits a cheerful man called Christopher Buckley, who tells me he is the author of a book called *Thank You for Smoking*. He is in a state of some excitement because the place card next to him reads 'Susannah York'.

To my left sits Garth Drabinsky, the legendary Broadway producer of *Showboat* and *Ragtime*, which has just picked up four Tony awards. The Drabinsky legend stems from his almost magical ability to stay financially afloat, confounding his many naysayers. He is a huge, darkly brooding presence, and seems depressed.

I feel depressed too. What did Dr Beth mean, 'You're certainly something but it's not pregnant'? I look around for Peter, who has been placed at a different table. Curiously, when I finally spot him, he is sitting next to Susannah York.

'Have you seen *The Horse Whisperer* yet?' asks Drabinsky morosely.

'Yes, very disappointing,' I start. 'What's Robert Redford's problem? How could he have cast himself as the romantic lead? He's far too old! His mouth's all lined,he looked ridiculous opposite Kristin Scott Thomas. And as for all those schmaltzy, sentimental shots of Montana . . .'

'Really?' he interrupts. 'I loved the movie.' He raises a heavy eyebrow. 'And I consider Robert one of my greatest friends.'

Monday, 18 May
Peter

I am not at my best at these society events. I seem to revert to my African childhood, dumbstruck and gauche, radiating rudeness to mask social incompetence. I tend to lean on Joanna, using her as a social battering ram, as she possesses complete candour and an effrontery to make me blush. Tonight, however, we are split up, but this is fine since Susannah York is at my table. In the course of the evening I do not manage to exchange a single word with her, however, so intense and exclusive is her conversation with the man on her left, apparently an old friend. Once I think she smiles at me, but I cannot be sure.

When we leave we are besieged by a squadron of publicity girls, who hover around the foyer to present us with our goody bags. I am still at a stage where I am enticed by goody bags. To me they are like unseasonal Christmas stockings. The prospect is exciting, though the contents seldom fail to disappoint. Tonight's freebies, which we examine in the cab on the way home, are the usual random medley of sponsors' offerings: a copy of the *New Yorker*, a volume of Shakespeare's sonnets, a tube of Callard and Bowser's liquorice toffees. On the drive home we declaim sonnets while chewing liquorice until our teeth have blackened.

The best gift is a small radio from Bloomberg, the financial rival to Reuters. But to our chagrin we discover that the radio has a strictly limited repertoire – it is permanently pre-tuned to Bloomberg's own station, and can receive no other.

Tuesday, 19 May
Joanna

After fruitless attempts to get through the voicemail, I make up my mind to go down and collect the second lot of results in person, when Dr Beth calls me.

'Joanna, it's Beth from Murray Hill, can you come in this afternoon? We need to talk. I've got your results back and quite frankly, Joanna, I don't mind tellin' you, I'm baffled.'

As I arrive, I see Donna the technician sitting on a low wall outside the surgery, smoking, a habit long since forbidden in New York offices. She gives me a thumbs up.

'Your numbers have doubled,' she says, drawing heavily on her cigarette. 'That's very good. That's what we look for.'

Buoyed up by this news, I sit patiently underneath the peaks of Yosemite waiting for Beth, who finally calls me in to tell me she is still baffled, but has booked me a sonogram. She leads me into a small white room, tells me to swap my suit for a paper robe and I lie back on a grey leather reclining chair.

The monitor flickers into life, she squeezes a transparent gel over my belly and I see a series of dark undulating lines, which she tells me is my uterus. The electronic wand hovers and she zooms in on a tiny dark spot.

'Mmn, a cyst,' she murmurs. 'Definitely an ovarian cyst.'

'Is that serious?' I ask, struggling to sit up.

She gestures me down and this time zooms in on an indecipherable white speck. She pulls one of her faces.

'A cyst is a symptom of pregnancy,' she says. 'Doctor to patient, it's too early to say. But woman to woman, I'd say you are pregnant, Joanna. Very, very early. But I don't think it's anything more serious.' She sounds disappointed. 'Congratulations,' she says flatly. 'You're going to have a baby after all.'

I manage a weak grin and, flooding with relief, make two instant vows. I will never come back to this surgery again. And I will never wear a turquoise pregnancy smock with white seagull-wing collar.

Tuesday, 19 May
Peter

My results are finally in. My time, it appears, is not up after all. There is nothing wrong with me. Nothing to explain the lump on my elbow. Dr Epstein sits across the desk flipping through the charts. He is bewildered.

'How's the writing going?' he asks, knowing that I am a writer.

I feel this is no time for small talk.

'Fine,' I reply, wanting to get back to my polyp.

'Still blocked?' he asks.

What is he, my agent?

'Well I had a bit of spurt a couple of weeks ago,' I admit, 'but it wasn't very good stuff.'

He asks to feel my polyp again and then his face lights up.

'I think you may have Carpal Tunnel Syndrome,' he says.

'What's that?' I ask fearfully.

'I think you guys call it Repetitive Stress Injury. It's caused by too much typing.'

I return to the apartment to break the news to Joanna.

'Turns out I'm fine,' I tell her. 'I'm not going to die after all. My test results are all negative. He thinks it's RSI. I must be the only blocked writer who has managed to contract RSI.'

Joanna doesn't seem particularly engaged by my relieved chatter.

'I got my test results too,' she says and hands me a package.

I unwrap it to find that it is a book entitled *The Expectant Father*.

Wednesday, 20 May
Joanna

Like most of my friends, I have put career ahead of children. In our twenties it seemed almost embarrassing to admit they were even a possibility. Now I'm suddenly aware of the explosive change that lies ahead. But instead of being scared, I find myself fizzing with elation – as though a secret trapdoor has sprung open to reveal a future quite different to the one I had been expecting.

I wonder, though, how my bosses in London will take the news of my pregnancy. I am currently the sole female staff foreign correspondent on the paper, and after only a few months I have fallen pregnant. This was clearly not part of their plan. I stare out of my greasy office window, trying to compose a memo breaking the news to the editor.

The truth is I am not a real foreign correspondent at all. I have no desire to zoom across the country clutching an overnight bag and a laptop, forever on call. I took this posting simply because I've always loved New York. As it turns out the job is largely office based, relying heavily on rewriting the New York papers and watching cable news. My colleague in Washington, Ed Vulliamy, calls it 'lift 'n' view'.

When I do try to engage in original journalism and hit the phone, no one has heard of the paper. This morning I am trying to get a comment on 'zero tolerance' from the NYPD press office.

'Hello. It's Joanna Coles from the *Guardian*,' I say.

'Where?'

'The *Guardian*.'

'La Guardia? The airport?'

'No. The *Guardian*. It's a British newspaper.'

'Really? Never heard of it.'

The bureau itself depresses me. Though I should not complain about the location, in midtown on 44th Street sandwiched between Fifth and Sixth Avenue, the office itself reminds me of the shabby sets invariably used in amateur productions of *Death of a Salesman*. The windows are so fudged with dirt that I can barely tell if it's raining. The glass top on the desk is shattered, its loosely arranged shards an industrial accident in waiting. The chair, a concave scoop of leatherette which has long since stopped revolving, has a two-inch nail sticking out of the left arm.

When I raise the issue with the foreign editor he is unsympathetic, assuming that I am exaggerating in the hope that he will allow me to refurbish with Philippe Starck accessories. Besides, he keeps reminding me, I am lucky to have an office at all. Most foreign correspondents are now required to work from a computer propped up in the back bedroom at home, something which would probably drive me mad.

Wednesday, 20 May
Peter

Joanna tells me that *The Expectant Father* will make me more understanding of what she is going through. I flip through the book and it falls open at an early page which advises me that the correct way to announce to my friends that Joanna is expecting a child is to say, 'We are pregnant.' I try saying it aloud. '*We* are pregnant.' 'We are *pregnant*.' It sounds absurd. I cannot bring myself to do this in public.

It is true however that I have been putting on some weight since the conception. John, also pregnant, has alerted me to Couvade's Syndrome, a condition suffered by fathers-to-be. Couvade comes from the French word, to hatch, and victims of the syndrome experience phantom pregnancies. I try out the idea on Joanna and she suggests that I might go to the gym more often.

I fall back on the thought that, rather like a beautiful Italian peasant girl who, having snared a husband, rapidly inflates into a moustachioed pasta pudding, I am perhaps relaxing into middle age, propelled by fatherhood.

Later I am consoled somewhat by a news item on the Rolling Stone, Keith Richards, the bad boy of rock 'n' roll.

It is reported that he has broken several ribs. This injury has not been inflicted in some night club brawl, however, or while trashing a hotel room. He has, in fact, sustained it in a nasty fall from the ladder in his library while trying to retrieve a volume from the top shelf. I wonder what the book was: Proust? Dickens? Or perhaps a leather-bound edition of the *New Musical Express*?

Eventually, it seems, a Rolling Stone does gather moss.

Thursday, 21 May
Joanna

My office is on the sixteenth floor and offers a Hopperesque view across the street and into the offices opposite, where I watch the other hunch-spined workers twisted over their terminals. I like being up high, but I worry about the bank of elevators, which, I have learned, sometimes stop unaccountably between floors.

The first time this happened was between the eighth and ninth floors and I was alone and felt reluctant to press the red alarm in case it triggered a general evacuation and froze the lift altogether.

After waiting about two minutes, I tentatively pressed the button. It gave an unimpressive little buzz.

'Hello,' said a bored voice through the intercom.

'I seem to be stuck,' I said, trying not to sound panicky.

'Yeah,' said the voice, pausing. 'You are.'

'Well, can you get it going again?'

'Yeah, the functions need resetting.'

'Well, can you sort it out?'

'Yeah, yeah. Don't panic.'

'I'm not panicking, I just want to get out.'

'OK, OK.'

Nothing happened so, assuming it might take some

minutes, I started on a muffin and opened the *New York Post*. I was reading the Page Six gossip column, which is usually in fact on page eight, when my eye slipped to a headline on the opposite page: 'WOMAN NARROWLY MISSES DROWNING IN ELEVATOR'.

I read on to discover that a woman and her Jack Russell terrier had been trapped in a lift after traipsing down to the basement to do her laundry. Unbeknown to her, workmen in the street outside had accidentally cracked a water main, which started flooding the basement and cutting the power. Eventually the water started creeping into the lift, where she was frantically pressing the alarm button. As the water kept rising she kept screaming, until her husband, worried at her delay, went down to investigate and finally heard her. By now the water was up to her neck. In order to save her dog's life, as the water rose, she had lifted him onto her head, where he had sat barking madly throughout their ordeal.

I pressed the button again.

'Yeah?'

'What's going on?'

'I told ya, I'm resetting the functions.'

'But how long is it going to take?'

'Another couple of minutes. I told ya, stop panicking, OK?'

Two minutes later the car duly jerked back into life and I ascended to my floor, where there was an exasperated voicemail from the foreign editor wanting to know where I was.

Thursday, 21 May
Peter

I have no inclination to read *The Expectant Father*, but am somehow drawn to it, almost titillated by the horror of what lies ahead. It warns me that Joanna may now exhibit violent mood swings as her hormones fizz with new life. My real worry is not the mood swings themselves, but her use of pregnancy as an all-purpose excuse for bad behaviour. She is already a skilful practitioner of pre-menstrual tension. By spicing it with the odd display of coquettishness and an occasional glancing apology, she can shroud bad behaviour for up to three weeks out of every four.

Now Joanna has nine months' access to the one excuse that tops PMT. I am filled with apprehension that she will seize upon her condition to behave as disruptively as she pleases. And though I'm determined to be stoical and tolerant, I suspect that this restraint on my part will only provoke her further.

Swallowing my panic at the turn of events, I grab my kit and head for the gym. I will exercise my way out of this anxiety. The lift doors part to reveal a neighbour who is an actor and his dog, a grinning Labrador with a red polka-dotted bandanna round its neck. The dog thumps its tail on the floor and, unsolicited, puts its paw up to be shaken. His owner and I exchange small talk. 'I'm up to my neck in Rosie's taxes,' he complains, patting the dog. 'I calculate that she's earned more appearing in commercials this tax year than I have. And there's only so many vet's bills and dog food that I can write off.'

At the Printing House gym, I gaze out over the West Village, while I pedal wildly, going nowhere on the stationary bike, and it occurs to me that I will have to earn more money if we are going to have a child. Hell, even our neighbour's dog earns more than I do.

Friday, 22 May
Joanna

I am running late to meet Meredith, a friend and investigative magazine reporter, in the Royalton bar. Despite the fact that according to all the pregnancy books, I should now be walking briskly twenty-five minutes a day, I can't face ten sweaty blocks of midtown crowds, so I hail a cab, which takes me twice as long.

'Darling, you're late,' she cries triumphantly as I finally spot her in the gloom squatting on a purple velvet pouffe. She pushes a clear cone of martini at me complete with bobbing khaki olive. It looks exquisite, a fringe of icy condensation slipping down the outside. I can't resist and take a small sip before declaring somewhat unconvincingly that I shouldn't really because I'm off alcohol at the moment. I haven't told her I'm pregnant.

'You, off alcohol? Don't be ridiculous,' Meredith scoffs and, grabbing a passing waiter, promptly orders two more martinis. 'With some of those outrageously expensive chips,' she yells after him, 'and we'll take a plate of aubergine caviar.'

I take another sip, planning to swap glasses when she goes to the loo, which she does a lot, not always, I suspect, for the actual purpose a bathroom is intended.

'So, have you heard about Kelly?' she says, leaning forward flashing her eyes in a way which signifies she has gossip. 'She's on Ritalin and she's had a complete personality change!'

'What?' I demand, wondering crossly why Kelly hasn't told me this herself.

'Ritalin, you know that drug they give to kids with ADD – attention deficit disorder.'

'But why? What for?' I ask, doubly cross that a close friend hasn't told me she's suffering from New York's most fashionable disorder.

'Says it helps her focus,' nods Meredith.

'Focus on what?'

'Everything! She says it's so good that yesterday for the first time in ten years she went out without any Valium at all. I mean she deliberately left her pill tin at home and, even when she was caught in a mob at Barney's sale, she didn't panic once . . .'

Given that I am reluctant to take even aspirin, I'm always impressed at the way New Yorkers pop pills. Kelly and Jeff's large bathroom cabinet, which I once secretly opened, resembles a RiteAid comfort station. Every shelf was crammed with brown glass bottles: Prozac, Zoloft, Valium and Lithium alongside the more mundane Tylenol 'Extra' and its rival Advil's response, Advil Extra Strength. Though they talk openly about self-medicating, I have no idea how much they actually take of the stuff.

Meredith goes to the loo and I switch glasses just as the waiter arrives with our next drinks and a white napkin envelope of home-made crisps and a plate of pitta slices, cut in the shape of triangles and arranged points-out in the shape of a star, to mop up a stylized taupe blob of mashed aubergine.

'Darling,' shrills Meredith, eyes flashing and sniffing like a bloodhound, as she returns. 'How are you?' As if we have just met.

Saturday, 23 *May*
Peter

At 3.45 a.m. I get up to go for a pee and on the way back I notice the bent figure of a tramp trundling a shopping trolley down Gansevoort Street. He parks it adjacent to the fire hydrant beneath our window and from the trolley's lower shelf he produces a long cast-iron tool – his own, personal hydrant spanner. He opens the hydrant, adjusting it carefully to allow a modest spout of water to flow. Then he goes about his ablutions. First, he fills up his three plastic water bottles; then he fussily rinses out a carrier bag, turns it inside out and vigorously shakes it dry. From his trolley he lifts out a tray of peaches and fastidiously washes them, one by one. After checking on his plastic bag again, which is drying, he eats two of his peaches, dabbing at his beard with a faded bandanna. He carefully eases the tray of remaining peaches into the newly cleaned carrier bag, ties its handles and gingerly places it back in his supermarket trolley. Then he washes his face over and over again and swills out his mouth.

From somewhere inside his grubby full-length gabardine coat he retrieves a little plastic box. I can't quite make out what it is. Tobacco? Snuff? Crack? Then he pulls something long and white from the box and breaks it off. It is a length of dental floss, and he proceeds to floss his teeth with great thoroughness.

In the gloom of the early morning Joanna appears, naked, on her way to the bathroom.

'Check this out,' I tell her. 'A tramp who flosses.'

Joanna observes the scene silently for a moment and then announces that her breasts ache.

'Look at them,' she murmurs, 'they're enormous.'

They loom, ghostly white globes in the half-light, and

indeed they do look considerably expanded. I reach for one and cup it in the palm of my outstretched hand like the Sikh cab driver did to Ru.

'Wow, that's some boob,' I exclaim, in what I hope is an admiring tone.

Below us the tramp closes the fire hydrant, replaces his spanner in the trolley, and trundles it slowly down Gansevoort Street, turning north on to the West Side Highway. I look at the clock. The whole ritual has taken nearly an hour.

Monday, 25 May
Joanna

. . . Though it is only 10 a.m. here, it is already 4 p.m. in London and I am in the office on deadline for a feature about Robert Downey Junior's persistent drug problem. I am distracted, however, by the frantic pitching coming through the thin wall. It is Ted, the elderly real estate agent in the next-door office, talking on the phone to a client.

'I'm going to have to push you, Frank, I'm sorry but I gotta know today,' I hear him say. 'Frank, if I could give you more time, then believe me I would. Believe me, I've been fighting for you, Frank, I've been fighting very hard. And I don't mind tellin' ya, they don't call me the Rocky-of-Real-Estate for nothing. Are you in with me, Frank? Do we have a deal here? I don't mind telling ya, ya won't regret it.'

Until two years ago the *Guardian* office in New York was staffed with thirteen people selling subscriptions for the *Guardian Weekly* edition. Then the paper's accountants in London caught up with this forgotten enclave and made them all redundant, shifting operations to Canada to cut costs. But they were unable to shift the unexpired Manhattan lease, and so for a while I worked in an eerily deserted office. Now the paper has managed to rent the remaining space to a trio of elderly real estate agents. They arrived one Monday morning with several boxes stuffed full of executive toys.

Ted is the most avuncular of the three. He has decorated his office with framed copies of the most lucrative deals he has closed over the last forty years. These are, I suppose, the real estate equivalent of Pulitzer prizes, though the small print makes them almost impossible to read. His favourite is prominently displayed on a separate music stand by his door.

'This', he told me, shortly after his arrival, pointing proudly to the cream paper filled with minute print, 'is for a helicopter landing pad I sold on top of the fourteenth tallest building in the city. And I tell ya, it was a lucky deal, lucky for me anyways!

'A month after I signed the contract, I'll be damned if a helicopter didn't topple off the edge of the Pan Am building, killing everyone aboard and some more underneath. After that, all helicopters were banned from taking off or landing on buildings across the city.' He gives a rueful laugh. 'Lucky for me, right? But God, was the guy who bought the landing pad from me pissed!'

In between the contracts he has slipped in the odd family photograph of a wife and scowling son, somewhere in his late teens, with a backwards baseball cap on his crown. In each of the photos he is also wearing Tommy Hilfiger jeans, with the crotch nestling between his knees, a trend, Ted explains, inspired by maximum-security prisoners whose trousers are always loose because they are not allowed belts.

The pride of Ted's executive toy chest is his wave machine. This is a glass box, a yard long by a foot high, filled with a viscous aquamarine oil. When switched on it simulates the ocean, only in slow motion. 'Very soothing,' nods Ted. One day, he says, he is planning to surprise me by changing the colour of the oil.

'I'll do it,' he threatens. 'Just see if I don't, I promise you, one day you'll walk in and I'll have changed it to purple!'

Under his desk he also keeps a wooden rod with an iron hoop, which looks like a metal detector.

'This is my "Bullshit Detector",' he announced within an hour of his arrival, waving it at me and making a high-pitched beeping noise. Whenever a client says something he doesn't agree with, he reaches for it, sweeps it towards them and starts up his high-pitched beeping.

Monday, 25 May
Peter

After consulting our battalion of liveried doormen, we have finally hired a cleaner. She is a short, hefty, middle-aged woman with brightly hennaed hair, called Margarita. Her work uniform is an appliqué T-shirt, black leggings, Nikes and dayglo pink rubber gloves. She arrives with another maid to negotiate her fee.

'Eighty dollars,' states her colleague baldly. 'That is the rate.'

This seems a little steep to me. In London we paid our cleaner £30. Given that Margarita says it will take three hours to clean our apartment here, $80 works out at nearly $27 an hour. The minimum wage in this country is $5.45 an hour, so we will be paying her almost five times that.

'Sixty dollars?' I suggest. 'That's twenty dollars an hour – a good wage,' I say hopefully. I am a terrible negotiator, the thrills of shopping at the souk are not for me.

But Margarita will not budge. There is to be no negotiation. The two women stand there arms folded over their bosoms regarding me sternly and I cave in. It's a deal. As they leave, Margarita's colleague informs me that laundry will be extra.

Margarita comes from Ecuador and though she has been in the United States for twelve years, she speaks no English. Well, that's not entirely fair. She speaks three words of English: 'No thank you.' She deploys this phrase in differing intonations, depending on the situation.

'Margarita, can you clean the windows?' I ask her, miming cleaning the grimy windows. 'No thank you! No thank you, Mr Peter!' she bellows back, nodding vigorously and smiling broadly so that her gold tooth winks in what little light has made it through the panes.

When I introduce Margarita to our stock of household cleaning materials and equipment – all the usual fluids and unguents and sprays, and my newly purchased vacuum cleaner – her brow knits in disapproval and she scowls. 'No thank you, Mr Peter!' she says firmly, and this time she means just that. I am mildly offended. I went to some trouble choosing the vacuum and it seems perfectly adequate.

'Look,' I appeal to her, 'it is the latest Panasonic, the Jet Flo 170. It's got 170, um 170 suck power, or something.' But she is not impressed.

Today Margarita arrives with her own preferred condiments of cleaning, evidently chosen with the loving care of a commando's specialized weaponry, and her own vacuum, all loaded on to a shopping trolley pushed by her taciturn teenage son.

'This,' he says, translating his mother's Spanish, 'this, my mother says, is a real vacuum.'

It doesn't look like much, an ancient beige drum vacuum,

its grubby plastic casing bound with masking tape. Margarita fires it up and sweeps the nozzle along the floor, where it immediately sucks most of a small kilim into its mighty vortex, and its tone changes to a strangled high-pitched scream. She rattles off another Spanish command and her son says to me, 'Go on, pull it. Pull the rug.' I grab hold of the kilim and tug it. Margarita takes up a wrestling stance and holds the vacuum pipe in both hands. We tussle this way and that for a while, but I am quite unable to dislodge the kilim until she switches off the power and I finally stagger backwards, kilim in hand.

'That's a hell of a vacuum,' I am forced to concede.

'No thank you, Mr Peter,' says Margarita graciously and smiles a victory smile garnished with another flash of gold tooth.

Tuesday, 26 May
Joanna

Tonight we attend the inaugural dinner of the American Friends of the Royal Court held at a grand townhouse just off Fifth Avenue.

It is run by a rather terrifying band of supremely confident English women who, among their other triumphs, are also accomplished fund-raisers. It's the first time either of us has been involved in anything like this, and it soon becomes apparent we are in way over our heads.

There are twenty of us altogether at the dinner and Stephen Daldry, the Court's artistic director who has flown in from London this afternoon specially to address us, explains what the theatre needs. Except that he is far too abashed to ask for money directly and, instead, keeps talking about 'raising the Royal Court's profile', so that it isn't entirely clear what he's actually after. Looking suitably perplexed, an American woman sitting opposite me suddenly pipes up, 'Well, what do you need? Would it help, for example, if each one of us sitting here were to write you a cheque for twenty thousand dollars?'

To my horror, several other people nod supportively. 'Good idea,' murmurs my neighbour, and one woman even makes as if to retrieve her chequebook from a small beaded handbag. Unable to catch Peter's eye, I sit frozen in fear of us being publicly humiliated as the only people round the grand candle-lit table unable to afford such a gesture. Fortunately, Daldry is so embarrassed at the idea that it is somehow lost over the dessert wine. Overwhelmed with relief, as we are leaving, I cheerfully sign up both Peter and I to attend a volunteers' meeting to explore ways of expanding the Royal Court's reputation in New York.

Tuesday, 26 May
Peter

Today I notice for the first time a disturbing tribe of women on the street — mothers with newborn babies. This tribe has apparently lost all dress sense and dispensed with sartorial vanity entirely, strolling along in lumpy sweaters, mismatched socks and untended hair. They converse in goo-goo talk with their little grubs, and wear beatific, gormless smiles. The only other place I've seen this foolish beam is on the faces of cult members. Will Joanna's brain also turn to mush? Will she too promenade in jumble-sale attire, with bad hair, chat entirely in infant gibberish, cease to call me by my name and address me as daddy instead?

Oh God, what have we done?

Wednesday, 27 May
Joanna

Someone has stuffed a flyer under our door advertising a playreading this evening at the local West Beth Community Centre. The reading has been arranged hurriedly by local actors and writers as 'the community's reply' to a rape in Horatio Street, which ended with a desperate girl flinging herself out of the bedroom window of her fourth-storey apartment. After the reading local police have agreed to address us about neighbourhood safety and how to protect ourselves.

By the time I arrive there are sixty or so women gathered in the hall and about a dozen rather reluctant-looking men. (Peter has refused to accompany me on the grounds that he is on deadline for a *Newsweek* column on Winnie Mandela, though I suspect the real reason is to do with 'Must See TV' night on NBC: *Seinfeld* followed by *ER*).

I take my seat towards the back of the audience and a large gentleman, apparently in charge of proceedings, steps up to the dais.

'Welcome,' he says. 'We're just waiting for our leader, who is upstairs chanting.'

'How very Greenwich Village,' mutters my neighbour, a blonde, bobbed woman with a complicated briefcase and tan legs which disappear into clumpy trainers.

The large man addresses us again. 'We realize we have had a terrible tragedy occur in our midst and this evening we want to bring a focus to this kind of violence.' He eyes us steadily as if one of us might be harbouring the suspect.

'You know,' he says slowly, 'there are people walking around who have done these things.' Several of the women nod knowingly, as Paul Benjamin, the playwright whose work is to be performed tonight, emerges from a side door, his chanting now apparently finished.

It is an adequate drama, notable mostly for the overwhelming earnestness with which it is read. The real drama, however, begins afterwards when the police officers address us.

Ronald Haas, a huge and rather comforting detective from the Special Crimes Squad, goes first. 'Obviously a heinous crime has taken place,' he begins. 'An individual was raped . . .'

'A WOMAN was raped!' shouts a furious girl in dungarees from somewhere on the third row. 'A WOMAN was raped.'

'A woman was raped,' the officer corrects himself. 'Obviously I can't give you specific details . . .'

'We don't want specific details,' calls another woman. She is gnawing a raw carrot. 'Just tell us what time it happened.'

'About eight-thirty,' says Officer Haas.

'Holy shit!' exclaims someone.

'The only other thing I can tell you', Haas continues uneasily, 'is that the assailant was a six-foot tall, two hundred and ten pound, black male with stubble.'

'Why have no police approached me to tell me to take care?' shouts another girl, this one in a denim smock.

'Because that's not their job,' cries a frail man from across the hall.

'Look,' says Haas, 'I care deeply about this community and I'm offended by this crime.'

'Well, what can you do about it?' demands an elderly woman, stroking a dachshund. 'Every time I walk down the street and see a black guy I'm gonna be scared now.'

At this point another detective, Merri Pearsall, who says

she has coincidentally just rented an apartment in the neighbourhood, takes over. 'My thought is, I might have prevented this,' she says wistfully, before running through some tips which might prevent us from being attacked ourselves.

'Get used to noticing details,' she says. 'Height, clothing, weight, hair colour.'

'How tall IS six foot anyway,' shouts the first dungaree'd girl. 'How can you tell for sure?'

'I have a dog and I always carry a can of Mace,' interrupts the carrot chewer, brandishing her carrot stick. 'Which is better? Dog? Or Mace?'

'I'd take a dog over Mace any day,' says Detective Pearsall. 'You can't use Mace if there's any wind and I've seen a room full of cops overcome by it in seconds. Definitely a dog.'

Dog over Mace, writes carrot woman on her notepad, firmly underlining each word three times.

As I gather up my things, preparing to walk home, I try to imagine a fear so intense that you would throw yourself out of a fourth-floor window. 'Is she OK?' I ask another woman, who seems involved in the evening.

She pulls a face. 'She landed on the second-floor fire escape and lost a kidney,' she says. 'But she's still alive, if that's what you mean.'

JUNE

The baby's brain, muscles and bones begin to form. The ball of cells growing inside your uterus – the embryo – is now the size of an apple seed.
BabyCenter.com

Monday, 1 June
Peter

236 days to go until the baby arrives. We have started calling it B-Day.

I mooch down Gansevoort Street in the simmering heat, past Judd Grill's gym, where I can see a trio of burly meat-packers building brawn on the bench presses; past Samba's Deli and the Maggio Beef Corporation, which is wedged beneath the amputated tracks of the old Manhattan Freight Line. Every lamp-post and street-sign reeks of vaporizing dog's urine. The very pavements themselves seem to per-spire. Through their cracks they ooze beads of greasy sweat from the city's foul subterranean bowels. I'm on my way to our local twenty-four-hour diner, Florent, for what has become my ritual lunch.

Outside on the broken sidewalk the restaurant has arranged a hopeful little cluster of fake marble bistro tables and green metal chairs under bright blue sun umbrellas. However, this venue has not proved popular with cus-tomers, who have to share it with a clutter of big red metal wheelie bins overflowing with bones, mysteriously dabbed with iridescent green paint, and listen to the insistent whine of band-saws cutting carcasses inside the Shuster Meat Corp – 'We specialize in boneless beef cuts'.

Florent looks like a diner. It is long and narrow, and has a mirror and red leatherette bench seats with chrome trimmings along one wall, and a white Formica counter down the other. But Florent is not a real diner at all. It is an ironic diner. A parody of a diner. It has quilted aluminium walls and a pink ceiling, from which hangs a slowly revolving disco mirror ball.

Above the cash register is an old-fashioned announcement board, the kind you used to see at convention centres, with individual letters pressed into plastic grooves to relay the day's schedule to delegates. The board has today's date followed by some helpful information:

The weather: Hot, hot, HOT!
Today 96°.
Tomorrow – Hotter 99°.

Underneath the heading 'Flo by Night' it suggests options for night clubs in the Meat Packing District, helpfully categorized:

Gay: Hell, Lure, The Anvil, Manhole
Lesbian: The Clit Club
Straight: Hoggs and Heifers
Or: Stay at home and read to each other

The walls of Florent are decorated with framed maps of various city centres around the world. But between these maps are fictional ones penned by Florent, who is evidently a fantasy cartographer. He draws the imagined layout of cities that might have been, with intricate plans of their docks and parks, bridges and graveyards.

Florent himself, who is seldom in residence during the day, is a gay Frenchman who arrived in New York about thirty years ago. He organizes the annual Bastille Day event held in Gansevoort Street. The highlight of the Bastille Day festivities is the Marie Antoinette look-alike competition, which a bewigged, powdered and bustled Florent always enters.

I haul myself up on a stool at the bar and flop the hefty bundle of the *New York Times* down on the counter. The Mexican busboy immediately slams down a glass of iced water, cutlery, a paper napkin and a paper place mat which is adorned with a map of Caribbean islands: Cuba, Dominican Republic and Haiti, Puerto Rico and Jamaica. At hand there is also a glass of wax crayons should I feel the need to doodle on the islands.

'Yo,' says Brigitte, the waitress, a cheerful TV editor from New Zealand working on her first novel, 'what can I get you?'

I do not need to see the menu, I know it by heart and have tried almost everything on it. The food at Florent is a peculiarly camp variety of diner food. So today my BLT comes complete with a fussy rocket salad and thin, delicately cut French fries.

I have with me part of the manuscript of my book and after a cup of stewed coffee I pore over the text.

'Hit a snag?' asks Brigitte, helpfully.

'Yeah, the voice isn't quite right. I'm thinking of moving it into the first person.'

Soon an informal writing workshop has convened with the waiters, Cedric-the-filmmaker, David-the-actor/playwright, and Brigitte-the-novelist, helpfully pointing out the advantages of an all-seeing third-person narrator over the 'I' word.

Sunday, 7 June
Joanna

I am still wondering how to tell the office about my pregnancy when Peter raises the issue of telling our respective parents. I know we must, but I am still apprehensive. His, I know, will be thrilled. Having spent their entire adult lives in the Third World, nothing seems to faze them and considering they are both now in their seventies they remain amazingly flexible in attitude.

I'm not worried about my father either – he is the most amiable, patient person I know and, after thirty years of trying to interest inner-city comprehensive kids in Shakespeare, he is resolutely unshockable. It's my mother who's the problem. My mother is a vicar's daughter and a former marriage guidance counsellor who is doing her best to reconcile herself to the fact that both her daughters now live with men to whom they are not married.

'Go on,' says Peter, pushing the phone across the dining table. 'Just do it, I'm sure she'll be over the moon.' It is 9.15 a.m. and we have just finished breakfast, so given the five-hour time difference I think they will have finished lunch in Yorkshire.

'I'll just tidy the breakfast stuff up first,' I say brightly, though our caffè lattes and warm blueberry muffins arrived in a bag from Barocco, one of a score of delis within 500 yards which deliver our breakfast, so there is nothing to wash up.

'Go on, stop playing for time,' he admonishes, hauling the *New York Times* onto the sofa and beginning to weed out the numerous sections we never read.

'Hello?' My mother answers the phone. She sounds suspicious, a tone which I've noticed has increased since she took over management of the local Neighbourhood Watch and now receives long recorded messages from the police about local burglaries, which she diligently transcribes by hand on her blue Basildon Bond pad and distributes to the neighbours.

'Hello, it's me,' I say.

'Hello!' she cries. 'Hang on, and I'll just tell your father to go and listen on the extension upstairs.' A good start; at least I've caught them together.

'I've got some news,' I begin awkwardly.

'Oh yes?'

'You're going to be grandparents.'

There is a pause and a sharp intake of breath.

'Oh,' says my mother. And then, with a small tinge of hope, 'I mean, well, I have one question for you. Does this mean you are finally going to get married?'

'No,' I reply slowly. 'I don't think we are. No.' I hope this sounds firm.

'How will you look after it?' she asks, sounding mildly incredulous.

'Mum, I'm thirty-six.'

'Congratulations, duckie,' my father's voice booms down the extension, valiantly trying to drown out my mother's apparent shock.

'I'm trembling,' my mother says, dramatically. 'Oh dear, I had no idea. I need to sit down . . .'

'I'm going to be a grandfather!' Dad says excitedly.

My mother interrupts him. 'Oh dear,' she laments again, and I can hear her struggling to say something encouraging. 'Oh dear,' she repeats quietly, 'I think I need a brandy.'

Tuesday, 9 June
Peter

Joanna has imbued our unborn child with its own character. It is that of a street-smart, super-competitive, gravel-voiced Manhattanite, already ashamed of its odd, foreign parents.

'Hey, Dad,' she rasps in imitation, 'how come you haven't got a real job?' The knowing foetus, her incarnation of it at least, is already withering in its take on our relative lack of financial status. 'Why haven't we got an Aston Martin like William's dad, huh?' it complains. 'And what's with this Village loft? It's pah-thetic! How come we don't live in a brownstone on the Upper East Side, like Gus?'

Joanna's name choices have become ever more bizarre and arbitrary. 'Obadiah. I like Obadiah,' she pipes up over supper at Florent, apropos of nothing in particular – pregnancy has made her a mental doodler. 'Or what about Zebedee?' She is deep into her Old Testament phase.

We return home to find our answer service bleeping with a message. It is from Andrew Solomon.

When we first arrived in New York we came equipped with an armful of introductions to people we 'absolutely had to meet'. Most of these meetings have proved rather awkward, contrived affairs, where once the subject of our mutual friend is exhausted, conversation becomes threadbare. So we have lost our appetite for this kind of entrée.

Andrew Solomon, journalist, author, socialite, art collector, is, however, in a class of his own. We have been furnished with his number by almost everyone we know in London. He has an astonishing social span – he is an international Zelig. I have met people in Botswanan game parks and on Caribbean beaches who, on hearing I live in New York, say, 'Oh, have you met a friend of mine, Andrew Solomon?'

The answer is no. It is not, however, through want of

trying. We have been playing phone tag with him for months now, but Andrew Solomon evidently lives his life according to an itinerary packed with ever more exotic and obscure locations.

'I'm afraid we've missed Andrew again,' I tell Joanna.

'Oh, where is he this time?'

'Nassau, Havana and Bogliasco.'

Thursday, 11 June
Joanna

Tonight we have supper with Larry and Nancy, two wealthy writers whose TriBeCa loft seems somehow far better designed for actually living in than ours. They too have been forced to partition space, but have chosen quiet wicker screens rather than our solution of messy book-shelves and desks. It seems a triumph of practical but stylish design and I am silently oozing envy as the door buzzes and supper arrives.

'Oh God,' I apologize, as Nancy starts removing the cellophane wrapper to reveal a huge platter of sushi, beautifully arranged with ginger roses and zig-zagged green papers to separate the portions. 'I should have told you, I'm pregnant, and raw fish is the one food which is supposed to be taboo.'

'Oh congratulations!' shrieks Nancy. 'Are you going to get married?'

As she heads over to the kitchen area to make me an omelette, their three-year-old daughter, Danielle, emerges from her wicker-screened den and Larry is instructed to put her to bed.

'Seriously,' Nancy continues, 'you are going to get married, right? I mean, if you don't it'll be tough on the kid at school.'

'Actually, I don't think we're going to,' I say. 'But it's a lot more common in Europe to have children without being married than it is here.'

'Oh, but you must get married,' shouts Barbara, another guest. 'I mean you must, for the child's sake. I've been married for thirty years and it just gets better!' Curiously, her husband is absent.

'Well, who knows?' I murmur, anxious to avoid further lecturing.

'Is Danielle in bed yet?' asks Nancy as Larry reappears, offering more wine.

'No,' he says calmly. 'She's watching cartoons and masturbating.'

Peter coughs on a prematurely smuggled sushi.

'It's a phase she's going through,' Larry explains jovially. 'She does it all the time.'

Saturday, 13 June
Peter

I log on to Amazon.com, the online bookseller, which has started carrying the sales rankings of the books they stock. This is fatal. You can now track the sales of your book on a daily basis – an agonizing process for us so-called 'mid-list' authors. Customers may also air their own reviews and bestow you with a star rating. Today my latest book, *Mukiwa*, a memoir of growing up in Africa, is the 20,181st best-selling book in American cyberspace.

While online I collect an e-mail from Amazon.com. It is an advertorial plugging new books on the subject of writing. I must have signed up for this electronic junk e-mail sometime by failing to tick the box declining it. I am very taken with an account by the children's writer, Maurice Sendak, best known for his fantastically fuzzy Wild Things, who says he's 'never spent less than two years on the text of one of his picture books, even though each of them is approximately 380 words long'.

Two years to do the words alone. All 380 of them. By my calculations he's polishing off 190 words a year. That's fifteen words a month. Say, a *bon mot* every couple of days, on average.

Go, Maurice! That's my man.

Sunday, 14 June
Joanna

Having checked in with my sister first, who assures me our mother is 'getting used to the idea', I phone Yorkshire again, hoping that the excitement of a first grandchild will have dimmed her moral disquiet.

'How are you? Oh, and the baby of course?' she asks, in tones which clearly suggest she's been got at by both my father and sister.

'We're fine,' I say, giving Peter a thumbs up.

'Well, I've stopped knitting blankets for Bosnian babies,' she says, sounding almost cheerful. 'Do you have any thoughts on what colours you'd like?'

Wednesday, 17 June
Peter

Margarita has come to clean, and I am tapping at my keyboard, trying to stay out of the way of her vacuum's mighty vortex, when a shadow crosses the light, and she approaches, clucking disapproval.

'Mr Peter, Mr Peter, no thank you,' she admonishes and, rather than feeling like her employer, I feel like a child who is about to be bawled out by a kindergarten teacher. In her pink dayglo glove she is clutching a pile of discarded mail, which she has retrieved from one of our waste bins. 'This, Mr Peter, no good. Very bad. No thank you.'

I look down at my desk, inexplicably ashamed of myself, though I am not sure what I have done wrong.

'Do like this,' she says, and begins to tear up the old press releases and credit card offers, and other detritus of the junk mail age, into smaller and smaller pieces. Then she deposits them in the bin bag with a flourish so that their individual shards scatter, making it impossible to reconstruct them. I am still uncertain of our sin, though I am beginning to suspect we have breached one of New York's arcane recycling regulations.

'Why?' I ask. 'Why must we tear up all our old mail?'

'Why?' She looks at me as though I am truly to be pitied. 'Because . . .' she struggles to find the word in her slowly improving English vocabulary. 'Because is dangerous.' And with that she retrieves some of the intact mail and pretends to be surreptitiously reading it, as though she is a spy. 'You see?' she asks. 'Is dangerous.'

I try to explain that we couldn't care less if strangers wish to peruse our old mail, but Margarita is unmoved and continues laboriously ripping up the letters. And in the end I cannot bear to witness this time-wasting exercise and I join her at the dining-room table tearing up inconsequential paper. Which is where we are found when Joanna returns from having her hair blow-dried.

Thursday, 18 June
Joanna

I am only nine weeks pregnant and already my wardrobe doesn't fit. This seems especially alarming because as I was flicking through Sheila Kitzinger's *Complete Book of Pregnancy* this morning I noticed the entry for sixteen weeks: 'Your waistline will be starting to disappear.'

It has already disappeared, completely. I begin a listless hunt through my wardrobe only to find myself, incredibly, fantasizing about wearing a comfortable turquoise smock.

Kelly has given me a book called *Pregnancy Chic*. Ostensibly a fashion guide, it is actually a vehicle to push leggings and spinnaker-shaped T-shirts manufactured by the authors. I can't work out what's worse, the jaunty illustrations of smiling women in caftans or the advice itself, which seems to concentrate largely on the many different things you can do with a scarf.

'Medium square: looks great tied loosely around your neck or shoulders over a tunic or a sweater! Pocket square: tied neckerchief-style with a tunic or button-down shirt! Oblong: looks best with a solid tunic, sweater or cardigan!'

I don't want to wear a neckerchief-style scarf, I want to be able to fit back into my Joseph bootleg pants, of which I have four pairs, and the size 4 jeans I bought in the Boston Banana Republic after losing half a stone covering the Louise Woodward trial.

I e-mail Jane in London, whom I cannot remember looking even vaguely pregnant during her ninth months carrying William. She sends back an encouraging missive, which she entitles, 'Sick Male Notions of Female Attractiveness'. 'Don't worry about buying maternity wear, squeeze into your old stuff and wear long jackets. Clothes are the least of your worries. If you haven't done so already, make sure you book a maternity nurse asap. All the best ones get booked fast and you won't get through the nights without one.'

Saturday, 20 June
Peter

216 days to B-Day.

I flop down on our vast bed for an afternoon nap after another noisy night of meat deliveries. It is the biggest bed I have ever slept in, a Serta Perfect Sleeper with an orthopaedic California King Sized mattress, six foot six inches wide, topped with a soft quilted upper lining, to give you the best of both worlds: firm support for your back and an inch of surface softness to snuggle into. With such vast dimensions, the California King Size presents various serious engineering problems, so, for example, our box spring base is in two halves, with extra legs in the middle of the bed to keep it from sagging. Of course, none of our English linen fits.

Our new bed feels especially luxurious given that for our first few days in New York we slept on a mustard-coloured sleeping Lilo that I had acquired at The Leading Edge in Whiteleys Mall on Queensway and shipped over with us on the *QE2*. The sleeping Lilo, according to The Leading Edge, which specializes in the latest gadgetry, was a breakthrough in somniac science, easy to store and transport, but with its own system of internal baffles, providing all the comfort of a real bed. Best of all, by simply altering the amount you inflated it, it could simulate a soft, fluffy mattress or deliver firmer support. In reality we found that every time one of us shifted weight the other was bobbed up on a swell of air pressure – it was like trying to share a trampoline.

The Leading Edge Lilo came complete with a foot pump and hose attachment. But it also came with a slow and unlocatable leak. Before we retired for the night, I would tread-pump the Lilo to full pressure. It would then slowly deflate until about two hours later, Joanna, a lighter sleeper than me, would awaken to the ungiving pressure of the parquet floor. She would elbow me and I would get up, attach the foot pump and groggily tread it for ten minutes until the Lilo had reinflated. I would repeat this performance every two hours, getting up to feed air to our bed.

This is what I now imagine having a small baby will be like.

The pleasure of our California King Sized Serta Perfect Sleeper is only ruined by the fact that every time I flop down upon its vast quilted acreage I am reminded that we paid too much for it at Bloomingdale's. I am taunted by the saturation advertising on TV by '1-800-Sleepys', and its rival, '1-800-Mattress, Leave Off the Final "S" for Savings' in their apparently cut-throat war to be purveyors of the best mattress deals to New York's fitful sleepers. Always an ex-post-facto comparison shopper, I have tortured myself by phoning both 1-800-Sleepys and 1-800-Mattress, to discover that the California King Sized Serta Perfect Sleeper, the exact same California King Sized Serta Perfect Sleeper, can be purchased from either of them over the phone, for $500 less than we paid at Bloomingdale's. And of course, both hyperdrive salesmen assure me, 'We deliver free! Guaranteed within two hours! Anywhere in the five boroughs!'

Monday, 22 June
Joanna

I am on my way to see my new accountant, a solemn-sounding man called Bob Green. When I phoned to make an appointment he informed me he worked from home, so I set off for his apartment on the thirty-eighth floor of a modern tower block overlooking the East River. When I arrive he answers the door, an unsmiling, middle-aged, black-haired man with his left shoulder wedging a phone to his neck.

His office is framed by huge, grey-tinted windows offering spectacular panoramic views stretching down past the solid towers of Brooklyn Bridge to the graceful columns of the World Trade Center. Directly below I can see a red helicopter taking off from the 34th Street heliport. It rises to the height of our window before swooping off across the East River towards La Guardia airport.

'What fantastic views,' I say as Bob reappears, neck straight and minus the phone. He nods silently, beckoning me into his office and reaching out to boot up a large desk-top computer, which emits the triumphant fanfare heralding the imminent presence of Windows '98.

He swings to face me and utters his first full sentence. 'I don't mind telling you, Joanna, I am going to be very aggressive on your behalf. Very aggressive indeed.'

From out of a drawer he produces a stiff pink bandage with cream Velcro straps which he proceeds to bind tightly around his right arm. 'Too much time on this thing,' he says gesturing at the keyboard. I commiserate as he swings back to the monitor and calls out, 'Full name? Address? Social security number?' As I answer, he pounds furiously at the keyboard.

For the next ninety minutes I produce endless, carefully collated receipts for restaurants, books, batteries, tapes and other journalistic minutiae as we examine my earnings.

My saving grace, he tells me, is the cost of setting up a household in New York, some of which I can offset against my freelance earnings, including a frenzied period of television appearances during the Louise Woodward trial.

By the end of our session the taciturn Bob is grinning.

'I think you can relax,' he says, scanning a column of figures he has printed out. 'In fact, I work out you overpaid already. The IRS owes you money. About eight hundred dollars in total.'

'Are you sure?' I ask, having earmarked my meagre fund of savings for the Revenue.

I thank him profusely, marvelling at how much more generous the US system seems to be to the freelance income. Bob smiles briefly and with a flourish extends his bandaged arm. 'Welcome to America, Joanna,' he says, with no trace of irony, shaking my hand for the first time. 'Welcome to America, land of the free.'

Sunday, 28 June
Peter

As good West Village citizens, we are watching the annual spectacle of Gay Pride. The floats progress slowly south down fifth Avenue towards the Village. Crowds of curious Mid-Westerners and outer borough suburbanites, the bridge and tunnel set, press against the blue wooden police trestles, snapping at the freaks with their Sureshots.

Behind an arch of rainbow balloons, the procession is led by a squadron of Lesbians on Harleys, dozens of them, built like beer kegs, inscrutable behind their Ray-Ban aviators. One gives a clenched-fist salute to the crowd, and is nearly unseated as her Harley hits a badly fitted manhole cover and fishtails crazily across the street before she manages to wrestle it back.

It is an astonishingly diverse assemblage: 'Puerto Ricans Against Anti-Gay Violence' saunter by, their sound system perched on a wheelchair; 'Latino Gay Men of NY'; Gay and Lesbian Arab Society; Bisexual Trekkies; one with a subsidiary banner proclaiming 'They say we don't fuck, We say Fuck You'; 'Come fuck with us – free your mind and your ass will follow.'

Dressed up as the Village People, 'The Clit Club' Lesbians are marching to the tune of 'YMCA'. The Gay and Lesbian Anti-Violence Project displays banners which entreat: 'Hang up on Hate, Give us a ring'. Their principal dancer protrudes from a giant pink phone on the back of a flat-bed truck and the whole float threatens to be borne aloft by a flotilla of pink balloons.

In front of me a transvestite rollerblader falls heavily on to her bum. Her companion, dressed in a sequined evening gown with a slit up one thigh all the way to her panty line and a gold bra with sharply conical revolving cups, brushes her off and helps her up. They curtsy briefly to the applauding onlookers and continue on their way.

A man pushing a trolley piled high with a teetering tower of pretzels eases it down the kerb ramp and joins a flock of anxious black-hatted Hasidic Jews as they dart across the road between floats. And then we catch sight of the ubiquitous Mayor Giuliani marching along between two hostile groups, but grinning fit to pop and dispensing royal waves this way and that to the crowd. Most boo back, a few cheer.

Some hours later and the fag end of the sweaty entourage is slowly straggling into Christopher Street, the final leg and their spiritual home, where the Stonewall Riots launched Gay Pride itself in 1969. A float blaring Schubert goes by bearing a bewigged look-alike who pretends to play a mock grand piano beneath the sign: Franz Schubert, the world's greatest melodist – one of our boys. Along the side, to ram the point home, it declares: Schubert is OUT.

Then along comes a dizzying selection of nationalities

just to prove that homosexuality is a truly trans-national, multi-ethnic, inter-religious state of being. Razem, Polish Lesbians and Gays, are followed by an ambiguous troupe of thick-set, heavily stubbled men in Doc Martens and white spangled tutus. 'The Russians are Coming' declares their banner. I wonder if this is the climax of the Cold War.

Along comes a woman gyrating on top of another flat-bed truck, her brief white singlet straining to contain two enormous orbs of evidently unnatural composition. From time to time she releases them from captivity, one at a time, fondling them affectionately as though stroking kittens, and makes as if to offer them to the crowd. Next to me a gay boy turns to his partner and sniffs, 'She's got *some* breasts going on there.'

Ahead the Lesbian and Gay Judges and NYPD Gay Officers are attracting thunderous applause, followed by the Gay Officers Action League, GAOL.

Gay bagpipers are up next, blowing 'Amazing Grace' through bloated cheeks, and then across my line of vision stroll two men in leopard-skin bell bottoms, with leopard tails arching stiffly from their bottoms up their backs and slung over their shoulders. They both wear rough straw hats on their heads and leather chaps on their thighs, and slung low on their slim hips holsters bearing not guns but Evian bottles.

The police are busy turning back pedestrians who have strayed off the crowded pavements on to the road. A lesbian is remonstrating loudly with a fat cop on behalf of her partner: 'She's having a panic attack, ya understand?' she pleads and the baffled cop lets them through.

NY Gay and Lesbian Physicians jostle for street space with Gay Vietnam Veterans and then things turn decidedly religious: Gay Quakers, Jewish Reform Synagogues, Presbyterians, United Reform Church, Gay and Lesbian Mormons. The Catholics' gay organization is called Dignity, and its leader, who has a papier mâché Christian fish on his head, is flashing his panties at the cheering crowd. From time to time he drinks deeply from a jewelled chalice.

New York Parents and Friends of Gays look predictably out of place – middle-aged straights, awkward and self-conscious but smiling bravely. They hold up a banner saying 'We Love Our Children'.

They are followed by a pair of identical twins, identically dressed, in neutral shorts and T-shirts, whose banner reads: 'I love my gay/straight brother. Can you tell which is which?'

At the end of Christopher Street the floats turn right into Greenwich Street, where a stone-faced marshal with all the efficiency of a prison warder is shutting down their sound systems and making the grumbling party animals disperse. Their grumbling is witty and restrained, though, and they are, in fact, incredibly well behaved. No one seems drunk or violent.

I sit at home that night feeling squarer than I've ever felt.

Monday, 29 June
Joanna

I've spent the last fortnight tracking down friends who have had amniocentesis. Of all the tests offered during pregnancy, this seems the most invasive, as they puncture the amniotic sac with a needle, and it carries the highest risk of miscarriage. Needless to say if I were two years younger I wouldn't have to think about it, relying instead on various blood tests. But at thirty-six, though I have no contra-indicators, I am automatically down on the chart as 'high risk' and now stand a 1/150 chance of having a

Down's syndrome baby. Another disadvantage to geriatric motherhood.

'Have you had a chance to think about amniocentesis?' asks my new doctor, Dr Levy, gently, as we sit in the cubicle, trying to decipher the latest blurry photo from the twelve-week sonogram.

'Oh God, is it really necessary?' I grumble. 'It sounds awful and I feel fine.'

'Well, it's entirely up to you,' he says smoothly. 'We would advise you to have it, but it's your choice. There's only one thing you need to think about seriously. Would a handicapped baby be deleterious to your lifestyle?'

Peter flashes me a look of alarm.

'If it wouldn't,' Levy continues improbably, 'then there's no need to have amnio, though you might want to have one just so you know. Some people like to know in advance, so they can prepare themselves.'

Prepare themselves? Ye gods, how exactly?

'But it sounds so risky,' I mumble.

He shrugs. 'It's not without risk and we go through that with you beforehand. Nationally the rate of miscarriage from amniocentesis is around 1/350. Anecdotally at Beth Israel, the hospital we are affiliated to, I can tell you it's a lot less.'

'How many have you done yourself?' demands Peter.

'About a thousand.'

'And how many have gone wrong?'

He puts his hands in his white pockets. 'Two.'

'What happened?' Peter persists.

'Well, one was an older mother, she was forty-two; and the other, she was about thirty-two, but there were other problems . . . Look, you don't have to make your mind up now. Take a week or so and call me back. We do it at fifteen weeks, so if there is something wrong . . .' He tails off, but we get the message.

I call friends in England. None of them has had amnio, not even Louisa, who's now at the same stage and same age.

'They said it was up to me,' she says dreamily, 'and I didn't feel like disturbing it.'

Regardless of age, an informal survey of my American friends turns up that they have all had amnio, some simply to find out the sex. 'It's fine,' urges Joyce, a brisk TV producer, sporting a floral sarong over her six-month belly. 'Besides, don't you want to know what sex it is?'

'Oh, John forced me,' cries Lisa, another friend, earnestly. 'He needed to know if it was a boy or a girl so he could prepare himself.'

They're incredulous when I tell them I don't want to know until the birth. 'It's like a magical riddle,' I say, as they laugh and swap uncomprehending glances.

Flora does at least admit she was terrified of miscarrying during the procedure. 'Make sure you have a doctor with steady hands,' she e-mails. I try to recall Levy's hands, they seem plump and creamy, I don't recall them shaking.

Monday, 29 June
Peter

Joanna has insisted that I accompany her to the obstetrician to check him out. I am there to give her a second opinion. He seems a bit young, in his late thirties, with an odd guffaw. His spiel is a dizzying recitation of the odds. This business is more like the tote than the practice of medicine. Now that Joanna is thirty-six, the odds of her having a 'normal' baby have declined to 150:1. The odds of amnio going wrong are 350:1. In the 1000 that's he's done, he's lost two babies, so his own personal odds stand at 500:1.

Dr Levy is evidently the bookmaker of obstetricians. I wonder if he takes side bets on his births.

As we leave he tells us that he will be away for the next two weeks.

'I'm going on vacation,' he beams.

'Where to?' I enquire pleasantly.

'Las Vegas.'

It figures.

Tuesday, 30 June
Joanna

My mother, now valiantly trying to adjust to the idea of a grandchild out of wedlock, advises me to have every test available. I call my proxy mother-in-law, a doctor in Zimbabwe. She advises me to ignore the test, stressing she had Georgina, Peter's younger sister, at forty-one and was fine. 'If everything's fine then my motto is "leave well alone",' she counsels firmly.

'But even if there is something wrong, I'll still love it,' I say, suddenly feeling weepy.

'I wouldn't be sentimental about having a Down's child,' she says quickly.

I remember something Professor Jack Scarisbrick, head of the Society for the Protection of the Unborn Child, once told me during an interview. A long-standing advocate of pro-choice, I had gone to interrogate him for the *Guardian* during the last attempt to reduce the limit on the abortion bill in 1996.

'People with Down's syndrome bring much joy,' he said, as we sat in his office surrounded by macabre plastic foetuses representing the various stages of embryonic development. 'They never murder or steal, they are loving and friendly and it's good to have people among us like that. They bring out the best in us.'

At the time I wrote his comments down, dismissing him as naïve. Now I'm pregnant, I can see his point. What if it does have Down's syndrome? And do we want to know in advance? Now I've seen it on the sonogram, could I really face a termination? What if this is my last chance and I'm too old to get pregnant again? Is this my choice, a Down's child or nothing at all? I pull out the blurry photo for the nth time and scan it for signs that something might be wrong. Pointless. I can't make out anything.

JULY

Eyelids are starting to form. The ears are developing
internally and externally. The finger buds are visible and
the toe buds will appear at the end of the week. The
elbows have appeared, but the arms will not lengthen
considerably. The spinal cord is evident, and vertebrae
and ribs are beginning to grow. Muscles and two layers
of skin are forming.
BabySoon.com

Thursday, 2 July
Peter

Since our visit to Dr Levy I find I have become mildly obsessed with odds and the science of chance. I have been doing my own calculations. If the national figure for amnios that go wrong is 1:350 and he's had two go wrong in the last 1000 tests, then by my reckoning he's due for another blooper by 1050.

The TV headlines are full of the local Lotto. Its prize money has reached $250 million, the biggest prize ever in the world history of lotteries. Joanna is tempted to take the ferry over the Long Island Sound to Connecticut – this Lotto is unavailable in New York State – to buy a clutch of tickets. But I point out that the chances of winning are apparently 1:14,000,000.

I feel if we live by the odds then we may expect to die by them too. We want 1:14,000,000 to come up in our favour, but are desperate that 150:1 go the other way. I have inherited my mother's superstitions about these things.

Sunday, 5 July
Joanna
Supper outside at Barolo, an Italian restaurant in SoHo, and one of only a handful of New York restaurants with a garden. Between courses I go to the loo and hear vomiting coming from the neighbouring cubicle. I hesitate, wondering if I should pass some paper towels under the door or at least offer to help.

'Are you OK?' I ask finally, tapping tentatively on her door.

'I'm fine,' she calls back. 'It's only bulimia.'

Monday, 6 July
Peter
I return red-faced from the Printing House gym and check for messages. There is only one, from my indefatigable, fast-talking American agent, Amanda 'Binky' Urban.

'Hi, Peeder. Binky here. How's the book going? Call me.'

I time the message with my old BBC stopwatch. It has taken her two seconds to utter ten words, eliding them together as mere syllables of one long word.

I have been in awe of Binky Urban ever since our first encounter in her seventeenth-floor office on West 57th Street. I was ushered in by her assistant to find Binky talking into a Madonna-style headset, negotiating a deal. She wore a black sleeveless shift dress and she strode across the room, the wing of her shining blonde bob swinging in time with her pacing. She paused from time to time to squirt mineral water from a sports-top bottle into her mouth. And every time she did so the toned polyps of her biceps twitched impressively. She motioned me to sit in the mahogany arm-chair, from where I gazed out at her view of Central Park while she cut to the nub of the deal.

'Listen,' she said authoritatively into her headset, 'I see no reason to drag this out past the weekend. You know the figure that will take this off the table. Match it and we've got a deal. Otherwise we open it to an auction. Let me know by Friday lunch.'

This was the sort of kick-ass agent I wanted working for me, I thought. An ultimatum-firing, hustling deal-maker, with an appetite for the fray. But I have been anxious ever since that I may not live up to my side of the relationship. I decide to put off calling her back until next week.

Tuesday, 7 July
Joanna

Browsing through the *New York Post* I chance upon the news that Andrew Solomon, with whom we are still play-ing phone tag, has received a $750,000 advance for a book about depression. 'Three-quarters of a million bucks!' I tell Peter, who claims this news is ancient. 'But surely such a whopping advance will make it even more difficult for him to stay in touch with his depression. I mean, it's got to be pretty cheering news. Enough to make you skip off down the street and toss your medication into the gutter.'

'Maybe the advance will block him. And he'll get depressed all over again,' suggests Peter. 'It might well have that effect – he gets a big book deal and then despairs of ever delivering a manuscript good enough to warrant the advance.'

I phone Andrew to congratulate him on his mega advance, but his machine reels off a complex African itinerary: Cape Town, Grahamstown, Johannesburg, various Zambian game parks, Victoria Falls, the Okavango Delta, Swakopmund, Ongava . . . I hang up before his tour destinations end.

Sunday, 12 July
Peter

We are touring the newly opened Thackeray Medical Museum in Leeds, on a twenty-four-hour stopover at Joanna's parents, part of a flying visit to England. We appear to be the only adults here but for a few harassed schoolteachers. The rest of the visitors are schoolchildren, hundreds of them in a mobile melée of screams and shouts. In such numbers they are quite frightening, and I am reminded of the terminal scenes of *Lord of the Flies*. The museum itself is actually quite fascinating and I am immersed in an exhibit which deals with an early Irish anaesthetist by the name of Abraham Colles who practised at St Stephen's Hospital in Dublin, where he tried to anaesthetize patients by pumping tobacco smoke up their rectums. As I study the blueprint for his patented Special Tobacco Smoke Enema Kit, Joanna appears to tell me that there is a whole section devoted to the mysteries of pregnancy and childbirth. It would be an excellent idea, she feels, for me to spend time there, to help me understand what she is going through.

I dutifully examine the various exhibits and wallcharts on fertilization and chromosomes until I reach a dummy of a pregnant women clad in a loose hospital smock, sitting in the gynaecologist's chair with her legs spread wide in the chrome stirrups. The wallchart explains the basics of the gynae's trade. No one else is in the room and I feel a little odd, as though I have burst in on this most intimate of examinations. The entire focus of the exhibit lies concealed beneath the folds of the white smock, and I can't help wondering whether, like the rest of the exhibits, this one too is a 'working model'. I sidle closer to the dummy patient intending to flip up the hem to satisfy my curiosity when suddenly there is a great roar all around me and I am surrounded by a posse of particularly aggressive schoolkids. I retreat and soon they are chanting, 'Ged-em-off! Ged-em-off!' and they peel back the smock themselves to examine the dummy's genitals. But an immediate groan of disappointment goes up and they roar off to the next room.

I am left alone in the room once more. Just me and the gynaecologist's dummy, with its smock now up over its head to reveal the source of their disappointment – a smooth, plastic, genital-free crotch. It feels wrong to leave the dummy in this desecrated position so I move in to pull the smock down again and make her decent. Just as my fingers close around the hem, I hear a gasp. It is Joanna's mother. She quickly moves away and I suspect she thinks I've been interfering with the dummy.

Hanging on a peg on the wall is a strange white cotton suit of some sort. I walk over to the panel, which explains its use. It is a pregnancy suit, which simulates the feel of being heavily pregnant. There is no one around so I quickly slip it on and Velcro myself into it. I walk about briskly to get the feel of it, and then, growing in confidence, I bend to try and touch my toes. Immediately I feel a small twinge of pain in my lower back.

I feel their presence before I hear them. The school party has returned. They are soon dancing around me, jeering and poking me in my false belly as I struggle out of my pregnancy.

Monday, 20 July
Joanna

Now in my third month, I am always hungry and, though eager to order in supper, am still working out my position in the Great Sushi Debate. Since arriving in New York we have eaten sushi take-out on average three times a week.

No one cooks in New York. It wasn't until British friends came to stay, several months after we had moved here, that we first opened our oven door. And that was only because they had offered to cook Sunday lunch. My friend Meredith, who has an acute storage space crisis in her small apartment, uses her pristine oven to store her jumpers.

But sushi, comprising as it does almost entirely raw fish, presents a problem for the pregnant. According to the American pregnancy bible, *What to Expect When You're Expecting*, sushi is 'completely taboo'. But this, though widely read, is a mean-spirited tome whose advice on how expectant mothers should treat themselves includes this: 'Before you close your mouth on a forkful of food consider "Is this the best I can give my baby?" If it will benefit only your sweet tooth or appease your appetite, put your fork down.'

I am thinking of mutinying against *What to Expect When You're Expecting*, as it seems to suggest one can only expect bad things pretty much throughout the pregnancy, so I call Dr Levy and ask his advice.

'You can eat everything,' he assures me. 'Just do it in moderate amounts.'

'Even sushi?'

'Well,' he hesitates slightly, probably weighing up the legal repercussions if he gets it wrong. 'I'd say probably no more than once a month.'

I call Helen, a writer friend, to ask her advice. Now on her second pregnancy, she is significantly more relaxed than I am and I was impressed to see her tucking into a large bowl of clams last week – another food strictly verboten by *What to Expect When You're Expecting*. She laughs and assures me her doctor has told her she can eat as much sushi as she likes. 'After all, Japanese women do,' she says.

'Well, Japanese women eat it all the time when they're pregnant,' I retort, when Peter protests at my suggestion of calling Sakura with our regular sushi order.

'Well, it's up to you,' he says, 'but imagine how awful you'd feel if you miscarried because of a piece of raw squid.'

I concede grudgingly and call our regular order in to Mama Buddha, our local Chinese, instead.

Wednesday, 22 July
Peter

I accompany Joanna to her amniocentesis tests under some protest and we are both squeezed into Jeannette Patrazzi's little office, high above Third Avenue on 17th Street. The notice on her door describes Ms Patrazzi as a Genetic Counsellor – an entirely alien concept to me – but then New Yorkers have counsellors for most things, so why not genetics?

She sits us down to interrogate both of us in turn about our families' medical histories, searching for any signs of inherited diseases. On her clipboard, with all the speed of a pavement artist, her pen flashes out our genetic heritage. It is a macabre family tree that is devised by cause of death. She quizzes us about our ethnic backgrounds with all the finesse of a Nazi purist, but explains that this is necessary because you can run but you can't hide from your genetic history. It will always catch up with you.

Each ethnic group, she explains, has its own special genetic booby trap, the downside of otherwise useful environmental mutations. Blacks have a hereditary predisposition for sickle cell anaemia (a condition causing severe organ damage and blocked blood flow) which is associated with heightened resistance to malaria. Ashkenazi Jews have a 1:200 chance of carrying the gene for Tay-Sachs disease, which is otherwise associated with resistance to TB, 'a serious killer in the East European ghettos', Ms Patrazzi reminds us. 'Babies with Tay-Sachs don't live beyond the age of three. They suffer from mental retardation, paralysis, dementia, blindness and cherry red spots on the retina.'

Caucasians' genetic cross to bear is cystic fibrosis, which causes abnormal secretions in the pancreas and trachea. Eventually, she goes on, infected bronchial secretions can block the lungs and can often lead to death.

When bombarded with the concentrated treatise of what may be wrong with our baby, it seems to me amazing that anyone ever gives birth to a normal baby. With my tendency to gloomy outlooks, I naturally become convinced that we cannot escape one of the thousands of cunning inherited diseases, each a deadly reef around which our genes must navigate.

Over tea later I am skimming idly through the *New York Observer* when I spot a full-page ad for Sloan-Kettering Hospital. It features a collage of sepia snapshots from a family album. A beaming baby romps in the foreground. Underneath the copy reads: 'You've got your father's eyes and your mother's sense of humour. But how do you know you won't get your grandfather's cancer?'

Wednesday, 22 July
Joanna

The actual amnio is booked at Beth Israel tomorrow, on condition we attend a 'genetic workshop' at the hospital today.

Our counsellor introduces herself as Elena. 'Now the first thing to remember is that amnio is optional,' she smiles, sizing us up. There are four of us altogether, me and Peter – the sole man; a homely looking black woman in an African print dress called Rita, and a large, dark-haired woman with fuchsia lips so startling in her whey-faced complexion that I can't stop sneaking glances at them.

'You're probably wondering what actually happens,' says Elena. 'We find the pocket of fluid known as the amniotic sac and extract some fluid with a needle. Ultrasound is used as a guide, so we don't hit the baby, and I should tell you to bring a bottle of water with you because a full bladder tilts the uterus and makes the ultrasound easier.'

'Last time I had an ultrasound', interrupts whey-face, 'they told me to drink eight cups of water in fifteen minutes. I told them they were going to have an accident on their hands!'

'Eight cups?' exclaims Elena. 'I think they meant eight ounces.'

'Well, they said eight cups,' whey-face insists defensively.

'Well, for amnio', Elena giggles, 'one glass is just fine.'

'Does it hurt?' demands Rita.

'No, an anaesthetic is not necessary, the abdomen doesn't have many pain receptors, it is mostly fatty tissue.'

We all nod in unison.

'Excuse me, but did you just say the baby is bathing in its urine?' interrupts Peter.

'Yes,' says Elena patiently. 'And drinking it.'

'Oh, gross,' says whey-face, discreetly unwrapping a boiled sweet, smuggling it to her lips and disguising the whole action with a cough.

'Maybe Sarah Miles is right,' whispers Peter.

Holding up a sheet headed 'Chromosome Abnormalities in Live Births', Elena battles on, explaining how the baby's cells are extracted from the amniotic fluid and cultured to see if all is well.

'Now, let's look at what might go wrong with the actual process,' she says gingerly, glancing round to check we're all still listening. I am frantically taking notes, Peter looks mildly embarrassed, Rita appears alarmed and whey-face, arms crossed belligerently, has mentally checked out from the whole process.

'One in two hundred experiences a complication, though that's a national figure, and here the risk is probably lower,' Elena continues. I jot this down, vaguely aware this doesn't tally with my doctor's figure. 'It's very rare, but the baby might be too active, in which case we would stop. And if the uterus is contracting, they may have to insert the needle twice.'

There's a scraping noise as Rita pushes her chair back and drops her head between her knees, moaning. Elena passes her a bottle of water. 'If the baby moves towards the needle they remove it immediately. Or the needle may get stuck.

'Any time a chromosome is missing there's going to be mental retardation,' she adds soberly. 'Down's syndrome occurs when there are three number twenty-one chromosomes. The legal limit for abortion in New York State is twenty-four weeks,' she concludes. 'We will support you whatever your decision.'

Of the three women I am the only one to go ahead and confirm my appointment for the next day. The other two both refuse to sign the consent form. 'It's selective breeding,' says whey-face, pursing her strange lips before commanding Elena to cancel her appointment and stalking out.

'Even if there is something wrong I couldn't have a termination,' says Rita, waving at her husband who has just arrived and is mouthing apologies through the glass door.

Thursday, 23 July
Peter

Joanna, true to her tendency to do things to excess, has followed the pre-amnio instructions too literally. Her sheet has told her to present herself with a full bladder. So at the Blue Water Grill on Union Square, where we treat ourselves to lunch, she absorbs most of a litre bottle of San Pellegrino, followed by a cup of mint tea. When the grainy sonogram takes shape on the TV screen above the examining couch, the obstetrician is taken aback.

'My God,' he gasps, 'that's one full bladder. I'm surprised there's room for the baby in there.'

Joanna is mortified. She is sent out to relieve herself and returns chastened.

The grainy image is back on the screen as the doctor runs the sonogram wand over her stomach.

'Ah, that's better. Do you want to know the sex?' he asks.

'No!' says Joanna vehemently.

Personally, I would rather like to know so that I can mentally prepare myself. And also so that I can refer to it as 'he' or 'she' rather than 'it'. But Joanna has read somewhere that knowing the sex beforehand increases the chance of post-natal depression by ruining the surprise of the birth. I would imagine that the birth itself is quite exciting enough without needing the supporting act of the gender lottery.

The flickering sonogram continues for a few minutes, its image updating every few seconds while both doctors stare intently at it. They appear to see something noteworthy and swap what look like meaningful glances.

Everything is now ready for the amnio itself. Joanna squinches her eyes shut in anticipation. I am sitting at the bedhead, peeping around the curtain. I swallow dryly at the ghastly sight of the other doctor fitting a foot-long needle to a big plastic syringe. He looks like a rifleman affixing his bayonet for an infantry charge. He approaches the tight little dome of Joanna's stomach with his gleaming spike and lifts it up to gain momentum for the downward stab. Joanna's belly looks as if it will pop like a party balloon. I feel rather woozy. The doctor glances up at the overhead screen to correct his aim, so that the needle will plunge into the amniotic fluid and not into the baby's tiny body. I think I am going to pass out. I imagine myself falling forward on to the theatre of operations and knocking the doctor off his aim, causing him to stab our baby.

As the point of the needle punctures the pale taut flesh my eyes close involuntarily for a second and I fall back heavily in my chair, exhaling loudly. When I look again the large plastic syringe is filling up with a liquid that appears to be diluted urine. It is agonizingly slow, but Joanna's eyes are still safely closed and she does not appear to be in any particular pain. Finally the plastic chamber is full, and the doctor withdraws the needle in a swift clean motion and dabs the entry wound with a cotton-wool swab.

With all the bogus bravado of the coward, I find myself enquiring nonchalantly about the technical details of the amniotic fluid. It is in fact urine, explains the doctor. He confirms that the foetus drinks and excretes it. We begin our lives drinking urine. And for that matter we spend nine months suspended in a sac of piss. It does not seem to be a particularly elegant way to arrive on this earth.

Somehow I know, even before the door is closed, that the cab ride home will be the ride from hell. The traffic is flowing strongly up Third Avenue, but even before Joanna is strapped in, the driver hurls the vehicle into the fray with only the merest flick of a derisive glance in his mirror. I lean forward, all fatherly concern.

'My wife', I explain, 'has just had a big operation. She is still very sick. Can you drive slowly, slowly.' He ignores me completely and turns up the Middle Eastern disco muezzin music. We begin one of those co-ordinated red-light crossings that can happen in New York if the timing is wrong. On the fourth early red he is forced to concede to a bus.

In my early days in New York I too was an exuberantly reckless cab passenger, never giving the seat-belt a second glance and urging my drivers to ever greater speeds. But, as well as Joanna's delicate condition, there is another factor which has converted me to the cause of safe cabbing. I have recently read a piece in the *New York Times Metro Section* that said that no tests have ever been conducted on the safety of the New York cab.

The problem is not with the vehicle itself. This model has been extensively tested at General Motors' crash labs. But when it arrives in Queens some contractor whacks in an armoured Plexiglass screen. No crash-test dummy has ever been put through its paces with this thick translucent husk. In the event of a crash, the human passenger's head smashes against a screen whose overriding design requirement is to stop the bullet from a handgun at close quarters. Terrible things happen to the human face when it is in unimpeded collision with such a material.

'Please?' I implore. 'We are not in a hurry.' I look at his New York cab licence photo, which by New York City law must be displayed in full view of the passenger. It shows a surly man, who bears an uncanny resemblance to the World Trade Center bomber. His name is Ahmet Dalliwhal, and he has, I imagine, probably picked up his driving skills on the Karachi turnpike, the most fatality-strewn stretch of road in the short but violent history of fossil fuels.

'Please, Ahmet,' I implore. Using their actual names is a trick that sometimes works for me, it somehow bursts through the thick cocoon of rudeness they learn at cabbie school. 'Ahmet, you go slow?'

He looks at me in the mirror with complete incomprehension and not a little disdain.

'Oh, leave it,' says Joanna crossly, scooting right down in her seat for safety.

Thursday, 23 July
Joanna

I decide to take the doctor's advice of bedrest seriously and retire with the cordless and my address book to make some calls. I ring David Usborne, my usually chipper rival on the *Independent*, to quiz him for gossip.

'I feel dreadful,' he says. 'I've got a hangover and last night I was refused entry after waiting half an hour in line at Mother, that night club round the corner from you.'

'Why?' I ask, envisaging perhaps a fight.

'It's so humiliating I can hardly bear to tell you,' he groans. 'It was because I was wearing a cardigan.'

Friday, 24 July
Peter

Not normally given to great acts of solicitousness, I am overly attentive to Joanna, treating her as though she is an invalid or a patient who has just undergone major surgery. Whatever the risks, Joanna evidently finds my behaviour irritating. She makes it clear that she isn't interested in me talking-the-talk. She wants me to walk-the-walk. This, she makes clear, entails delivery of tea and any other required refreshments to her bedside, a general lack of personal criticism for the foreseeable future and uninterrupted possession of the TV remote control. If I comply in these, and various other ways that may make themselves known to her in due course, I will be able to prevent her from some terrible side-effect.

'Digestives,' she moans, propped up magisterially upon our California King Sized Serta Perfect Sleeper, 'I must have digestive biscuits.'

I am soon cruising the muggy lengths of Seventh Avenue in pursuit of the elusive biscuit. It takes me some time to realize that in the United States digestives are called graham crackers.

'Look,' says Joanna when I return triumphantly bearing her biscuits – she has apparently lost all interest in my bounty – 'look at the picture, isn't it sweet?'

She holds out the sonogram photo of our child. I look at it for some time. It is completely indecipherable to me. I can't make out what species it is. I can't even make out which is top or bottom.

'Look, there are its eyes, there's its nose, its little ribs just like a tiny toastrack.'

I feel as though I'm looking at one of those pointilliste games and if I stare long enough the shape of a baby will suddenly become apparent to me too. At least I should be able to clock the toastrack. But there is still nothing.

'Aahh,' says Joanna, going all soppy. 'I think it's smiling for the camera.'

I look and look some more and slowly a vague form does emerge. It appears to be a malevolent hamster. Then its shape changes. It is now a thin-faced, beaky bird: Whatever it is, it is definitely scowling.

Saturday, 25 July
Joanna

My friends with babies have all eagerly warned me about the pain of delivery, recommending epidurals at the first contraction. I'm sure I'll follow the path of least resistance, but I am currently obsessed by the tale of a New Jersey schoolgirl, who is awaiting trial for murder. She delivered her own baby in a college bathroom in total silence before returning to the dance floor.

According to reports, Melissa Drexler, a quiet, hardworking student hoping to study design at university, arrived at her school prom at 7.30 p.m. At 7.45 p.m., after complaining to her boyfriend of 'women's problems' she disappeared into the loo, only to emerge half-an-hour later with fresh make-up, her delivery over.

She then danced for two hours until a cleaner, dispatched to clear up blood in a toilet cubicle, found the baby's body, which Drexler had strangled before dropping in the trash can. Finally, a teacher deduced what had happened and confronted her.

I am staggered by this story. How could Drexler have given birth so quickly and in silence and still had energy left to go dancing? I suppose her seventeen-year-old body was in better shape to attempt this feat than mine. Though

I am fit, I am still thirty-six and in medical terms am now referred to as a 'geriatric prima gravida'. However much I prepare myself and however short my labour, I can guarantee it will not be in silence.

Sunday, 26 July
Peter

We retreat to the Hamptons on Long Island to wait for the test results. Like Paris in August, New York feels deserted in the summer; many of its residents retreat from the oppressive heat by migrating to the mountains or the seaside. I tend to think of New York as a temperate northern city, when in fact it is on the same latitude as Lisbon.

We have rented a summer place in East Hampton. There is one fact about East Hampton that tells you most of what you need to know. It has no launderette. This is the place to come for a lingering death by a thousand social comparisons. This is where celebs come to breed. It's the summer home to Calvin Klein, Ralph Lauren, Donna Karan, Lauren Bacall and Steven Spielberg. This is a place where ordinary millionaires feel poor and envious.

What on earth are we doing here?

We live in a rather grand shingled house on the Circle, close to the centre of East Hampton, the most moneyed and the most expensive of the series of manicured villages and towns that collectively make up the Hamptons. How can we afford such a desirable house? We can't. Some time ago the owner divided it into four apartments, two on the ground floor and two upstairs. And we share one of the small two-bedroom 'garden apartments' with another couple, Dani and Michael, friends from Manhattan. The idea is that we rotate weekly with them during the summer, but often we all pile down together and squeeze into the flat.

Although we like being at the seaside, we are embarrassed by our modest digs. They are smaller than most servants' quarters in these parts. In fact we go to great lengths to conceal our minute dwelling from visiting friends. We endeavour to arrange to meet them at restaurants or at the beach. We never invite them back or entertain at home. But despite our attempts at domestic quarantine, one couple in particular, smelling a social rat, has inveigled our address and ambushes us. Through the window of our little kitchen I spot Henry and Amy, an intense Wall Street couple, who are summering here. I sound the social alarm and we rush out to head them off at the door.

'Wow, that's quite a place you guys have got there,' Amy remarks admiringly over dinner later. 'Traditional shingle like that, so central, big garden, all-year rental. That must set you back a bit?'

I shrug noncommittally, realizing that she is under the impression that we rent the entire house but doing nothing to disabuse her of her upward appraisal of our financial standing.

'Your last book must have sold well,' she continues, with a probing laugh.

'Not bad. Not bad at all,' I say equivocally.

That night as we lie cramped in our tiny double bed, I am overcome by cabin fever.

'Why didn't you tell them that we just rent the flat?' Joanna asks. 'Then we wouldn't have to keep up this ludicrous charade.'

'I don't know,' I say miserably. 'I knew she'd say something condescending.'

Why did I do it? Probably because she'd already sneered at our hire car, an ugly Japanese compact with a prematurely crimped tail, like buttocks defensively clenched after an unwanted pinch. It is painted in the gruesome shade of avocado green inexplicably popular in 1970s bathroom suites.

'We journalists and writers are the court jesters to those with real money,' I complain. 'We dance around on the social periphery, performing for their entertainment, until they tire of our company and rusticate us.' And I remind her of a story told by our friend John, a columnist for the *New York Times*. He was at dinner at the house of a wealthy banker friend, plying them with anecdotes and witticisms, when the hostess turned to him and patted him on the arm. 'That's why we like you, John,' she tinkled. 'You're one of our *interesting* friends.'

As opposed to one of their peers, on the same economic level.

Joanna is snoring lightly.

Wednesday, 29 July
Joanna

We are lounging listlessly on our wooden-slatted Adirondack chairs on the porch in East Hampton waiting for the phone to ring. At the hospital last Monday Elena told us it would take six to eight days to get the results of the amniocentesis and it is now exactly a week later. I have been trying to factor in the effect of a weekend on the tests. Do weekends count, or are the six to eight days only working days?

'If the news is good,' Elena told us during the workshop, 'then we just leave a message saying congratulations! If the news is bad we leave a message asking you to call us.'

I wonder if I should phone to check if the results are in yet, but she did say 4.30 p.m. and I should probably keep the line free. The last time I can remember feeling like this was waiting for A-level results.

I can't imagine how we will react if, instead of announcing in a jubilant tone that everything is fine, they ask us to go in and discuss the results. How exactly will they word it? I suppose they must be trained to give bad news. I will, of course, insist on knowing what the results are over the phone, but what will we do if it does have Down's? We have already decided that we would insist on a second opinion, though they told us they always grow two sets of cultures, just to be certain.

Thursday, 30 July
Peter

'Which is it: Sean "Puffy" Combs or Sean "Puff Daddy" Combs?'

'I dunno. And it's pronounced "Coombes", anyway,' replies Joanna, deep in her copy of *Hamptons*, the glossy freebie that runs nothing but group pictures of society revellers.

'God, look at us!' I bluster, startling Joanna out of her magazine. 'Discussing the name of a rapper with all the exacting pedantry of a Debrett's sub-editor ensuring the precise honorific of an hereditary peer.'

'Well, at least Puff Daddy worked to get where he is,' says Joanna.

It's a fair point. Puff Daddy Combs, a black rap artist who now has his own successful record label, has exploded onto the Hamptons' social scene this season with all the finesse of a cluster bomb. He has purchased a grand manor and taken up residence there with a large retinue of flunkies, quickly becoming a fixture at major Hamptons' events, to the consternation of the Old Money set, a set that has been on the decline for some time here, vanquished by Wall Street Masters of the Universe, and Hollywood Show-people on furlough.

'Look, he's on the List,' says Joanna, once again nose in glossy.

The List is an apparently arbitrary catalogue of names of people-on-the-Hampton's-scene, selected at the whim of Jason Binn, publisher of *Hamptons*. Our fellow summer tenement dweller, Ron, who lives upstairs with his psycho-therapist wife Betsy in what is probably the only apartment in East Hampton smaller than ours, has recently unsettled Joanna with the news that he has been featured on the List no fewer than three times.

I suspect that Joanna secretly covets a place on the List, if only to call people's attention to the fact by affecting embarrassment at having appeared on it at all.

Friday, 31 July
Joanna

Everything feels on hold.

'We could tell the Schiffrins I'm pregnant, they should be back from Europe by now,' I say to Peter, as we toy unenthusiastically with eight-dollar ham and salsa sand-wiches from Barefoot Contessa – possibly the most expen-sive deli in the world.

'Why don't we wait until tomorrow?' Peter replies calmly. 'Just in case . . .'

At 4.30 p.m. precisely the phone rings. It is a researcher from the Leeza Gibbons talk show. I am strangely fasci-nated by the glamorous figure of Leeza Gibbons. The spell-ing of her name, for one thing, the ostentatiously phonetic 'Leeza'. And the fact that she was once married to Brian, the famously wooden son of Ivy Tilsley from *Coronation*

Street. Like most of Britain, I'd been amazed when Brian, aka Christopher Quentin, announced that he was getting engaged to Leeza, and giving up this prime part to follow her to the USA, there to pursue his own acting ambitions. Sadly, both the marriage and his career quickly foundered.

The researcher wonders if they could fly me to Los Angeles to talk about Princess Diana's legacy. I tell her curtly that I'll call her back.

Peter has emerged from his desk and is sitting silently on the sofa. We agree to wait until 5 p.m. and if we've heard nothing by then we'll go for a walk along the beach. If it's good news we agree to go to the local toy shop and buy a first toy.

At 5.10 p.m. there is still no news. We go to the beach.

AUGUST

The foetus now has a definite chin, a large forehead, and a button nose. *His eyelids have begun to develop across his fully formed eyes, and he is beginning to respond to external stimuli – if his mother's abdomen is poked, he will try to wriggle away.*
Dr Miriam Stoppard, *Conception, Pregnancy and Birth*

Saturday, 1 August
Peter
We have developed a routine of working in the morning and cycling to the beach in the late afternoon on our Hampton Cruisers, old-fashioned sit-up-and-beg bikes with wicker baskets, back-pedal brakes and no gears. Until we purchased these bikes we had been under the impression that the Hamptons were flat. We now know better.

After trying several beaches we favour Two Mile Hollow, a particularly beautiful beach, which curves in a shallow blond crescent in each direction. The light here is magical, soft and refracted, and it's easy to see why the Hamptons were first colonized as a summer resort by New York's painters.

Joanna claims that the adverts for the unisex perfume, Eternity, by Calvin Klein (who lives opposite Georgica beach nearby in a stunning traditional grey shingled house with its own windmill) were shot on this beach, but I'm not sure she can stand this up.

Two Mile Hollow beach is finely calibrated into very particular comfort zones. Gays to the far left, lesbians straight ahead, straights to the right, straights with kids to the far right. By and large these zones are self-enforced, though it is permissible to stroll along the water line through alien zones as long as you do not appear too shocked at anything you may witness there. Most of the potentially shocking stuff takes place to the far left in the male gay zone, but high up in the dunes, well out of casual view. In fact there is little public nudity. What exposure there is, seems to be age determined. The older you are the more likely you are to strip off.

Though the beach regulations state that dogs may only be on the beach before nine and after five, Two Mile Hollow is a popular dog hang-out all day, and the various sexual sub-tribes appear to have quite divergent tastes in canine companionship. The gays favour miniature breeds; Jack Russells, Maltese poodles and fox terriers. Lesbians tend to like bigger dogs, German shepherds, Dobermans and mastiffs. And the straights go for Labradors, the cardigans of the canine world.

Saturday, 1 August
Joanna

The President has taken time off from Monica problems to visit East Hampton for a frenzy of fund-raisers, organized by the local celebs. All week Secret Service helicopters have been hovering over Georgica Pond scoping out the approaches to Steven Spielberg's post-modern barn, where Bill and Hillary are staying. The Spielbergs have even erected a temporary indoor riding arena to provide entertainment in case it rains, though the weather promises to be excellent.

I have spent all week trying to procure an invitation to a Clinton bash, any Clinton bash. The most realistic chance I have is for Kim Basinger and Alec Baldwin's event, which is brutally tiered by ticket price. Those who have forked out $5,000 each get to shake hands with Bill and Hillary and sup in the Baldwins' dining room on seared tuna, serenaded by Hootie and the Blowfish.

A thousand bucks gets you into a marquee on the lawn, and a buffet salad, made with 'local Hamptons potatoes'; and for $250 you can stand in the outer reaches of the garden nibbling a 'locally baked doughnut' and slurping a paper cup of 'locally produced cold corn chowder'. If you're lucky, you might catch a glimpse of the President as he arrives and hear the distant strains of Hootie and his Blowfish.

It is the first time a standing President has visited the Hamptons in living memory, and the locals are demonstrating an exaggerated ennui by moaning abut the traffic congestion it is causing. Chief Inspector Stone of the East Hampton Town Police had contributed significantly to local alarm by issuing an apocalyptic warning that this weekend the three-hour journey from New York will take *twelve* hours – in the event the roads are so deserted that the journey time is cut to an hour and a half.

My contact on the Democratic Party committee, a local worthy on the board of the East Hampton Ladies' Village Improvement Society, ultimately fails to come up with the Baldwin tickets. They are in such demand, she apologizes, that she couldn't even secure one for her own daughter, who has come up from Florida specially. I have no joy playing my foreign press card. No one cares what the British media think.

I toy with the idea of gatecrashing another event, Jonathan Sheffer's afternoon cocktails, not least because I am curious to observe his garden. Mr Sheffer is the conductor of the New York chamber orchestra, Eos, and is so excited to be hosting a presidential party, with his partner Christopher, that he has had his entire lawn sprayed green. It was green before, but he wanted it greener.

The real power party was held last night at the $9 million Cranberry Dune, belonging to financier Bruce Wasserstein, who had his '16th century Scottish barn' transplanted from Europe, stone by stone.

Kelly has badgered the supposedly secret menu out of the caterer: a starter of smoked salmon in cucumber cup with caviar mousseline, duck prosciutto and white peach chutney on a corn crêpe, followed by lobster and squid salad with Louisiana shrimp, served with avocado, hearts of palm and roasted tuna wrapped in bacon with roasted asparagus.

For this, diners paid a cool $25,000 a throw, slightly outside the *Guardian*'s budget.

Sunday, 2 August
Peter

It is the last day of the President's visit to East Hampton and since Joanna has failed to inveigle her way into any of his functions I am trying to be dismissive of his presence, pretending that we are above the hullabaloo. It is my way of being supportive. We stroll into town to pick up provisions from Barefoot Contessa, only to find that Newtown Lane has been cordoned off by the EHTP so that the President can do a walkabout and gladhand the local shopkeepers. I harumpf about it, as though I am a long-time resident.

As we are returning home, waiting to cross Main Street,

the presidential cavalcade drives by. Security vehicles pass first and then the convoy slows to a halt just as the President's limo draws opposite us. We are the only pedestrians there and the President leans forward to peer at us. Up close, his grey-flecked head is enormous, as though already carved into Mount Rushmore. His features are marooned in the large puce terrain of his face. He waves tentatively, and Joanna and I look at each other, astonished, and burst out laughing. The President also seems to find some amusement in our sudden traffic-enforced intimacy and he laughs too. For an elastic moment we are suspended in this impromptu one-on-one waving session and then he is borne away by a tide of yowling sirens and strobing lights.

Sunday, 2 August
Joanna

I am beginning to develop a soft spot for Sean Puffy Combs. The ultra-conservative *East Hampton Star* has run a piece blustering with outrage about a recent raucous party he hosted at his mansion. It is reported that guests were served platters of steaming hot marijuana brownies. Apparently the EHTP are on the case. Luckily the President was not on Sean Puffy's guest list, or he'd have to swear that though he might have chewed, he didn't swallow.

Monday, 3 August
Peter

As the wait for the amnio results continues, we are becoming more irritable. We are both finding it difficult to sleep now. And the tiredness is accumulating. After watching a *Seinfeld* repeat, we crawl to bed at midnight fairly weeping with exhaustion, only to lie awake under the gently slapping ceiling fan. In the far distance the horn of the train sounds mournfully, the Long Island Railroad on its way out to Montauk. It sounds romantic, I imagine, like some sad clarion call for an unremembered age, an age before we lost the equilibrium of our existence.

Finally I fall gratefully into a deep, dreamless sleep. Then, as if there has been no perceptible passage of time, I am sitting upright in our cramped double bed – awake. It cannot be morning yet? It isn't, it is still quite dark and we are being bombarded by the big band sounds of wartime favourites. It is insomniac Eunice, the retired estate agent next door, whose entertainment centre is thoughtfully located against our thin, common dry wall. Our bedroom buzzes with the chorus of the 'Boogie Woogie Bugle Boy of Company B'. I check the time on my new luminous Seiko watch. It is 3.30 a.m.

'This is outrageous,' I say in my best censorious headmasterly voice. 'Unacceptable,' I add for emphasis.

'Well, do something about it!' says Joanna crossly, pulling her pillow over her head.

'I will,' I say defensively. I take up a kneeling position on the bed adjacent to the common wall and after a couple of practice, phantom knocks, I rap urgently on the wall.

'There,' I mutter. 'That ought to do it.'

We wait for a response. Is it my imagination, or does the big band sound grow perceptibly bigger? I rap again, but nothing happens.

'Oh, for God's sake,' says Joanna, emerging from beneath her pillow with all the menace of a scorpion appearing from under a rock, 'do it properly.' She reaches down to her bedside and retrieves a bulky Birkenstock, which she smashes furiously against the wall half a dozen times. The most immediate effect of this, admittedly, unequivocal communication of disapproval, is the thud of *Flowers on Provençal windowledge by Polly Carter, 1981* upon the sea-grass. The picture bounces and hits the bedstead, smashing its glass into the intricately woven crannies of the matting. Then the big band sound mutes.

In our aural war with Eunice, it is but a small victory. At 6 a.m. I am lying awake listening first to an advert for Saturn cars and then to the NBC early morning news. In the background of the anchorman's pumping newsdrive, I'm pretty sure I can hear Eunice's contented bourbon-fuelled snores. In the weak dawn light I notice what look like black tyre tracks upon the wall. They are Birkenstock treads. I get up to go to the loo and stand on glass shards from *Flowers on a Provençal Windowledge*.

Tuesday, 4 August
Joanna

Still no news, though I am feeling less anxious as various friends have been phoning to reassure us that this is just the way the American medical system works. It worries you unnecessarily, then gives you all sorts of tests you don't need.

At 5 p.m. I phone the genetics department. Contrary to my assumption, the receptionist tells me that it actually takes six to eight working days, so today is the earliest we could have heard anyway. I hear her flicking through papers. 'No, we don't have nothin' for you yet.'

Unable to concentrate on work, I reach for my Filofax to make some distraction calls. It falls open on 'S' so I try Andrew Solomon, but he is away again. He may be reached, says his message, at numbers in Charlottesville, San Francisco, Davis, LA, Taipei, Kyoto, Beijing, Ulan Bator and Moscow. 'Until August 13th,' his recording continues, 'I will be, variously, in the Gobi desert, on the steppe, and sailing up Lake Khövsgöl Nuur with the Mongolian navy. In an emergency it may be possible to reach me via my translator's mother at (976–1) 454.379 or (976–1) 325.723 – but don't count on it.'

Tuesday, 4 August
Peter

To take my mind off the wait I accept an invitation to play tennis at the renowned Meadow Club on First Neck Lane in Southampton, one road back from the sea. Across the street is Woody Allen's beach-front mansion. The Meadow Club has more grass courts than Wimbledon. It is a vast quadrangle of pristine playing lawn, some forty-five courts in all. Today four courts are in use. On the training courts a Serb instructor is trying to teach an elderly American woman to serve. It is not going well.

'All the coaches are Serbs at the moment,' observes my partner, Henry, the investment banker. We knock up for a while and then he suggests we play for real.

After bouncing the ball expertly up and down on the grass a couple of times, showing admirable hand-eye co-ordination, I toss it high into the famous, ethereal Hamptons' light for my first serve. I am young. I am fit. I have not bothered to warm up. As my raquet head whips down to slap the monogrammed ball in for a certain ace, I feel a rip across the muscles of my back. I am too embarrassed to own up to my pulled muscle and soldier on through two desultory sets, going down 6–2, 6–1. My opponent is exultant.

Later I drive slowly down the five miles of Meadow Lane, a narrow spit of land bounded on one side by continuous beach pounded by Atlantic breakers, and on the other by what they call in these parts, a 'pond', a sheltered lagoon.

As I drive I gawp at the single row of houses, some of the most expensive real estate in North America. Seldom has so much money been spent with so little taste. It is a gruesome accumulation of architectural follies on a grand scale – the full extent of the kitsch and the eclectic and the bastardized, tee'd up on the dunes for the merciless dissection of passers-by. Spanish villa style abuts French château and the avant-garde. One house is a dead ringer for a stealth bomber, its dark matte shingle eaves soaring and then swooping down to the sand as though trying to evade enemy radar. Dragon's Head is the first among equals, bustling to the front for the sheer enormity of its misconception. It is famous in these parts because it was retrospectively denied planning permission. A dizzy of turrets tops acres of smoked plate glass, busy little porticoes and walls of grey granite blocks, built with all the finesse of the jailhouse. It is a cautionary example of what happens when you allow the client to wag the architect.

Thursday, 6 August
Joanna

Five p.m., still no news. If we haven't heard by this time tomorrow, I will phone again. In fact, I will just check the Manhattan number in case there is a message.

There is: 'Hi, Joanna and Peter, this is Jeannette from Beth Israel. I'm calling with good news, your test results were negative. Congratulations. I repeat the test results are negative. Call me if you want any more information. This is Jeannette at Beth Israel.'

Thank God. I play the message back to Peter, who makes a whooping noise and gives me a high five.

So now we have jumped the hurdle of amniocentesis

we face, in Elena's words, 'the same risks as the general population'.

We go to the nearest toy shop, Victoria's Mother on Main Street, and have a row about whether to buy a small velvet dog or a fluffy bear in a stars and stripes jersey.

Thursday, 6 August
Peter

We go out to celebrate our amnio results at Babette's, an East Hampton restaurant that greatly excites Joanna for its frequent sightings of Steven Spielberg. He is reputed to order nothing but scrambled tofu. We order from a menu that is so pretentious it is completely incomprehensible. It turns out to be an unimpressively mushy dinner, whose constituent parts seem embarrassed to share a plate, and detract from the taste and texture of one another. I gain a new appreciation of Spielberg's tofu habit.

The couple at the next-door table have a baby capuchin monkey, which the entire kitchen staff parades up to admire.

'He is called Benjamin,' explains his owner, a thin-faced, dark-haired Colombian. 'We call him Benjie.'

Benjie is clinging to a frayed teddy bear. The staff coo and Benjie surveys them with a hostile glance. According to his mommy he is, apparently, taking a break at the Hamptons from his usual habitat, a SoHo loft. He eats angel-hair pasta and smoked tempeh and Portobello mushrooms from a saucer, palming it all into his little muzzle with tiny black fingers.

Benjie is secured by means of a collar of ribbon attached to a thin red velvet cord, a tiny-calibre version of the velvet rope used to cordon off VIP areas at night clubs. But there is considerable slack in the cord and I notice he is regarding my turkey bacon with close interest. He flares his nostrils at it. I feel sure that Benjie has had enough of tempeh and angel-hair pasta and diced Portobello mushrooms, enough of being a vegetarian. Benjie wants my meat. We lock eyes across the table and he regards me with frank hostility as one primate competing with another for scarce resources. I bare my teeth at him, surreptitiously, so the Colombian won't see. I have read somewhere that this is how alpha male primates see off competitors, by unsheathing their canines. To my disconcertion, Benjie bares his teeth back at me.

'Ah, sweet,' the kitchen staff chorus. 'He's smiling.'

Smiling? Like hell he is.

Monday, 10 August
Joanna

It is 10.40 a.m. and back in Manhattan, I have now been waiting at the doctors' surgery for fifty-five minutes. I have finished a long and much-talked about piece in the *New Yorker* entitled 'Why Parents Don't Matter', which instructs parents to stop blaming themselves if things go wrong with their children. And I have flicked listlessly through *Parents* magazine, which says that if anything goes wrong then it is all the parents' fault.

Another woman whose appointment was, I am convinced, later than mine, has been called before me to see the same doctor and I wonder if I should make a fuss. I hate doing it, but I have been advised by all my friends that when dealing with American doctors you have to show that the patient is boss.

'Always let them know you have access to a good lawyer,' Dana has counselled me. 'And let them know you'll sue.'

100

I wander up to the receptionists' desk, where the three of them are squabbling in Russian.

'Is there a problem? Why is my appointment running so late?' I ask nicely. They stop arguing and stare at me.

'Name?' asks the youngest of the three, bored and chewing, with Slavic cheekbones so fierce they look like offensive weapons.

I give it as she glances at her appointments schedule.

'There's no problem,' she says, sulkily getting up and squeezing out of her booth to place my chart in a wire holder. 'It'll be 'bout five minutes.'

I stalk back to my seat and snatch up a leaflet entitled *The New Mommies' Network* offering a selection of seminars including *Early Discipline: Setting Limits for Baby!* and *Toys as Developmental Tools.* I stuff it in my bag and gaze round the surgery wondering, not for the first time, if I should change doctors.

Unlike England, where one takes what one is given, the trouble with being able to choose your doctor is that the onus is then on you to be sure you make the right choice. Staring at the surly coven behind the receptionists' desk, I am convinced I have failed. Choice brings responsibility and I have not lived up to mine. I did not, as one should do, inspect the surgery before I made my first appointment and I certainly didn't interview each of the three doctors before signing up to their practice.

More to the point, how can one tell if someone is a good doctor? Should I ask for a list of statistics? Demand to know the survival rate of the babies they have delivered?

Then there's the address: Murray Hill. Who runs a surgery stuck out here in the boondocks of Murray Hill? Geographically, it might consider itself an exclusive arrondissement of midtown, but medically it might as well be in Minsk. Why aren't I sitting in a plush reception on the Upper East Side?

I am suddenly overcome with fury. Another ten minutes have gone and I am still here, while the woman who arrived after me has already left, grinning at me on the way out. I know they've confused our appointments, but won't admit it. Flushed with hormonal rage I feel like screaming, 'Look, I'm paying four hundred dollars a month for this, what's going on?'

'Ms Coles?'

Brandishing my chart, a short nurse beckons me to follow her into one of the small cubicles. 'Are we having our test for Down's syndrome today?' she smiles, as if talking to a child.

'Well, that would be rather pointless, given that I've already had amniocentesis,' I reply tartly as she flicks open the chart and bothers to read it.

'Oh yes, and everything was OK?' she asks, gesturing me towards the scales.

'Yes, it was fine.' I take off my jacket and shoes and step on to the scales as she fiddles about with the weights to make it balance.

'Ooof,' she scolds. 'Who's put on too much weight then? Eight pounds since the last visit. You need to halve your calories!'

'But I missed a visit,' I protest, 'so it's eight pounds over two months really.'

'Look,' she snaps, back in adult-speak, 'I'm not saying this to hurt your feelings. You've put on more than you should have and it will make it harder for you to get thin again after the birth.'

I'm almost certain she's wrong. I have been reading

Miriam Stoppard and Sheila Kitzinger so obsessively I can recite whole passages from memory and, considering I had lost weight during the first trimester, I know an eight pound gain is within the limits.

'Have you done a urine sample yet?' she asks, back in her baby voice as I smoulder over my weight gain.

'Perhaps that will take a couple of pounds off,' I mumble, disappearing into the bathroom to take aim into the tiny plastic cup. As I shuffle back into the cubicle, Dr Sharon has arrived.

She is the second of the three doctors in the practice and it's surgery policy that you have to see all three because you don't know which one will be on call when you come to deliver. I had imagined a somewhat older and reassuring figure, with whom I could swap amusing birthing anecdotes when the time came. Instead, Dr Sharon is probably not yet thirty, with a bush of uncombed hair and big unpainted toes. She looks nervous and as she pulls the tops of my leggings down I know instinctively that this is not a woman in whose presence I can lose control and lie screaming with my legs apart.

We listen to the baby's heart, which is thundering like zebras' hooves across the Serengeti, and she assures me that all is normal.

'Was there a problem this morning?' I ask, as I swing off the bed.

'How do you mean?' she says, folding her arms defensively.

'Well, I had to wait fifty-five minutes, yet the surgery didn't seem very full,' I grumble, remembering Dana's advice about the patient being boss, but feeling myself go red.

'I feel I saw you in a timely manner,' she says curtly.

'Sometimes they have problems with finding a chart. I'll make sure to bring it up with the reception staff.'

'And another thing: your nurse tells me I'm overweight, but according to my calculations, I'm completely on track.'

She glances at the notes, then looks me up and down. 'Yes, everything looks fine,' she says, arms crossed. 'Anything else?'

'Well, yes, I notice from the websites that Roosevelt appears to have much better birthing facilities than Beth Israel,' I say defiantly. I have spent the previous evening surfing the web, moving between the sites for Beth Israel, where I am booked to deliver, and its sister hospital, Roosevelt. According to the pictures on www.wehealnewyork.org, Roosevelt looks far more comfortable than Beth Israel.

'Each bedroom in our Birthing Center has hardwood floors, a large double bed, a rocking chair and a fully equipped bathroom with hydrotherapy bath,' it offers. 'Partners are welcome to stay the night and the mother can keep her baby with her at all times. Mother and baby will not be separated.'

'Well we only deliver at Beth Israel,' says Dr Sharon, adding with a slight note of menace, 'to go to Roosevelt you would have to change doctors.'

'And is that hard?' I ask.

'Not hard at all,' she smiles coldly, grabbing my chart and sweeping out of the room.

Wednesday, 12 August
Peter

I'm late for a lunch with another transplanted London writer, Joe O'Neill, who has trumped our West Village loft by renting an apartment in the Chelsea Hotel, where Sid

Vicious lived up to his name and stabbed his consort, Nancy Spungen, to death. And because I'm late I break my new economy pledge to go everywhere by bus or subway, and hurl my arm out at a passing yellow shoal of cabs. A particularly desperate cab cuts across three lanes and screeches to a halt in front of me. On its roof it bears a large internally illuminated plastic sign which reads: *Who's the Father? 1-800-DNA TYPE.*

We lurch off up Eighth Avenue, and as the driver clicks on the meter a sultry pre-recorded message advises me, 'This is Eartha Kitt. Meeeouvw. Cats have nine lives, but you only have one, so buckle up.' When Eartha has had her say, the driver, Harris Fleur, according to his Taxi and Limousine Commission ID, turns up the radio. It is tuned to WQEW, and is belting out old Peggy Lee tunes: 'Alone'; 'Misery Loves Company', and Harris Fleur is singing along lustily in an Afro-Caribbean accent. He knows all the words.

We stop at a red light and my nostrils twitch as an acrid urine smell infuses the cab. I look outside to locate the source of the offending odour until I realize that the windows are closed and the aircon turned up. Then I hear a great sigh of relief from upfront, and hear the splashing. I crane forward. Harris Fleur has fed the crinkled snout of his substantial brown penis into a waxed juice carton and is pissing noisily. He catches my eye in the rear-view mirror. 'Nowhere for cab driver to take a piss in this town. Nowhere at all,' he complains.

The light turns green and cars behind us begin honking. 'OK! OK!' yells Harris Fleur, and stabs a bird at them with the middle finger of his free hand. He flicks the cab into gear and draws slowly away. His other hand is still clutching his cock, still feeding it into the spout of the carton clasped between his thighs. Though his driving becomes much smoother, I can still hear the piss sloshing around in there.

When we reach our destination, and I have alighted, I glance back to see him leaning out of the open driver's door, holding the carton low and emptying the last dribbles of piss onto the steaming tar.

Wednesday, 12 August
Joanna

I phone Dana again for advice on doctors. 'I just don't think I'd trust Dr Sharon in a crisis,' I say, wondering if, perhaps, I have a problem with female doctors. 'If she told me to push and it didn't feel right then I wouldn't.'

'Then you must change and hang the expense,' cries Dana, with all the financial confidence of someone whose husband has recently pulled off a significant movie deal on his latest novel.

'If I was in your position, I would shop around,' she advises. 'You have to remember that obstetricians are not plastic surgeons; this is not the glamorous end of the medical market. The thing to look out for when you're interviewing them is the address. It's *got* to be the Upper East Side.' And she gives a quick laugh. 'That strip between Madison and Fifth on East 85th Street is extremely exclusive, it's near the Metropolitan. I'd try for anyone up there.'

I call our insurers, asking them to send me their latest directory, and make a note to cross out all those with addresses below East 70th.

Thursday, 13 August
Peter

I'm at Marylou's, a late-night bar on West 9th Street, with Toby, a pugnacious English writer, who has taken me out to celebrate the amnio 'all clear'. 'God has green-lighted your project,' he tells me.

We are both drunk on Martinis, the quickest way to get plastered known to man, and Toby is deep in a pidgin English conversation with a rather glamorous oriental woman. I am left twiddling with the olive in my drink when I am startled by a low moan to my left. It has been emitted by a raw-boned woman in a patchwork leather jacket and a face that serves as a cosmetics palette.

'Ohhhh,' she repeats, apparently in pain.

'What is it?' I ask, alarmed. It is my secret fear that one day I will be called upon to do the Heimlich manoeuvre, something which I have never mastered despite the fact that, by law, every restaurant and bar in the United States has a large poster with step-by-step instructions. Rather like the laminated emergency procedure cards in the seat pockets of aircraft, I have never bothered to read it.

'I ham sooo unhappy,' she complains, in a heavy Russian accent. I lean back on my bar stool to size her up. Her hair is a coarse candy floss of flax gooed together in a stiff blonde halo.

'Why are you unhappy?' I ask. It seems ungentlemanly not to enquire.

She looks me in the eye. 'Sooo many things,' she says significantly.

'Oh?'

'Many *complicated* things.'

'Really?' I say, but she refuses to be drawn further.

I try another tack. 'What would make you happy, then?'

'Money,' she says immediately. '*Money* will make me happy.'

Her occupation penetrates my Martini'ed stupor.

'You know, it might work better for you if your approach was more subtle?' I suggest benignly.

'Subtle?' she repeats suspiciously. She is unclear that I have taken it upon myself to advise her about the defects of her pitch.

'Yes, subtle. Customers – clients,' I say, quickly correcting myself, 'clients might like the pretence of romance, the illusion of love. Otherwise it's all a bit depressing, just a commercial transaction – soulless.'

Her eyes brighten with comprehension.

'You think I ham hooker?' she screeches, scandalized. 'I'm no whore!'

And with that she turns to the man on her right and begins to proposition him.

'I ham sooo unhappy,' I hear her say before I relinquish my bar stool to go to the lavatory.

The men's room is a one-at-a-time affair, useful in ensuring privacy for substance abuse. A long queue has formed outside it, curling back into the dining room. I wait in a drunken blur as the pressure in my bladder grows more urgent. The line shuffles forward very slowly, but at last I am next to go when a man appears at my side. He is wearing a white linen suit, spats, a string tie and a pencil-line moustache, a parody of a 1930s pimp.

'I need to go so ver badly,' he insists pleasantly with an Hispanic lisp. 'You let me in first. OK?' He is clearly drunk, even drunker than I am.

'Hell, we're all desperate here,' I counter. 'Go to the back of the line.'

His bonhomie evaporates at this and he fronts up to me.

'Ya let me in first, OK.' It is no longer a question. I try to size him up as an opponent. He looks like the kind of guy who might pack a flick knife. But I'm bursting to pee, and this need overwhelms my natural caution and my preference for conflict avoidance.

'No fucking way,' I say.

He approaches, getting so close I can see two fertile shrubs of dark hair sprouting from his nostrils.

His voice rises an octave in exasperation. 'Man . . .' he says, trailing off, and I can't work out if he's threatening or pleading. His ringed fingers grasp unsteadily at the lapels of my leather jacket. It is a new jacket, three-quarter-length deerskin, purchased only this morning after weeks of agonizing and comparison shopping, and I don't want it grubbied up by this incontinent pimp.

'Leggo,' I complain and I push him back. It is not intended to be a serious shove, just a 'get out of my space' sort of a shove, but he staggers backward, unable to regain his equilibrium, tottering further and further away from me, until his backside lands on a big round table. It is populated by heavy-set swarthy men with gelled hair and thick wrists, around which glitter broad gold-link chains. The men are interspersed with brittle, bottle-blonde women. The pimp sits heavily on the table, some central bolt gives out with a groan and the whole thing collapses in a crash of crockery, enfolding him in a messy mummy of linen. All is screams and hoarse shouts as the enraged diners spring out of the way of splashing wine and water and saucers of olive oil.

Just then the loo door springs open and I rush inside, seeking sanctuary. I take a long, satisfying pee and then sit for another ten minutes on the toilet lid waiting for the commotion to die down. Then I quietly unlock the door and, after a precautionary peep, I rush through the dining room. From the corner of my eye I see that a generalized fight seems to have broken out, but I dart right past it and burst out into the muggy street, where the Russian hooker accosts me again.

'I am so unhappy,' she croons, beginning her pitch from the top. She has clearly forgotten that she's already targeted me once tonight. I brush her off and set course for home, walking fast, head down.

Friday, 14 August
Joanna

Kelly phones from the Hamptons to report interesting new developments. Sean Puffy Combs's interior decorator has stormed off after irreconcilable aesthetic differences. She could tolerate the rap star's ubiquitous gold and green colour scheme, but drew the line at Puff Daddy's obsession with his monogram. He insisted she emblazon it in gold letters not only at the bottom of his heated swimming pool, but also on the bottom of his five baths, on the rim of his jacuzzi and on every towel in the $2.5 million house, including those reserved solely for beach use. Apparently, the final straw came when he told her to have it inscribed on every single kitchen dishcloth too.

'Do you think his mongram is just SC?' wonders Peter. 'Or SPC? Or even SPDC?'

Friday, 14 August
Peter

According to Radio 10-10 WINS, it is touching 100 degrees in downtown Manhattan, with humidity in the high 90s. As it is Dani and Michael's turn in our shared Hamptons' cottage, we are roasting in the city. I stroll down by the Hudson River, hoping vainly for a sea breeze and shady bench on which to sit and read my book and recover from my pounding hangover. Maybe even see a bird. So far I have not spotted a single bird in New York that is not a pigeon or a seagull. I consult the tiny map in my Manhattan diary and head for Battery Park, which, it transpires, is being dug up. A large sign informs me that the park is built on a giant pier and that the wooden supports for the pier are being snacked on by small fish called snail darters. The irony is that the snail darter had become almost extinct in the Hudson River and has only reappeared thanks to the efforts of local conservation groups in cleaning up the water. And to show its thanks the snail darter immediately set about devouring the park that is the centrepiece of conservation efforts.

I find a corner of the park that is not yet a building site and flop down on a bench, besieged by the judder of jackhammers and roar of cement mixers and compressors. Above me are the glass towers and atriums of Battery Park City and in front a flotilla of luxury yachts bob gently in the marina, their rigging tinkling like wind chimes on a Thai veranda. The biggest yacht is a sleek royal-blue sloop. Lashed to its helipad sits a small helicopter with a plastic bubble cockpit and rotors folded back like a dragonfly at rest. The yacht is owned by the business magazine, *Forbes*. Its name, scrolled proudly on its prow, is *Capitalist Tool*.

I sense rather than see someone joining me on the bench and I look up from my book. It is a human cigar – or at least a man in a velveteen cigar costume. He is impersonating a Partagas cigar, according to the strip around his barrel. His brown-clad arms reach up and slowly twist his head, representing the burning ash at the tip of the cigar. He wrestles mutely to detach it and I consider offering to help. Then it comes off with a plop, to reveal a sodden, red-faced Hispanic man with tousled damp black hair.

From a small brown furry rucksack, the cigar man retrieves his lunch – a pastrami sandwich and a can of soda. He scoffs down the sandwich, glugs the soda and belches loudly. Then he replaces his head, and flips a flyer at me from his bundle. I thank him gravely and he bows his ash in acknowledgement. Then he pushes himself up off the bench and moves away very slowly, taking tiny, mincing steps as his legs are restricted within the barrel of the cigar suit. Over and over again, as he disappears from sight, he offers flyers to pedestrians and rollerbladers, but they ignore him.

Saturday, 15 August
Joanna

I have developed a heightened sense of alertness where baby stories are concerned and am haunted by a terrible tale from Illinois that Kelly claims to have seen in the papers recently. It's so chilling that at first I dismissed it as an urban myth. But Kelly is adamant, so I do an on-line search of the *Chicago Tribune* and sure enough it is true.

Two years ago a couple shot dead a friend of theirs, an eight-month-pregnant woman and, performing their own C-section, sliced open her belly and cut out her foetus. When the police raided their house, they found the baby fast asleep under a clean blue blanket, in perfect health. The couple, who were black, confessed and were both jailed for life. It seems they had always wanted a pale-skinned child of their own.

Monday, 17 August
Peter

It is late morning and I have finally roused myself from an unproductive torpor to go to midtown and meet Tom, a lugubrious friend from *Newsweek*, for an expense account lunch at Osteria del Doge on 44th Street. So I'm sitting on the 1 train, in a busy carriage examining the adverts overhead. It seems that no bodily problem is too intimate to be canvassed among complete strangers. 'Call 1-800-Nasal Polyp' entreats the ad directly in front of me. Next to it, I am advised to ring '1-800-Anal Wart'. A woman sitting across from me follows my eye line to '1-800-Anal Wart' and I quickly look away, fearing she might think I am in need of this service.

A man bursts through the interconnecting doors from the next car. He is about forty, shabbily but not trampishly dressed.

'Good morning, everybody!' he announces in a surprisingly strong, mellifluous voice. 'My name is Steven, I'm HIV Positive, and I'm certified legally blind.' He doesn't have sunglasses on and I look at his eyes trying to work out if he really is blind. He looks right at me, and I find myself waving my hand quickly from side to side to see if he notices. His supposedly sightless gaze follows my hand for a moment before resuming its studied vacancy.

'I'm homeless as well,' he continues. 'I'm also hungry and I'm trying to raise three dollars to go to McDonald's. Can anyone spare any small change?' He passes slowly up and down the carriage, but no one can. For Steven, it seems to me, has made a fundamental tactical error in his guilt trip. He has taken on blindness, so he cannot look at us or shame us; he does not 'legally' see us at all, so we may ignore him with impunity. We do not have to stare down at the floor to avoid his accusing gaze, we do not even have to mumble a rejection as he looks beseechingly at each one of us in turn.

Bad gig, Steven.

Monday, 17 August
Joanna

Peter has been trying to shame me into using the subway more often. So today I take the 9 train into midtown. I'm sitting in a fairly empty carriage when a grizzled man sitting opposite in sandals, shorts and an Aloha shirt produces a pair of nail clippers and begins to clip his toenails. Several other passengers look aghast, but no one speaks up.

Then an errant nail clipping shoots up in a parabola and lands on the pages of a newspaper being read by a woman in a smart business suit.

'Oh, gross! That's *disgusting*!' she shrieks. 'You pervert. You should do that at home, not here.'

'What's yer problem, lady? I'm not hurtin' anyone.' He looks around for support. 'She uptight or what?'

Nobody replies and he bends down to clip his other foot. The woman leaves the train at the next stop and I slip quietly down the carriage, out of range of any further flying shards.

I take a cab home.

Tuesday, 18 August
Peter

I have developed some odd white blotches on my chest, which I think might be some sort of heat rash from too much time on the beach. I describe my symptoms over the phone to my mother in Africa, and she recommends something called Miconazole nitrate cream, an all-purpose anti-fungal cream which, she assures me, will cure it. Miconazole, she promises, is available over the counter without need of prescription. On my way back from the gym I drop into RiteAid and, overwhelmed by row upon row of medicines, I seek out the pharmacist for directions. Various

customers are lounging around waiting for their prescriptions to be filled when I arrive at the counter. I check the scrap of paper on which I have printed the drug's name.
'Where can I find Miconazole cream, please?' I enquire.
'Miconazole?' she booms in a voice that carries across the vast hangar of a store and out on to Seventh Avenue. 'For vaginal discharge?' The desultory customers perk up.
'Uh, well, no, I think it's for general fungal infections,' I say.
'Well, our Miconazole is over there in aisle two and it's for vaginal infections.' She stresses the word 'vaginal' unnecessarily and I flee down aisle two. Sure enough, the packet warns, in red capital letters, that Miconazole is 'FOR VAGINAL USE ONLY'. There is no room for ambiguity here. I conclude that at seventy-three my mother has finally lost her medical marbles.

Tuesday, 18 August
Joanna

I need another new bra. I am outgrowing them at a rate of one every three weeks. And my nipples have grown enormous. Men stare at them on the street. As Yorkshire folk would say, they stick out like chapel hat pegs.

Wednesday, 19 August
Peter

I phone my mother to query her prescription, and also to wish her a happy seventy-third birthday. And I recount to her my mortifying Miconazole hunt.
'Well,' she says indignantly, 'any pharmacist should know that there are different preparations. If a man asks for Miconazole, they should assume it's the general purpose cream, or at least they should enquire.'

I tease her that I'd concluded she was medically confused.

'I'm not past it,' she retorts. 'Let me tell you how I spent my seventy-third birthday: I was in at work by six forty-five a.m. By twelve noon I'd seen thirty-five patients. I then went to the dentist and had root canal work. Then I went over to ward twelve, the mental ward, and certified four patients in need of psychiatric admission. I'd like to see *you* doing that when you're seventy-three.'

Hell, I'm still four years off *forty*-three and I couldn't do that.

Thursday, 20 August
Joanna

'You know we are going to have to move?' I murmur over our decaff cappuccinos and 'apple crumble muffins', which I was persuaded to try for a change when I phoned in our regular order of bagels and scallion cream cheese to Barocco.

'They've no fat, no sugar and they're fifty cents off!' enticed Rosita, who takes the phone orders.

'This is disgusting,' says Peter, pushing his muffin away. 'What is it again?'

'I told you, it's apple crumble, it's good for you. It's got apple but no sugar and no fat.'

'No sugar, no fat and no taste.'

'It's such a shame,' I say, looking round at our hopelessly impractical forty-foot-long sitting room with its view onto the Hudson. 'But this is so not an apartment for babies.' Today, tidy after a whirlwind visit by Margarita, it looks like something out of *Architectural Digest* with its gleaming wooden floors lethally polished to skating standards, and stylish Roman columns installed as an ironic feature by Stephen and Christopher, the gay couple who rented the place before us.

'I suppose we could get some wicker screens like Nancy and Larry and partition off a nursery space.'

'I'm not going to be able to work with a baby bawling away behind a wicker screen,' says Peter, trying a conciliatory nibble at his muffin. 'Mind you, I can't work anyway . . .'

'I think we're talking about a boring apartment with proper rooms,' I say sadly, my vision of us living on a Woody Allen filmset finally slipping away.

'We could always put the baby in the closet room,' Peter observes, polishing off the muffin, his hand now creeping over to my plate to start mine. 'I mean, when Martin Amis was a baby he slept in a drawer and it didn't seem to do him any harm.'

Monday, 24 August
Peter

I have been strong-armed into accompanying Joanna to her doctor's appointment. What worries me, as we sit in the reception, is that nothing is alive in here. The flowers in the vases are paper hydrangeas and silk stargazers. The cylindrical glass aquarium, which stands like a transparent column stretching up to the ceiling, is in fact dehydrated. It has an arrangement of shells, several fake pink jellyfish hanging by clearly visible fishing line, a scattering of gaudy rubber frogs and a solitary plastic turtle. The aquarium sits on top of a wide, circular chrome base which reflects our images. It is like looking at yourself in the back of a spoon. We are broad and distorted and ugly. We are grotesque and now we are breeding.

Over the speakers of the muzak system comes Eric Clapton's song 'Tears in Heaven'. Written to commemorate his toddler, who fell to his death from their high-rise New York apartment, I feel it is not necessarily the most reassuring of soundtracks for us would-be parents.

Behind the desolate aquarium, displayed along the counter side, are the icons of modern payment: Visa, Mastercard, Diner's and Amex. And above them a large angry sign which declares, 'A CHARGE WILL BE MADE FOR ALL BROKEN APPOINTMENTS.' This rule apparently applies in only one direction, however. We have now been waiting for an hour past our time slot. On the door I notice another sign: 'NO news is GOOD news – you will be notified only if your pap smear is ABnormal. Please DON'T call us, we'll call you.'

Out of boredom I eavesdrop on one of the receptionist's telephone conversations. '. . . Sexual relations, that's how it passes back and forth,' she says. 'I'm gonna give you seven pills. Take one a day.' She listens for a while, before interrupting again. 'OK, honey, it's Flagil. I just wanna be sure you're not infecting each other.'

Listening with me is a Hasidic Jew in his regulation black suit, his sideburn coils trembling at his cheeks like two black springs. He purses his lips in disapproval and his eye line disappears beneath the broad rim of his black hat. Next to him sits a heavily tattooed woman, chin on chest, snoring gently.

We are finally ushered into the cubicle where the sonogram is to take place. Joanna changes into a white disposable paper robe and lounges on the examination chair beneath a pine-scented Magic Tree. I notice that the soles of her feet are filthy from padding about our apartment barefoot and I point this out. She tries to angle her feet down so the nurse won't notice. The nurse is Luba. She is stout with tight poodle curls.

'You English, yes?'

We nod.

'I'm Russian,' she says, rolling the 'r' for a lengthy breath. 'I left eighteen years ago from Moscow, under Brezhnev. I'm Jewish so I got a visa for Israel, but I came straight here. There are too many Jews in one place in Israel, it's no good. See, there's its leg,' she says, pointing at the sonogram image on her screen. 'Its toes. Its heart. Let me see if it has all chambers. One, two, three, four. Yes. Pulse one-fifty, normal. Let me see if its spine is all joined up. Yes? Mmmm, yes. See, look baby's waving, heh, heh, heh. You sure you don't wanna know sex?'

'No!' says Joanna, starting out of the chair.

'OK, Joanna.'

Afterwards, we both claim to have spotted the tell-tale signs of its gender.

'I saw a little penis,' I say.

'Well, I spotted the ovaries,' insists Joanna.

Tuesday, 25 August
Joanna

Peter has gone to Washington to discuss Zulus with *National Geographic Magazine* and I have decided to take advantage of his absence to do some initial apartment hunting. Though he has volunteered to traipse around the city with me and has already begun scanning the rental ads and drawing up lists, I would far rather do it on my own. The thing is Peter is completely unable to make a consumer decision. This tendency was well developed in London but has become far worse since we moved here, so much so that I can now barely stand to go shopping with him, either for clothes or food.

As soon as we get into a shop he is overcome by an

almost pathological gloom. Even if the expedition is his idea, after five minutes he will announce he has developed a headache or become silent and unresponsive until I suggest he goes and finds the in-store café or waits outside.

I think it comes from growing up in Africa, where he had no consumer choice, but he has no ability to commit to a purchase. He will also debate buying an item for weeks until he has battered any enjoyment from the event. Recently it took him several weeks to decide between two almost identical leather jackets and, of course, once he had finally settled on the deerskin jacket the shop had run out of his size and he had to wait another six weeks, fretting that he had made the wrong choice, until the new stock arrived.

He's just as bad with food. Last week I asked him to buy some supplies for supper and he returned triumphantly from D'Agostino's brandishing a solitary tub of potato salad and a packet of weary smoked mackerel as if he'd bought enough supplies to last a serious snowstorm. He seems permanently surprised that food we bought a week ago is no longer in the fridge.

'But we've got loads of salad stuff,' he protested last week, when I asked him to pick up a bag of 'Pre-sliced, Pre-washed, European-Style Salad' on his way back from the gym. 'No,' I remind him, 'we bought and ate it last week.' No matter how many times I point it out to him, he seems genuinely astonished that buying food must be done on a regular basis. On the rare occasions we do venture to D'Agostino's together, we only avoid a row if I take charge and ask him to find specific items, like a jar of capers or Carr's Water Biscuits. Only then, oddly, does he seem to enjoy himself.

SEPTEMBER

The baby is now completely formed. From now on its time in the uterus will be spent growing and maturing until it is able to survive independently. Lanugo (fine down) is starting to form all over the baby, following the whorled pattern of the skin. The baby is 6¾ inches long and weighs nearly five ounces.
Sheila Kitzinger, *The Complete Book of Pregnancy and Childbirth*

Saturday, 5 September
Peter

It is Labour Day weekend and we rent a car and drive down to Maryland for a pig roast, to be held at the house of a tugboat captain on the Chesapeake Bay. We have been invited by Tom, my laconic friend who works for *Newsweek*, but whose real passion is the saxophone.

The pig weighs in at 260 lbs. It lies belly down and legless on the griddle of a pig roaster made of oil drums welded together. There it sizzles for most of the day, its molasses-dark juices draining through a small hole in the griddle into a tin below. Much to the children's squealing delight, steam issues in a strong jet from the pig's cored anus. After several hours its eyes shrivel up – tiny dried peas that slide slowly down its blistering cheeks, like two last tears. Its ears swell until they are like two inflated balls. From time to time someone uses a floor mop to baste the beast. Finally its back sags and its leathery hide wrinkles into dark brown ripples as it transforms into crackling.

It is a strange cast which has gathered here on the grassy banks of Chesapeake Bay, around an original nucleus of friends who all lived on the same block in downtown Philadelphia. There is Neil – a Falstaffian character – with a rotund belly, a black beard, trousers that hang loosely by their braces, and a non-stop chatter, interrupted only by his own appreciative laughter. Neil runs an outfit called the Dumpster Divers, who scavenge for antiques and collectables at construction sites and abandoned buildings.

'Our drama group in Philly does a solstice play every year,' he tells me later as we swim in the muddy bay. 'We did one called *The Berlin Wall*. It was the year the Wall came down. We inverted the ''W'' of wall so it became *The Berlin Mall*.'

He begins singing in a rich baritone to a syncopated beat:

'They came,
They saw,
They did a little shopping.'

'That', says Neil proudly, as the words float out across the bay to the yachts on the sound, 'was the opening chorus.'

Also among our number is Talane, a thirty-something, apple-cheeked blonde. She used to be Tom's bank manager in Manhattan but is now a personal coach. 'Not a trainer,' she quickly corrects me, 'a life coach, someone who helps people achieve their goals.

'It's not like therapy,' she explains. 'I don't deal with unresolved problems of the past, I deal with the goals of the future.' She trained at Coach University, an institution which exists only on the Internet. After a six-week course she was ready for business. Her clients fill out a lengthy questionnaire, in which they must note down and prioritize their goals. But first they have to practise attaining more modest, easily achievable tasks.

'I give them homework,' she says.

'Homework – like what?' I ask incredulously.

'Like – "Go clean your closet." You see, everything you have takes up energy, so before you start on something new you have to get rid of some of the old stuff, stuff that's cluttering up your life – to make space.'

She coaches her clients on e-mail and via half-hour weekly telephone calls. Price? $50 an hour.

Sometimes she works with 'clutter consultants', who are an even newer profession. For a fee they will come in and sort out your cluttered life.

Bob the tugboat captain has rummaged through a chest and produced a British ensign. He tacks it to the side of the house next to the Stars and Stripes and the flag of Maryland. It flaps over the porch as the children swing in the hammock, as the adults munch on corn cobs and soft-shell crabs and tear at great slabs of roasted pork, and as we get slowly drunk on bourbon and beer, and a blues band blasts its music out across the wide Chesapeake estuary.

Neil joins me as I survey the scene of plenty.

'You know they had a competition once to think up a motto for America,' he says, tugging on his braces.

'Yeah, and what won?'

'I don't remember. No one remembers. But I do remember the motto that came second: "America – more of everything."' His big belly shakes as his baritone laugh booms out again over the water.

Tuesday, 8 September
Joanna

I have been advised by Kelly that the best real estate broker in the city is Feathered Nests. I call them and am put through to Inez, a proficient-sounding woman who claims she has several 'perfect' properties in our price range or, rather ominously, 'maybe just above'.

'OK, OK, I need details,' she says. 'First, you know we charge a broker's fee which is fifteen per cent of the first year's rent?'

'Of course,' I say, realizing we probably did know but had forgotten to factor it into our costs.

'Then you must be ready to fax me bank details, employment details, social security details, two personal references and one professional reference as soon as I tell you. Oh, and bring your passport. Now do you want pre- or post-war?' she asks. 'Downtown, uptown or midtown? Apartment building or brownstone? Doorman or non-doorman? Pets or no pets? Outside space important? View? Where are you now?'

'Um, well we're currently in a loft in the Village, but we're having a baby, so we need somewhere with more rooms . . .'

'You want to see a selection maybe? I can do you a selection. In fact I have a loft in SoHo which would be perfect for a couple with a baby. Perfect.'

'I'm not sure we want another . . .'

'What, you think I've been a broker for twenty-five years and I don't know what people want?'

'No no, I . . .'

'I think this property would suit your parenting needs,' she says aggressively. 'But you'll have to make it by first thing tomorrow morning. Eight a.m. Greene Street.

Perfect location. Perfect. Lots of cafés, film companies, you can mix with arty people. You're British, right? I thought so. You'll love it, it's a very European scene. Meet me there. Don't be late because I don't know how long it'll stay on the market and then you'll be disappointed and blame ME.'

At 3.30 p.m. when Peter phones from the Washington shuttle, I announce to him that I've arranged to view an apartment in SoHo.

'SoHo? How many rooms has it got?' he asks dubiously.

'I'm not sure.'

'Well, didn't you ask?'

'Um, it's sort of a loft, but the broker says it's definitely OK for a baby,' I say quickly, drawing the conversation to an end.

Tuesday, 8 September
Peter

'You didn't go *swimming* in Chesapeake Bay?' asks Jeff, interrupting my report of our weekend pig roast.

'Sure. Why not?'

'Why not? Because they've discovered a brain-eating microbe that hangs out there. That's why not! It's been chowing down on fishermen's brains.'

It is true that my memory has been even more faulty of late. And Joanna's has almost ceased to function altogether. I had put this down to pregnancy, but maybe . . . I hurry home to research the deadly lergy.

I log on to the *New York Times*'s website in search of the details and sure enough my search delivers a piece from April, alarmingly headlined: 'Fears of Deadly Organism Cast Shadow on Chesapeake'. But the site will provide me with no further information unless I am a registered subscriber.

Another piece from August is headlined 'Fish-Killing Microbe Is Found to Cause Serious Harm to People'. 'A toxic microbe blamed for killing millions of fish in the Chesapeake region', I read, 'can cause a serious but reversible neurological syndrome in humans, researchers from the University of Maryland say in a new study. The single cell microbe, *Pfiesteria* . . .'

Then the text runs out. This is all I am allowed to peep at without being a subscriber. I hurriedly register, but at the very end of the tedious process it rejects my English credit card and I am left again to nurse my burgeoning fears.

'Serious but *reversible* . . .'

Wednesday, 9 September
Joanna

Inez is waiting outside the apartment as I arrive, full of hope. Perhaps there really are child-friendly lofts and we are not looking down the barrel of suburbia in Brooklyn or Connecticut. Greene Street, like most of central SoHo, is beautiful, a corridor of grey and white six-storey buildings, zig-zagged with fire escapes. Formerly factories, most of them have now been converted to swanky loft apartments with pressed-steel ceilings, central columns and wide wooden floors.

'Joanner? I knew it was you already, even as I saw you turn the corner, I said to myself, "That's Joanner." Come, *come*,' Inez cries, pressing the apartment number and pushing the heavy grey security door as the buzzer sounds.

She's about forty-five, skinny as a starling's rib with dyed tufts of black hair, a short black suit, flat black pumps and tired, pale-blue eyes. I follow her into the industrial-style elevator, sliding the grille behind me as she grapples with the old-fashioned handle, which has to be eased slowly to the side as if pulling a pint of Tetley's.

I try to grin optimistically as we wheeze up the three floors. 'Great location huh? Isn't it? *Isn't it?*' insists Inez. I feel exhausted by her manner already. 'And I have two more for you to look at nearby, straight after this.' I nod as we judder to a halt. The door slides open directly on to the apartment, but before we can release the grille a woman of about fifty has pressed her face and wild shaggy hair against it.

'Are you a lawyer?' the woman demands suspiciously.

'Er, no,' I reply.

'No lawyers, OK?'

'I'm British,' I volunteer, hoping this detail will divert her from asking my occupation, journalism rarely scoring higher than the law in most people's estimation.

'Oh, British?' She seems momentarily nonplussed and nods permission to Inez, who slides open the grille. We find ourselves standing in the quintessential Manhattan loft: bare brick walls, hardwood floors, Sixties tie-dye wall prints and one massive window at either end.

'It's beautiful,' I murmur, briefly forgetting that it is even less practical than our present place on Horatio Street.

'Yes and we have some famous people living in this building,' the woman says proudly, 'though I can't give you their names for security reasons. How-do-you-do,' she adds formally in a mock British accent. 'I'm Renée.'

'Joanna,' I say, extending my hand, which she takes and, instead of shaking it, squeezes wetly. 'I love your apartment,' I say politely.

'Oh, everyone loves this apartment,' says Renée waving her arms expansively and laughing in a strange way. 'The trouble is, I don't like everyone.' Inez makes a little snorting noise and goes off to investigate the bathroom.

'What sign are you?' asks Renée.

'Sign?'

'Star sign. Durr. You know, zodiac, astrology, the cosmos.'

'Oh, sorry. Aries.'

'Aries is good,' says Renée, clapping her chapped hands. 'Aries is very good. And your husband?'

'Sagittarius.'

'Very compatible, very compatible, if you'd said Scorpio I'd have said no way. Rent my apartment to a Scorpio? Get out of here! Now what about your actual birth date?'

'April 20th,' I mutter, hoping that her birth sign expertise stops short of the knowledge that I share this birth date with Adolf Hitler.

'Oh, you're on the cusp with Taurus, also good,' she says. 'Very good. Now what about your moon?'

'My moon?'

'I have to know where your moon rises.'

'How did it go?' asks Peter, who is back at his desk when I return.

'Hopeless. The loft was nice but even less practical than this place and the woman who owns it was a nutter. I looked at two other places and both were completely unsuitable. I'm exhausted and I'm never going to use that broker again. I don't know, maybe we should stay here until the baby's born at least.'

Wednesday, 9 September
Peter

Over lunch today, at Vong on East 54th Street, my friend Alan Charlton announces that after ten years in Manhattan media he's finally decided to move back to London.

I know I should be telling him how we'll miss him, but he and his family live in a lovely pre-war 'classic six' on the Upper West Side, overlooking Riverside Park, and I find myself blurting, 'What's happening to your apartment?'

'Yeah, I'll miss you too,' he says sarcastically. 'Why is that all anyone wants to know? You're like a bunch of vultures circling overhead.'

When I get home I mention to Joanna that the Charltons are going home.

'So what's happening to their apartment?' she asks quickly.

Thursday, 10 September
Joanna

I am poking hungrily around the kitchen to make myself a snack when I discover a loaf of bread with the sell-by date of 24 August – seventeen days ago – which we have forgotten to throw out. But when I come to examine it, it appears to be perfectly fresh and surprisingly springy to the touch.

American food lasts much longer than British food. I am suspicious of this, but as long as you don't make a habit of studying the sell-by dates, it can be rather useful. A neighbour in Horatio Street once told me that she was convinced the reason so many Americans get colon cancer is because the food here is bursting with preservatives, which the stomach is unable to break down properly.

Dismissing this theory, I spread the antique bread

with marmalade and find that it tastes really rather good.

Thursday, 10 September
Peter

The discount electrical store, The Wiz, has, I notice today, unveiled a new slogan. The old one was: 'NOBODY BEATS THE WIZ!', but since going into chapter 11 voluntary insolvency, to obtain protection from its creditors, that slogan has become inappropriate, it seems. Now its windows are populated with huge red letters which demand: 'ARE WE HAVING FUN YET?' The question immediately begins to haunt me. It pops back into my mind unbidden throughout the day, as I walk down the street in a state of some melancholy. ARE WE HAVING FUN YET? Well, *are* we?

I think that this would have made as good a national motto as 'America – more of everything'.

Friday, 11 September
Joanna

'Uh oh, bad news for Sean Puffy Combs,' says Peter, scanning Page Six, the *New York Post*'s gossip column. 'He's been dropped from the new Oliver Stone baseball movie.'

'Oh, why? Did he have a row with Stone?'

'No, says here it's because he "threw like a girl".'

Friday, 11 September
Peter

I have been nagged into accompanying Joanna to the first session of her Maternal Fitness course at the New York Sports Club on 34th and Fifth Avenue. Our instructor, a sporty, twenty-something blonde in a grey Kansas University sweatshirt and white Lycra shorts, points to the self-conscious men: 'You', she yells, 'are the foetus police. It's your job to ensure that your wives do their daily exercises. It's like training for the New York marathon – the marathon of labour!

'The main point of all these exercises', she continues, 'is to keep your recti muscle – the one down your belly – short. Now remember a *short* muscle is a *good* muscle! I've seen some women whose recti muscles have separated so badly that I can fit my fist in the space between them. Their bellies have gotten so flabby and pendulous, that there are pockets in there and their bowels can bulge into that space. But not you, right?' The women look aghast.

'You'll be told later by your Lamaze labour coaches to bear down as though you're having a bowel movement. So everyone bear down now like you're going to the toilet.'

Fifteen people sitting against the wall all strain. I sit there, refusing to participate.

'Now, it's time to do those kegels. I want you all to *squeeeze* your vaginal sphincters.' She eyes the mutinous men. 'You have pelvic floor muscles too – come on, everyone, *squeeeeeeze!'*

I decide this is to be the last time I attend Maternal Fitness. Empathy can only go so far.

Saturday, 12 September
Joanna

Though we are keen on inheriting Alan and Sophie's rambling apartment with its extra room for a baby, we have only ever been there at night and have reservations about the area. Do we really want to swap our trendy West Village location for the Upper West Side?

'Darling, the Upper West Side is so over,' proclaims Meredith in alarm, when I mention our plans.

131

She, of course, is safely installed in a rent-stabilized, child-free, TriBeCa loft across the block from JFK Jr, his wife and their mongrel, Friday.

'Oh, no way,' I say defensively.

'*Way.*'

The truth is that neither Peter nor I have ventured much beyond Café Luxembourg on West 70th Street. And Alan's apartment is another thirty streets further north.

'It looks OK,' I say, unfolding my laminated *Streetwise Manhattan* map. 'I mean, how bad can it be? It's got Riverside Park right next door, and Central Park ten minutes east, and the Columbia campus is just up the road on 115th.'

'Why don't we take the C train to 96th and do a recce of the neighbourhood?' says Peter. 'And look, we can walk through here.' He jabs his finger on a grey square bordering Central Park, called Park West Village. 'That sounds pleasantly bucolic. Maybe we could grab a latte there.'

But when we leave the subway it becomes clear there is nowhere to 'grab a latte'. Park West Village turns out to be a series of high-rise, low income apartments, proving once again the unwritten law of public housing – that the more urban the estate the more rural the name.

The only store in sight, a small food shop, has its grey metal grille semi-drawn, as if ready to disappear within it like a nervous armadillo. On the corner of Columbus, a gang of black youths in puffa jackets, swollen-tongued trainers and sail-wide jeans are strutting and shouting. Across the street a dozen Hispanic teenagers, all wearing CD Walkmans secured by red bandannas, are performing wheelies on mountain bikes, yelling obscenities at the black gang.

'This isn't quite how I imagined it,' I say.

'Mmm, it is a bit grim,' admits Peter, as we cross Columbus and pass two overweight NYPD officers leaning against the bonnet of their patrol car, sipping Diet Cokes and eyeing the rival gangs.

We turn right up Amsterdam, past a row of scruffy bodegas which look as if they have never known direct sunlight.

'It's true what they say about Manhattan changing block by block,' sighs Peter as we slip west onto 99th Street and then hit a bustling Broadway, where every shopfront seems to offer cheap take-out.

We head west until, finally, we arrive in front of Alan's building on West End Avenue, quiet and genteel as a maiden aunt. With no commercial zoning, the solid, middle-class apartment buildings stretch for more than thirty blocks.

'It reminds me of Budapest,' says Peter, as we give our names to the liveried doorman, who buzzes up to announce our arrival.

Alan greets us at the door.

'Bloody hell, the area's a bit dodgy,' says Peter.

'Which way did you come?'

'We walked from CPW through Park West Village.'

Alan snorts with laughter. 'No wonder, man, you should never go east of Broadway that far north. Anyway,' he continues rather archly, 'if this block's good enough for Richard Dreyfuss, I'm sure it's good enough for you guys . . .'

The apartment, with its warren of separate rooms, is far better suited to a baby than our loft and we agree to take it, notwithstanding the fact that it is poised on the edge of the badlands.

'Wow, I can't believe Richard Dreyfuss lives here,' I exclaim in the lift on our way out.

'It's only Richard Dreyfuss,' grumbles Peter. 'I bet you can't remember anything he's done since s.'

'*Close Encounters*,' I retort. 'And he was brilliant in *Whose Life Is It Anyway?* He'd be handy for an interview.'

Saturday, 12 September
Peter

I return somewhat unnerved from our recce of the Upper West Side. It's not so much the fact that we will be nudged right up against the ghetto. It is the preview of domestic life that the visit to Alan and Sophie's has offered. The image I have taken away is of Alan sitting on a plump Shabby Chic sofa, while his two high-spirited young daughters stand on either side of him using the sofa as a trampoline. On every downward bounce they pat their daddy on the head, while he struggles to talk as though nothing distracting is happening. Tiring of this, they then embellish their move by yelling; 'Pee-nis head! Pee-nis head' on the downward bounce. Alan gamely chats on, ignoring them, while I struggle to keep a straight face. Is this what fatherhood has in store for me, I wonder? Reduced to a penis-head in my own home.

Monday, 14 September
Joanna

I am using our move to change obstetricians for a third time. I'm fed up with the squabbling Russian receptionists in Murray Hill and still smarting from the nurse's accusation that I've put on too much weight. So I plump for an all-female practice on Central Park West with a low C-section rate, the medical equivalent of a Michelin star.

After checking out www.wehealnewyork.org again, I

am now certain that I want to give birth at Roosevelt Hospital, on 59th Street and Tenth Avenue.

'Excellent, both Elle McPherson and Uma Thurman had their babies there,' says Meredith, who attaches great importance to such celebrity endorsements. 'And I heard that when Uma was in labour she was so hungry the doctor accompanied her and Ethan Hawke to a Chinese restaurant across the block and they all had dim sum.'

My new doctor, who has privileges at the hospital, recommends I sign up for one of Roosevelt's birthing courses.

'When are you due?' asks the course director when I phone.

'Oh, not until late January.'

'Oh, you've left it kinda late,' she says. 'I'm not sure we have anything that soon.'

'But it's still four and a half months off.'

'Most people book up as soon as they know they're pregnant,' she scolds. 'Let me see, November's full, December's full . . . The only thing I have left is the Weekend Intensive Lamaze at the beginning of January. But that may be leaving it too late. Do you want to risk it?'

'Well, if it's the only thing left . . .'

'It's all Saturday and Sunday, nine-thirty to five p.m., and you bring a packed lunch.'

'All weekend? I thought it would take an evening.'

She laughs. 'Oh no, we like couples to earn a minimum of nineteen and a half hours' credits.'

'Nineteen and a half hours?'

'Plus there's a film night we like you to attend. Your instructor will be Sigrid, you'll find she's one of the best in Manhattan.'

135

Monday, 14 September
Peter

I am wrestling grimly with my novel when I am saved by the ring of the phone. But it is a false salvation, for I am greeted by the voice of Amanda 'Binky' Urban, my American mega-agent, who wants to know how the book's going. I should really admit to her that my book is not going at all well. The problem, I have decided, is the research. I have done too much of it. I can talk knowledgeably about sexing a hyena, about the cannibalistic, post-coital foibles of the praying mantis, and antisocial behaviour in teenage orphaned elephants, in particular their worrying propensity to rape rhinos.

What I cannot do is make my two main protagonists fall in love, though this is essential to the plot. One is a forty-seven-year-old game ranger based in South Africa, a sort of Inspector Morse of the bush. The other is a thirty-five-year-old advertising executive and environmental activist from New York. Though the ranger can be quite charming, in a gruff, acerbic sort of way, he unaccountably begins to behave badly as soon as he has to share the page with her. Understandably, she finds him truculent and unappetizing. Nothing I can write seems to be able to thaw the emotional ice between them.

'It's going great,' I tell Binky. 'I'm really very pleased with it. Just smoothing out a few last things now.'

'When can I expect to see something?' she asks.

'Well . . .' I try to think of an arbitrary date sometime quite soon. 'Christmas. You can expect the first draft by Christmas.'

Tuesday, 15 September
Joanna

'Where's the *bloody* phone,' asks Peter irritably, searching for the cordless. 'You had it last. I *wish* you'd put it back on its base when you've finished with it.' He dials our number on the other line so that the ringing will reveal the hiding place of the missing handset. 'I mean is that really *such* a difficult thing to remember?'

'Shhh. You'll frighten the baby,' I appeal. This is my standard riposte now whenever we are heading for a row. But today my nagging that Peter should read my pregnancy manuals rebounds on me.

'Oh, it won't frighten the baby,' he says, picking up a copy of Miriam Stoppard's *Conception, Pregnancy and Birth*. 'In fact, rows are good for it.'

'Don't be silly.'

'Listen to this.' He starts reading from a chapter called 'In Touch with Your Baby'. 'Short periods of intense anxiety or anger (caused by . . . an argument with your partner, for example) do not appear to have any long-term negative effect on your unborn child. *In fact they may even be beneficial as they help her begin to develop the ability to cope with future stressful situations.*'

'See?' he says triumphantly. 'Far from hurting the kid, it does it good. In fact, I think we should row more often.'

Tuesday, 15 September
Peter

We are idly watching the *Robin Byrd Show* – a hard-core sex programme that takes over the neighbourhood public access Channel 35 late each night.

About twenty years ago, Robin Byrd, then a pneumatic blonde, pioneered the TV sex show. Now she is well into her fifties, and looks like a cross between Suzi Quattro and Rod Stewart, with a 1970s feathered blonde fringe drawn low over her forehead. She appears in a crocheted bikini, and looks rather out of place among the porno actors who parade across her show. Neither does she have anything much to add by way of commentary, besides her catch phrase, 'Lie back and get comfortable,' which she repeats interminably. Occasionally she cackles with random laughter.

Next up it's Holly Wood.

'Holly would if she could, eh?' More crazed cackling from our hostess. 'Holly Wood features in this month's issue of *Bust Up* magazine.'

Holly Wood has breasts like inflated airbags. Her head looks tiny in comparison. The scars from her boob job are plainly visible as she sashays earnestly to Madonna's 'Like a Virgin'.

Next up is Crystal 'all the way from Kentucky', where she is a 'feature dancer'. In no time Crystal has her kit off. She bends over to touch the tips of her shoes and the camera zooms in until the screen is entirely filled with bulging pudenda. She looks back at the camera and winks, then begins pursing her pubic lips in time to the music.

'Well, she's certainly got her kegels off pat,' says Joanna.

Robin announces that she wants to perform a number called, '"Baby Let Me Bang Your Box" – a little song that I sing about a piano.'

The show cuts to commercials.

'1-888-557-SLUT. Are *you* ready to rise to the occasion?'

'1-888-874-SUCK. Oooh! Yesss! *Please* call now!'

'1-800-TVTS. The original Chicks-with-Dicks, for the best of both worlds.'

'1-888-970-STIL. For spiked heels and more!'

'And now back to the show. First up is Kaylin Cleavage . . .'

Wednesday, 16 September
Joanna

I am staring out of the window watching a black transvestite and a young, bald, white man furtively negotiating sex behind a meat dumpster, when Peter comes up behind me singing the Lou Reed transvestite classic:

'A hustle here, a hustle there,
New York City's the place where,
Hey babe, take a walk on the wild side,
Hey Jo, take a walk on the wild side.'

He is singing it to annoy me, since I was dispatched to interview Lou Reed shortly after we arrived here and failed absolutely. He was supposed to be promoting a re-issue of his single 'Perfect Day', but in New York parlance, we had a disconnect.

I'd read in previous interviews of his tendency to be awkward, but often the people with the worst reputations turn out to be the most interesting. From the start, though, it was clear that his rap was not a bum one. He hated Time Café on Seventh Avenue South, the meeting place arranged by his PR, and insisted on trekking over to Les Deux Gamins, a cramped French bistro nearby.

'Do you live around here?' I asked, making small talk as we set off.

'That's your first question,' he said, looking at his watch, 'You've got twenty-nine minutes left.'

Once we sat down, I produced my tape recorder. 'Why are you using that piece of crap?' he asked. From then on he either repeated my questions blankly back at me or yawned as if he hadn't heard them.

After ten minutes, I'd had about as much humiliation as I could take. 'Look, this isn't going anywhere,' I said and got up to leave. As I fled, he called after me, 'I'm sorry.' Then he added penitently, as if we were lovers just splitting up, 'Can't we at least be friends?'

Wednesday, 16 September
Peter

I am puzzled by our local Pakistani newsagent. He has been consistently unfriendly to me, though we spend hundreds of dollars with him, and pay our account on time. It's not as if this is a natural coolness on his part, for he bequeaths loquacious smiles to almost anyone who comes into his cubby hole, and dispenses chirpy inconsequential chit-chat quite liberally. Just not to me. I have tried on many occasions to improve relations – trailing many conversation openers, from Test Match scores, to Benazir Bhutto's latest travails, the Indo-Pakistani nuclear race, law-and-order problems in Karachi. And I've been careful never to display an opinion in these gambits. But he just glowers at me suspiciously from behind his old-fashioned till, or starts sorting out his cigarette packets. I think I may have inadvertently offended him in some way and I am on the verge of asking him point-blank.

But today he provides the answer himself. Hardly has the chime of the security bell stopped than he is greeting me effusively by name, producing the latest issue of the *Spectator* and the *London Review of Books*, which he says he's been saving especially for me.

I can hold back no longer. 'You seem a lot friendlier, all of a sudden,' I venture.

'Yes,' he happily admits. 'This is true. I was very afraid of you, Mr Godwin.' Then he gives an embarrassed little laugh. 'You see, I thought you might be Mr Godwin, the escaped murderer. But now I checked with the police and now I know you're not!'

'What are you talking about?'

'Well, one of my hobbies is amateur sleuthing. So many people come through this shop every day, and I have an excellent head for faces, so I check all the reward notices – just in case. Some of the rewards are extremely generous. I could retire, you know. Anyway, I thought you were Glen Godwin, you look quite like him. The FBI are offering $50,000 for his capture, you know. Go and check on their website if you don't believe me.'

Later I do just that and discover that the FBI has a website of its Top Ten Most Wanted. Someone called Glen Godwin currently sits at number three. He is an escaped murderer serving twenty-five-to-life in Folsom State Prison. At least he was until late June 1987, when he became one of only three people to escape from that penitentiary, by crawling out of a storm drain down to the American River, where a getaway raft was waiting. The FBI believes my namesake to be armed with handguns and a nine millimetre rifle, and is indeed offering $50,000 for information leading to his capture, although they warn reward hunters that the fugitive is extremely dangerous and on no account to be approached by any member of the public.

I scroll down to see that the newsagent is right. Apart from the same surname, Glen Godwin is exactly the same age as me and of similar weight and height. There follows a photo gallery of Glen Godwin, in various poses, and he does look unnervingly like me.

I briefly consider getting a laissez-passer from the FBI,

assuring any party who challenges me, that I am not Glen Godwin the former construction worker turned dangerous fugitive, but Peter Godwin the former journalist turned blocked writer; that I am unarmed and relatively unthreatening unless relentlessly provoked.

Thursday, 17 September
Joanna

We are becoming infected with the American idiom. This morning at breakfast I hear myself using the word 'conflict' as a verb. 'I'm conflicted over what to write this week,' I moan.

Predictably, Peter, who is more of a linguistic purist, rounds on me. I defend myself by hailing the great messy potage of current English – which thrives as a welcoming stew, absorbing all manner of grammatical gristle, street slang and newly invented vocabulary.

But the truth is I started doing it just to annoy him and now I seem to have lost control of the process. Yesterday I caught myself describing how my pregnancy 'has impacted on our relationship' and then a bit later on I heard myself describe how my London flat had once been 'burglarized'. I have even begun saying zee instead of zed.

But Peter 'has issues' with even the most obscure of Americanisms. He is irritated, for example, that Britain's shish kebab has, on its trip across the Atlantic, reshuffled itself into 'shish kabob'. 'Why?' he keeps asking whenever he sees it on menus. No one seems to know.

Thursday, 17 September
Peter

I am on a Marmite run in Myers of Keswick on Hudson Street in the West Village. It is a strange little establishment, an English general store circa 1950, faithfully preserved in expatriate aspic, patronized by immigrant Brits, ex-Rhodes Scholars and Anglophilic gays. In the window stand pyramids of canned Heinz soups and baked beans, Bisto, Dettol, Lucozade, HP sauce, Golden Syrup, Nescafé Gold Blend, McVitie's Ginger Nuts, Vanish stain remover, Robinson's Barley Water, Ambrosia rice pudding, Yorkshire Tea and plain old Typhoo – all the foibles of the peculiar British palate.

It was from Myers of Keswick that Fergie, already the spokeswoman for Weight Watchers, apparently ordered four sausage rolls, prompting the *New York Post* to speculate that she was bulimic. The next day, one of Fergie's assistants rang the *Post*, insisting on a correction to make it clear that three of the sausage rolls were for her friends.

Inside the gloomy shop the walls are decorated with tea towels bearing the Union Jack and the Welsh Dragon. The owner, who originally ran a butcher's shop in Keswick in Cumbria, sits working at his paper-strewn desk in the corner of the shop, like some Dickensian clerk.

I come away with not only my Marmite, but a Scotch egg, a box of custard creams and a packet of Wall's pork sausages.

Back home I present my bounty to Joanna.

'Why on earth did you buy this?' she challenges, snatching the Scotch egg and brandishing it angrily. 'It's things like Scotch eggs that made me leave Britain.'

I have no idea now why I bought it.

Friday, 18 September
Joanna

This morning I determine to solve the mystery of where Margarita goes. She turns up early, bins the trash and does a few other cursory tasks, and then loads our swollen bag of laundry into her battered shopping trolley and disappears. She does not burst back into our space until about one p.m., when she wheels in our cleaned and folded clothes, fretting about terrible queues in the basement laundry. Then she sets to the apartment with her formidable turbo vacuum, sucking up admirable amounts of dust and various baubles besides.

'Listen, I don't care how long the bloody queues are down there, it can*not* take *four* hours to do the washing. She's just taking the piss,' complains Peter.

So today, after she's been gone for a couple of hours, I wander down to the laundry room myself, seeking an explanation for her prolonged absences. I peep through the window pane of the door to see her darting between teetering piles of alien washing and the long bank of humming washing machines and dryers. She has all the synchronized efficiency of a magician spinning plates.

It becomes clear to me Margarita is in fact running a laundry business, mostly on our time.

Friday, 18 September
Peter

Panting slowly along the Hudson on my thrice-weekly jog – now that I have given up rollerblading – I approach a small dog of indeterminate breed, wearing a Black Watch tartan coat. Its owner, an elegant middle-aged man dressed in a peppercorn tweed suit, accessorized with a gold fob watch and a Leander pink paisley hanky peeping from his top pocket, has hoisted the dog up by the tail so that its two rear legs are several inches off the ground, and he dabs fastidiously at its bottom with a rolled-up ball of tissue.

A gaggle of toddlers mills by and one little boy yells out in astonishment, 'Look, mommy, a doggie getting its butt wiped!'

I notice that the dog wears an expression of resigned humiliation.

Saturday, 19 September
Joanna

Peter has read somewhere that it takes seven minutes for the average person to fall asleep. He's now perturbed that it takes him far longer than that and decides to time himself. But I point out there is a practical difficulty: he will fall asleep before he has done the final clocking. I refuse to lie awake timing him, which leaves him the option of setting the alarm – to see if he exceeds his seven minutes. But that seems counter-productive, even to him.

In any case, he worries about the Heisenberg uncertainty principle – that by studying something, you inevitably change the thing you study. The very act of trying to measure the time it takes him to fall asleep will in itself distort that time. He falls asleep almost immediately pondering this problem.

Saturday, 19 September
Peter

I am shopping in D'Agostino's, incredulous as ever at the sheer swollen size of everything in American supermarkets. It is as though an entire culture is on steroids. Orange juice comes in gallon containers, chocolate in slabs the size of roof slates. As I wander down the aisle, tubs of something called 'I Can't Believe It's not Butter' compete with neighbouring vats of 'Move Over Butter' for my shopping dollar.

On my way home I wander absently through a fair in the street neighbouring ours. There are bright pennants fluttering in the breeze and music and crowds and stalls, people eating candyfloss and corn on-the-cob and drinking out of beer bottles concealed in brown paper bags. But two yards in I realize that this fair is not as other street fairs: everyone is in black, many with studded bodies. Some wear spiked dog collars. And the stalls are selling bondage gear; whips and cuffs and giant, gnarled plastic dildos. I am wearing shorts and a T-shirt and deck shoes, carrying my grocery bags. I smile brightly as I walk through, nodding companionably like a country vicar negotiating a ghetto.

Sunday, 20 September
Joanna

'I'm going to change the light bulbs,' says Peter, bursting into the sitting room dragging our red stepladder behind him.

'But we don't need new bulbs,' I say mildly.

'This is no ordinary bulb,' he says, holding it up against the window as if it's a glass of fine claret. 'This is a full-spectrum bulb which mimics natural sunlight. It will stop you being depressed,' he promises.

'But I'm not depressed,' I protest.

'Well, I think that we may both be suffering from early SADS, seasonal adjustment disorder syndrome, it's caused by lack of exposure to natural sunlight,' he carries on, wobbling from the top of the stepladder as he unscrews the old bulb.

It is true that, while our loft is wide and high, it only has windows at one end, and the further you penetrate into the interior the darker it becomes, requiring lights on throughout the day.

'I saw this news story about an old people's nursing home where both the staff and the inmates, even those with Alzheimer's, were hugely rejuvenated after full-spectrum bulbs were installed,' says Peter.

To my amazement he has purchased an armful of these bulbs, at $10 a piece.

'Much cheaper than a shrink,' he says. 'Right, now I'll go and change the one in the kitchen. Can you try and observe if it makes any difference?'

Sunday, 20 September
Peter

Susan, a New Zealander web designer, a friend-of-a-friend, has set up a website for my last book, *Mukiwa*. She has connected it to various search engines so that it can be tracked down by people interested in Africa. The site itself has various click-on links, a blurb about the book, a specimen chapter and a rather blurred picture of myself, trying to look contemplative and authorial, but managing to appear, it seems to me, faintly phoney.

It also has a guest page. So today, as I do every few days, against my better judgement, I log onto the *Mukiwa* site to see if anyone has left a message on the guest page. After an initial flurry of comments, mostly from old school-friends trying to contact each other and hurling jocular abuse at themselves and me, the page has become sadly inactive of late. It now appears to be stuck on guest number forty. My habit of checking the clearly moribund web page is now verging on self-flagellatory, but I can't seem to resist these futile peeks. And I wonder about all the forgotten websites that orbit unvisited through the great galaxy of cyberspace, like ghostly outer planets on which all signs of life are absent.

Monday, 21 September
Joanna

'How are you feeling?' asks Peter. I suspect he's being unusually attentive because he's about to leave for Africa.

'Fine,' I say. 'Why?'

'D'you think the full-spectrum light bulbs are making any difference?'

'Um, not yet.'

'No. Neither do I.' He looks crushed. 'But perhaps the Heisenberg uncertainty principle has distorted our judgement?'

'It's only been twenty-four hours, maybe they need a big longer to take effect.'

Monday, 21 September
Peter

I am on my way to South Africa on assignment for *National Geographic Magazine*, cruising at 35,000 feet, thinking about my life. Not the mundane 'to-do' list of everyday existence, but the grand organic sweep of it all. This happens every time I take a transcontinental flight. Cocooned in a protected capsule, soaring and uncontactable – I am provided with a spiritual enema. I measure my life in these solitary aeroplane journeys, as close to God as I now come.

I have begun to think of aeroplanes as flying cathedrals, or at least in the way that secular folk use cathedrals – as catalysts for contemplation. Even the layouts are similar. The aisles are naves and the altar is the cockpit. The priests are pilots and the stewards and stewardesses are altar boys and girls. And just like cathedrals of old, some pews – the ones endowed by the wealthy – are closer to the altar than others. First-class seats are always closest to the cockpit.

We, the passengers, are on a journey from one place of being to another. And rather as rival religions offer us spiritual flights to essentially the same Nirvana, so competing airlines hustle to take us to the same destinations. Regular churchgoers are rewarded just as frequent fliers are, with grace, which serves as religion's airmiles.

Tuesday, 22 September
Joanna

I am lying in bed in my room at the Tower Hotel in the shadow of Tower Bridge, staring at the brown bend of the Thames. I should be sleeping but for the last hour I have been hunched in the bathroom being violently sick. In four hours' time I am supposed to go and finalize the details of my new job at *The Times* but feel so ill I cannot imagine ever leaving my bed again. In front of me stretches an intricate series of appointments which I will now have to unravel.

In desperation, I contact the hotel doctor.

'I'm pregnant and I've just been very sick,' I moan.

'Well, up to the sixteenth week it's quite normal to be sick,' he says wearily, evidently fed up at being roused for an apparently routine query.

'But I haven't been sick at all throughout my pregnancy, this is the first time,' I blub.

'Well, as I say, it's quite normal. I wouldn't worry.'

'I think it might have been the baked potato with tuna,' I speculate. 'I live in America and I'm already high risk, I'm thirty-six.'

'That's not considered high risk in England,' he mutters. 'You may have mild food poisoning then, but in any case

there's no danger. Call me back if you feel any worse.'
Terrified I may have poisoned the foetus, I lie in bed and weep.

Friday, 25 September
Peter
One of the main attractions of writing for *National Geographic* was to avoid the bustling deadlines and occasional danger of hard news.

But my plan for a safer, more in-depth journalism seems to have rebounded. On this trip I've been shot at several times, mostly in fairly ludicrous circumstances and mostly unintentionally: A fusillade in honour of an assassinated Zulu warlord went awry when a stoned gunman lost his footing on the freshly dug grave soil and scattered bullets at head height. Then a traditional Zulu stick-fight turned anarchic when a warrior walloped the referee, and a general fire fight ensued. And this was supposed to be a safe 'anthropological' story.

Saturday, 26 September
Joanna
Back in Manhattan Meredith calls to suggest supper, to cheer me up in Peter's absence. 'But we'll have to go Chinese,' she says, 'I'm only eating lightly steamed vegetables.'

I've grown familiar with Meredith's food fads, which usually stem from passing allergies, and decide not to pursue this one. But she's determined to tell me anyway. 'I've discovered I'm allergic to dairy,' she continues.

'How did you find out?' I ask.

'Oh it's kind of obvious. I've been feeling toxic for some time,' she says vaguely. 'You know, bloated and nauseated and, well, I went to see Madonna's herbalist last week and she said I was suffering from yeast-takeover.' She stops and then whispers conspiratorially, 'Meat is truly poison, darling, and so is dairy. From now on I'm only eating living foods.'

'Living foods?'

'Raw things, darling, uncooked fruits or very lightly steamed vegetables and I'm really into tofu. You should try it. Really. It would make you feel so much better.'

Saturday, 26 September
Peter

I arrive in Miami at dawn and am bounced from the immigration line and sent for 'secondaries'. I am getting quite experienced at the dreaded secondaries, and obediently follow the sign to a great hall presided over by immigration officers, who sit behind a counter elevated out of punching reach, so that I have to stand on tiptoe to hand up my documents. Then I sit for several hours, among large, remarkably patient families of Mexicans and Colombians, Haitians and Brazilians, waiting to be grilled further on our intentions, should we be permitted to enter the USA.

Eventually my number is called and I am directed to a glass-walled office in which sits an immense female Latino officer.

'Good morning,' I say.

She nods without looking up as she frowns over my dog-eared letter from the US Embassy, explaining that I am in effect the 'common law' husband of a resident alien.

'The Federal Government', she explains, as many immigration officers have done to me before her, 'recognizes no such thing.'

I nod meekly.

'It's simple,' she says, as though addressing a backward child. 'Either you're married or you're not. Which is it?'

'Not,' I admit.

'Then ya gotta problem,' she says, tapping her biro on her intricately doodled blotter. 'Ya can't just keep on comin' in an' out as a tourist. I mean you're practically *livin'* here!'

'Well, I thought the letter from your Consul in the London Embassy explained the situation.'

'Yeah well, *that's* the State Department. *This*', she says tapping the badge pinned to her blouse, 'is the Immigration and Naturalization Service. We got our own rules.'

'My girlfriend is six months pregnant,' I appeal.

She shrugs, unmoved, and I realize that this woman has probably heard every single species of hard-luck story and special pleading imaginable to humanity. I cannot compete with refugees and torture victims. Nothing I say is going to have the slightest effect on her. I decide that my best hope is to play a waiting game. The hall behind me is filling up with what appears to be most of the contents of a flight from Bogotá, and the officers have to keep the line moving along – quotas to maintain, performance goals to achieve.

'Well?' she says, almost disappointed that I don't seem to be dancing the tacitly agreed steps of our immigration tango, where I beseech and she ruminates. Instead I affect resignation.

'Well, of course, it's up to you,' I admit.

I begin idly to flick through the pages of my passport, examining the stamps and noticing that the smaller and less important the country, the more florid and attention-seeking the stamp.

'Oh, all right,' she humphs. 'I'll give you six months, but you sort this out, right?'

I thank her and shoulder my way through the teeming

ranks of the Third World, many of whom, I fear, are as close to their American dream as they will ever come.

Sunday, 27 September
Joanna

We are pursuing my fantasy of renting somewhere warm after the baby's birth, somewhere to recuperate in the sun. But we are constrained by all sorts of limits: we must stay in the USA, where our health insurance works, and we must be somewhere accessible by land, as my doctor has frightened me with new evidence linking early air travel with infant cot death syndrome. And it must be somewhere warm in January. So we settle on Florida, a twenty-hour train journey by Amtrak Sleeper.

My current plot is to rent a small conch house in the old town of Key West. I have never been there, but I imagine a month of lazy days with the baby strapped to Peter's chest, gurgling contentedly, while we breakfast over the newspapers in an open-fronted café on Duval Street, a favourite hangout of Hemingway's in the 1930s. In the afternoons I intend to swim my way back to pre-maternal trimness in the warm turquoise shallows. My chief influence for Operation Key West is Alison Lurie's novel, *The Last Resort*, in which everyone seems to live in pastel-painted wooden houses weighed down by crimson boughs of bougainvillaea.

Key West's added attraction is that it's always been a writer-rich environment – home to more Pulitzer Prize-winning authors than anywhere in the States. At least that's what people keep telling us, but other than Hemingway we've had some difficulty finding out just who these other writers are. The only writer mentioned in my Florida guide-book is the poet Robert Frost, who used to spend his summers there in a small cottage, which is now a Heritage House Museum.

Peter has agreed to Operation Key West on condition that we do a recce first. So after spending several hours on KeyWest.com, I have set up a series of meetings with real estate agents, all of whom claim to have exactly what we're looking for. Now I am in Miami waiting for Peter to join me en route from Africa. There is only one problem: Hurricane Georges has arrived in the Keys to meet us.

Tuesday, 29 September
Peter

We are in South Beach, waiting for Hurricane Georges to blow itself past the Keys, so we can drive down there to find somewhere suitable for Joanna to stage a warm-weather postpartum recovery. Our gilded cage is the Delano Hotel, the twenty-storey temple of South Beach Art-Deco, swathed in the all-white velvet bondage of its over-designed confines. In our small corner room the floors and walls and curtains are white, the bedspread and towels and robes are white, the TV and hi-fi are white. White, white, white. This is what it must be like to go snow-blind.

In the late morning we take the ghostly red-lit lift to the white mausoleum of the lobby and pick up the newspapers at the hotel shop. There, in amongst the emergency toiletries, Joanna discovers a small box labelled anal floss. She thinks it must be a joke, but this is South Beach and I'm not so sure.

We stroll down Ocean Drive to the News Café, to breakfast on eggs and home fries and large glasses of juice made from pulped Florida oranges. The sound system throbs with Vivaldi and Debussy. It is barely ten a.m. and the electronic billboard on top of a nearby high-rise tells us that the temperature is already 93 degrees.

As we read the papers over coffee, sculpted youths with bare midriffs and bodies pierced with jewellery, rollerblade or scoot on skateboards down the avenue of palm trees. Convertible cars with their tops peeled down cruise slowly by, once, twice, their occupants absorbing glances gratefully. Even the huge chromed tractor unit of a juggernaut joins the passing parade, looping back to make several unnecessary passes. It is a boulevard of attention seekers.

We walk back to the Delano, crossing the sidewalk to seek out the broken shelter of the shady side. Back at the hotel we descend to the pool, which is lined by squads of white-uniformed waiters and attendants. Beyond is a wooden fence and the beach, but few feel the need to venture out there, content to wallow here, in our own amniotic sac.

Our companions are hard-bodied gays, and louche, overweight middle-aged businessmen, whose skins are irradiated to carcinogenic ruddy brown husks. They are escorted by much younger gum-chewing girlfriends, who sport artificial breasts which rear up from their lurid bikini cups like clenched buttocks, and lone tendrils of tanga strap which snuggle in the clefts of their real bums. Their nails are long and curved and painted to match the colour of their bikinis, lime green or candy pink. Their hair is big and aggressively blonde. The girls seem perfectly comfortable being ogled by the rest of us. They float on Lilos around the pool languidly exhibiting their wares. One of them, I notice, has a tattoo on her calf and I swim closer to examine it. It is a bank of roses, and under them the word 'Princess'.

Next to the fat men there is an absolutely vast young man, a great pear of a body layered by a black suit and tie and wrap-around Ray-Bans. He is obviously a bodyguard and he sits in the sun fairly spurting sweat.

So our day passes, as we wait for Hurricane Georges to clear the Keys and make Key West accessible again. The news reports say that no one is being let in, except for locals.

Wednesday, 30 September
Joanna

It is so hot I can hardly bear to leave the air-conditioned sanctuary of the hotel. Peter has insisted on booking a convertible, imagining he is something out of *Miami Vice*, but every time the automated roof yawns open I nearly pass out with the heat. So we cruise around with it tightly battened down and the air-con on full blast. To make matters worse my only summer maternity dress is lined with acetate, which sticks to my thighs every time we go out.

Miami is America's most popular location for fashion shoots and skinny Ford models mill around the hotel lobby and out on the veranda, giggling like schoolgirls, their jumble of long loose limbs held together only by their string bikinis. I feel more pregnant than ever, among these gambolling sylphs. Lounging under an umbrella by the green Gunite pool, I realize we haven't seen a single child, either at the hotel or strolling down Ocean Boulevard. Miami Beach is even less of a breeding ground than the West Village.

Wednesday, 30 September
Peter

We leave early in the morning to see how near Key West we can get before we are turned back. The drive seems interminable, through the suburban sprawl of south Miami, but at last we are in the Keys, with the blacktop road rollercoasting up over causeways flanked by azure seas – real azure, not touched-up, brochure azure. Soon signs of the hurricane damage appear; posses of cherry pickers poke up at the fractured technological tentacles of overhead electricity cables and telephone wires; broken branches and trees line the roadside. We pass a trailer park which has been splintered and torn and splayed open like a wound for passers-by to peer inside.

Then the traffic slows to a halt and we are at the police cordon. I open the window to let the muggy air pollute the chilled recycled air inside and hand our press cards to the black state trooper. He scans them through the narrow slit between the rim of his hat and the top of his Ray-Bans, and compares us with an expression of incredulity that anyone would voluntarily go to Key West at a time like this. Then he waves us through.

OCTOBER

The baby now has eyebrows and some hair on her head,
and she is continuing to gain weight.
If the baby is a boy, his testes have formed
and are beginning their descent out of his body
and into the scrotum, but they are still located
inside the abdomen.
Now that the baby is about five months old,
she will be able to use her own immune system
to help defend herself against infection.
BabySoon.com

Thursday, 1 October
Joanna

After cruising the chaos of Key West the only accommodation we find open is the Southernmost Guest House. It is a grand, grey-fronted Victorian house, trimmed with filigree, run by a garrulously hospitable grandma. She is wearing a V-necked black net top, exposing a good deal of improbably pneumatic cleavage.

'Surgically enhanced and why not, hey?' she laughs gaily, squeezing her shoulders together proudly to give us the full effect, before reaching for a key on a huge wooden fob. 'Welcome to the only house on the street to have electricity!'

We follow her up the stoop and onto the first-floor balcony, past a wooden love seat swinging lazily from the eaves. The tiled room is excessively fussy, with lacy tablecloths draped across every surface. Empty champagne bottles – the souvenirs of many a honeymoon – line the bookshelf, next to vases of silk flowers. On the table sits a giant brandy snifter, in the bottom of which languishes a china mouse, presumably trapped. But we notice none of these things, just the welcome roar of the air-conditioner and the deliciously chilled air.

'Seventy-five bucks, that's half my normal rate, plus breakfast, well, coffee and cake downstairs,' she offers. We take it.

Thursday, 1 October
Peter

Most of Key West is still without electricity and the town is filled with the din of dozens of mobile generators and freezer units on refrigerated trucks, and the noise of pumps, and cranes and bulldozers clearing the debris, and the buzz of dozens of chainsaws being used to cut the hurricane-felled palms into smaller clearable chunks. There are great mounds of stinking seaweed in the streets, and dead birds everywhere.

The shops and restaurants and many houses are boarded up, often with defiant if banal messages to the hurricane spraypainted on the shutters. 'Go away Hurricane Georges!' 'Key Westers say NO to Georges.' 'We HATE hurricanes.' On the shutters of a sunglasses shop is the message, 'Shades is closed till further notice – you don't need sunglasses in a hurricane.'

The town itself is almost entirely depopulated. Only a few hardy eccentrics remain, defying the warnings to evacuate. A black woman with a bleached blonde Afro, purple bell-bottoms and white patent-leather platforms, cycles up and down, one hand on the handlebars, the other making frantic signs of the cross.

And later, on the boardwalk at the marina, we run into a one-legged, one-armed, drunken Ahab figure. 'You'll see, this will come to no good!' he warns us in the tones of a Doomsday prophet.

The only place we can find to eat is Mangoes on Duval Street, which Amy, its indomitable owner, has kept open throughout the hurricane, as an emergency cafeteria. But we must get there for supper by 5.30 p.m. and be gone before 7 p.m. when the curfew kicks in and the National Guard begin patrolling the town for looters.

As we scuttle up the unlit street from Mangoes back to the Southernmost Guest House just before curfew, Ahab bursts out of a side street. 'Your stars are ill-placed!' he bellows, brandishing a bottle of rum and giving us both a tremendous fright.

Back at the Southernmost Guest House the electricity has finally gone down. The big white air-conditioner stands silent and the temperature steadily rises while we try to judge the moment when it will be cooler to open the windows to the steaming doldrums outside and lose the largely illusory remnants of refrigerated air within.

Friday, 2 October
Joanna

Our forays into Key West's rental market have not been successful. We soon discover that most of the real estate agents have scarpered and only two of our viewings have survived. The first I have arranged with an absentee landlord, whose apartment I found posted on KeyWest.com.

Though the apartment is advertised as 'classic Key West architecture', we arrive at a gated complex of modern white wooden houses. A wiry walnut of a man in his

160

seventies, dressed only in micro cut-off denims and a sea captain's hat roosting on the back of his head, strolls out to greet us.

'Hi there, people, I'm Argo and you must be the Brits to see Otto's place,' he says, hand outstretched. His chest is trellised with a froth of grey hair, and a thin stream of sweat emerges from under the peak of his cap, along his bushy right eyebrow, and down his cheek. His little brown dugs tremble as he bids us follow him up the stairs to a second-floor apartment. It is tiny, a fact the landlord has tried to disguise with a multitude of angled mirrors and smoked glass. 'It kind of reminds me of the Middle East,' says Argo sincerely. 'Not that I've ever been there. But Otto has.' We are in and out in four minutes.

Our second appointment is with Keith, a grey-faced young agent. He insists on firing up an ancient moped and leads the way, weaving erratically in and out of the fallen trees.

Our first stop appears to be the conch house of my dreams. Pale lilac with a little stoop, it is midway down a charming street in the old town, with a courageous palm tree still standing in its little patch of garden. 'It sleeps nine,' says Keith, having some difficulty propping up his moped. He fails to mention that all nine would sleep in narrow dorm beds squeezed into two small bare rooms and that the place has clearly been repeatedly trashed by shifts of freshmen for the last ten years.

His final suggestion turns out to be a huge concrete development on the edge of town, built in a horseshoe around a pool now bobbing with driftwood and seaweed. Circa 1970, it has all the appeal of a penitentiary with long, bare concrete corridors which eerily echo our conversation. 'This is awful,' murmurs Peter and we make our apologies.

'I'm not sure a twenty-hour train ride with a baby *is* such a good idea anyway . . .' I start.

'If we set off now, we could get the last flight back from Miami to Manhattan,' he says quickly. We leave Keith at the gate to Key Alcatraz, frantically pumping his kickstart.

Friday, 2 October
Peter

We pack our bags, settle up with supergran, and set off on the four-hour drive to Miami. As we negotiate around another pile of fetid foliage, a piece of it detaches itself, and rolls down in front of us. It is Ahab, our personal doom-monger, come to bid farewell. He stands up in front of the car, his beard and clothes festooned with bits of seaweed and palm fronds, and gives the bonnet a tremendous thump with his old wooden crutch. 'You are blighted!' he rages, shaking his bottle at the now sunny skies. 'Calamity is upon you!'

I hoot and he staggers away, throwing himself back on to the great mound of fly-hazed seaweed from which he becomes again indistinguishable.

Monday, 5 October
Joanna

Back in Manhattan I am now suffering from heartburn and unable to sleep. I lie in bed surfing aimlessly through the seventy-six channels we receive via Time-Warner cable.

On Channel 2 David Letterman is reading a news item about students in a social-studies class whose teacher had set them the arduous task of biting slices of toast into the shapes of American states.

Over on Channel 34, public access television, a man in sunglasses is introducing a photograph of his own misshapen penis, which twists like an 'S'. This, he explains solemnly, is a symptom of Peyronies's disease, then he tries to sell his own patented technique for penis enlargement. Twenty minutes later, when I flick past again, he's still there, with the same photo of his unusual penis displayed onscreen.

Tuesday, 6 October
Peter

I try Andrew Solomon again. His answer message informs me he's away on another trip and furnishes me with contact numbers in London, Istanbul and Patmos. 'Until the 11th,' says his message, 'I can in principle be reached on a Turkish boat phone, number (7-095) 969.74.39, though I am mistrustful of both that redoubtable technology and our captain's language skills.'

Wednesday, 7 October
Joanna

Though they are usually keen to recommend local services in exchange for a tip, the doormen are unable to suggest anyone to help us move apartment, so I resort to looking in the back of the *Village Voice*.

'Don't worry, lady, this is a small job for us,' says Ira, of GV-Moving-For-All-Your-Needs. 'We'll deliver the packaging materials in advance and our men will arrive on the dot of eight a.m.'

The packaging arrives as promised and I am rather impressed to find there is much more of it than I had ordered.

'They're clearly used to people underestimating how much stuff they've got,' I rationalize to Peter, who is silently assembling cardboard boxes of various sizes.

'That's what I like about American companies, they seize the initiative.'

'It'll be rip-off,' says Peter. 'New York movers always are.'

By 9 a.m. the following morning, I have phoned Ira twice and both times I've been fended off by the voicemail. I leave a message on a random extension and eventually a woman calls me back to assure me a truck is on its way but has been delayed due to the terrible traffic. 'But you're only in SoHo,' I protest.

'The office is in SoHo, but the truck is coming from New Jersey,' she says.

At 11 a.m. it finally arrives with a crew of five, headed by a twitchy redhead who introduces himself as 'Your foreman, Isaac, I am Israeli.' For the next two hours they proceed to wrap everything we have not already packed in vast swathes of bubble wrap, including the bed and sofas, though we assure them that wrapping them in blankets would have been fine.

'We don't want any tears in the fabric,' warns Isaac, winding vast straps of masking tape round and round the mattress.

'He seems very cautious,' I whisper approvingly to Peter. By 2 p.m. we are done and hail a cab to the Upper West Side.

An hour later there is still no sign of Isaac and his gang.

'They've probably stolen all our stuff,' says Peter gloomily.

'Of course they haven't,' I say, but I'm privately relieved to see the truck finally straining up West End Avenue. As Peter shows two of the men to the service elevator, Isaac pulls me to one side, fidgets quickly on a notepad and presents me with the bill. It is for $1,839.

'You pay me now,' he says. 'Cash only.'

'But that's *three* times the original quote,' I exclaim. 'I'm not paying that.'

'It's the packing materials,' he says rudely, shoving the figures at me. 'You used twelve rolls of bubble wrap. And we've used sixty rolls of masking tape, twelve wardrobe boxes, forty book boxes, six hi-fi boxes . . . Then there's the three hundred dollar service charge.'

'But no one told me I had to pay for those separately,' I start, suddenly realizing how naïve I've been. 'And no one told me about a three hundred dollar service charge.'

'Well, it's compulsory,' he shrugs, folding his arms across his sweaty grey Gap T-shirt. 'Sixty bucks per worker. Then there's the travel time because the traffic was so bad it took us three hours to get to you this morning. Then another hour to get here from the Village . . .'

'But why did no one tell me about this? That's why I got a quote from Ira.'

'Ira, schmira,' he says. 'It's not my fault.'

He kicks the side of the van, where our possessions are still hostage and I stomp off to the cashpoint to get more money.

When I return to the apartment, I wait for them to unload our belongings. Then I slip into the kitchen to phone Isaac's boss. He claims to have no record of my original quote.

'But Ira faxed it to me,' I say, waving the fax at the phone.

'Ira doesn't work here any more.'

At this point I fall back on the phrase I have found most useful since living here. 'Look,' I say in what I hope is a calm but menacing voice, 'I feel it's only fair to tell you at this stage that I am a lawyer and your company has already violated several state regulations ... In addition I have a quote on paper ...'

'OK, OK,' he says quickly. 'Fifteen hundred dollars.'

'Twelve hundred,' I counter. 'That's still twice the original estimate.'

'OK, OK,' he says again, wearily. 'Put Isaac on the phone.'

The two of them then have a screaming argument about the service charge, which Isaac has clearly invented.

'I wasn't going to take it anyway,' he shouts at me, flinging the receiver down. I hand over the $1,200 cash and he storms off, his four silent cohorts trailing sullenly behind.

'Never mind,' says Peter as I slip the deadbolt on the door. 'At least it's all over and we're here now.'

It isn't over. Ten minutes later the boss calls back to say he has decided to sack Isaac for imposing the bogus service charge.

'Well, that's your decision,' I start, when Peter starts frantically mouthing, 'No, no, don't get him sacked, he knows where we live!'

And so I spend the next few minutes ludicrously trying to defend the surly crook who has just tried to rip us off.

Thursday, 8 October
Peter

I am walking up Broadway, north from 96th Street, returning with Joanna from a trip she has forced me to take to a local grocery she has been recommended, the Gourmet Garage. On the window it calls itself 'a working-class deli', but in fact it is full of yuppies buying mesclun leaves, unpasteurized manchego cheese, white truffle oil, and organic granola with dried strawberries.

The Sherpas of Broadway throng about us, hardy delivery men from Ecuador, Peru and south China who live frugally in rooming houses and remit most of their pay to families in their distant homelands. Short and wide and sturdy, like tough little pit ponies, they haul groceries and take-out food on their bikes, riding on the sidewalks, where they slalom through the pedestrians and careen the wrong way up the street, fearlessly dodging the heavy, erratic traffic. They chatter to each other in harsh mountain Spanish and in ejaculatory Cantonese diphthongs, unseen and unheard by the middle-class residents of West End Avenue and Riverside Drive. It reminds me of South Africa in the old days, where blacks were socially invisible to whites.

Friday, 9 October
Joanna

Brunching with Kelly, Jeff and several of their friends I recount our experience with Isaac. They are unsurprised. Our story, it turns out, is a standard tale of Manhattan moving, if not a rather lame offering. Meredith announces that last time she moved apartments her possessions were safely in the truck when the foreman demanded to know how much tip she was planning to give him.

'I don't know, it depends on how much gets broken,' she joked, having set aside $40 for each of the three men.

'Well, lady, how much gets broken depends on the tip,' he leered, sticking his unshaven chin alongside her cheek. 'I usually recommend a hundred dollars a man or it's not worth our while. If anything gets broken, you can always claim on insurance. Do we understand each other?' She ended up forking out $300.

We spend the rest of the day unpacking boxes, keeping an uneasy eye on the door should Isaac suddenly make a reappearance, wielding a crowbar or worse. Around 8 p.m., exhausted, we flop down and start channel surfing until we hit *20-20*, America's equivalent of *Watchdog*, presented by Diane Sawyer, famous for her low but alarmist tones.

'In tonight's show, *20-20* goes undercover to expose bogus moving companies who move your belongings right out of your sight and right out of your state!'

Several people describe their possessions vanishing for ever. 'I realized the truck was moving off in the wrong direction for our new house but I never realized they were robbing us,' sobs one woman. 'I just thought they knew a quicker way to get there.'

'The advice from the experts', Sawyer concludes, 'is never select a moving company from the back pages of a newspaper or magazine. Only go for established companies and always ask for personal recommendations. And now, the man who hired one of the country's top paediatric surgeons to help his crippled pug dog walk again! We'll be right back after these messages . . .'

Friday, 9 October
Peter

At a book-launch party today, where the VIPs all had to wear name tags, I notice a genial chap labelled Maurice Sendak. The name is familiar but irritatingly unplaceable. And then, on the way home, I remember that he is Maurice Sendak, the-slowest-writer-in-the-world, the one who snails along at 190 words a year. I have missed my opportunity to congratulate him on this feat.

Saturday, 10 October
Joanna

Unwilling to leave her flourishing launderette business, Margarita has refused to work for us in the Upper West Side, so I have been touting for cleaner recommendations from residents in our new block.

Today I am sitting wrestling with a column when there is a rap on the door and through the spyhole I see the telescoped face of a brightly henna'd woman staring at me.

'Hello,' she says in an Eastern European accent, when I open the door. 'I am Sofia. I hear you look for cleaner. I am cleaner. Good cleaner. Mallory in 13D recommend me. I am Albanian. I clean for you?' And reaching for my hand, she says, 'You show me apartment, I tell you how much. Yes?'

Impressed by her efficiency – I only asked Mallory if she could recommend someone yesterday after bumping into her in the lift – I obediently give Sofia a quick tour, during which she whistles at the scuffed wooden floors. 'Apartment, bad condition, very difficult to clean,' she says finally. 'I think five maybe six hours' work. One hundred dollars.'

'I'll have to think about it,' I reply, baulking at paying $20 more than we paid Margarita and realizing that I should at least ask Mallory for a reference.

'I am Albanian,' she says again. 'My family? I don't know where they are.' And to my horror she starts to cry. 'I don't know where they are,' she shudders again. Unable to go back to my work, I make us both a cup of tea and try, without much success, to follow a complicated narrative which ends with Sofia's arrival, alone, in New York.

'Four years,' she says holding up four bitten fingers. 'I have been here four years. I wanna go back, but now not possible.'

I listen with a mixture of guilt and irritation at Sofia's distress and my ignorance of the internal politics of Albania and Kosovo. I give what I hope are supportive but noncommittal sounds.

After about twenty-five minutes of this, she perks up. 'Mondays is good for you, yes?'

'Let me talk to my boyfriend,' I say weakly. 'Give me a number to call you.'

'No number,' she says, rising decisively from the table. 'I come back tomorrow. OK?'

'OK,' I say, with a non-specific sinking feeling, realizing it will be more or less impossible not to hire her.

An hour later, in pursuit of a Starbucks' decaff, I bump into Mallory again in the lift. 'Thanks for sending Sofia round,' I say. 'Is she reliable?'

'What? I didn't send her round.'

'Well, she just came to see me on your recommendation.'

'But she's terrible,' Mallory exclaims. 'Goddamn it, she must have seen a note I put on my desk about you. I've been trying to get rid of her – she's lazy, she's always late and she's expensive. I hope she didn't spin you all that Albanian bullshit. I can't believe she told you I recommended her.'

'Is it bullshit? She seemed terribly upset.'

'Perleeze,' she says, rolling her eyes. 'She told you her family were missing? Yeah, right! They all live in Brooklyn. Listen, my uncle has a cleaner who he really likes, I'll get her number for you. But don't take Sofia.' And she stalks crossly out of the lift and into the back seat of a chauffeured Lincoln town car, throbbing patiently at the kerb.

170

Saturday, 10 October
Peter

Joanna is complaining that I snore – an allegation which I hotly refute. She says that she wouldn't mind if it were a regular, comforting snore which she would find almost sweet, but that I emit arbitrary snores of varying durations. She claims to be worrying that I may be choking in my sleep, or even that I stop breathing for unnaturally long periods. In order to clear up this matter, we agree to place my tape recorder beside the bed, set on its voice-activate function.

Sunday, 11 October
Joanna

Meredith phones and offers to give us a housewarming.

'I can't face it,' I say, 'we've still got tons of boxes to unpack and we haven't got enough furniture.'

'What's to face?' she laughs. 'Think of the gifts. Everyone brings gifts to a housewarming.'

'But we don't really need anything except big stuff, like another bed,' I say, adding ungratefully, 'and I don't want loads of knickknacks.'

'No, no, you need a theme for gifts,' she says, ignoring me. 'What about bar tools?'

I cringe. 'Meredith, we don't even have a bar!'

'Oh, everyone needs bar tools, darling,' she scolds. 'Ice tongs? ... How about a crystal bowl with special ridges to hold lemon slices? Tell me, do you actually *have* one?'

'No, of course not.'

'For drinks parties I find mine indispensable. I know,' she cries. 'Marquetry!'

'Marquetry?'

'Yes,' she laughs expansively. 'Picture frames, mirrors,

171

inlaid wooden trays. Darling, it's perfect. *Everyone* loves marquetry.'

Sunday, 11 October
Peter

Over breakfast I rewind the tape and play it back. The sound is a long continuous roar, like a large antelope in pain. Joanna laughs so hard she almost falls off the kitchen stool. But I point out that the continuous roar is a distortion caused by the tape switching on for a snore and off again as soon as silence reigns. 'It discriminates,' I complain. 'It doesn't give me credit for the silences – there could be hours in between these individual snores when I was breathing quietly.'

Later I look up snoring in my *Merck Manual of Medical Information*, only to discover an appalling complication: sleep apnoea. 'Because symptoms occur during sleep,' explains the *Merck Manual*, 'they must be described by someone who observes the person sleeping. The most common symptom is snoring, associated with episodes of gasping, choking, pauses in breathing . . . In severe cases, people have repeated bouts of sleep-related obstructive choking . . .' Other side-effects of sleep apnoea are 'Headaches, excessive daytime sleepiness, slowed mental activity', all of which I suffer from. Eventually, warns the *Merck*, sleep apnoea can result in heart failure. The treatment ranges from trying to sleep on your side to wearing an oxygen mask in bed and, finally, a tracheotomy, where surgeons drill through your neck to gouge a permanent hole in your windpipe.

As I cannot trust Joanna to give an accurate report of my sleeping habits, I am thinking about booking into a sleep lab for overnight polysomnography, where they will attach electrodes to my head and measure the 'physiological parameters' of my slumber. Will my insurance cover this? I wonder, as I fall asleep.

Monday, 12 October
Joanna

Unable to face Sofia, I retreat to my study and tell Peter I won't answer the door.

'You have to deal with her,' he says. 'Otherwise she'll just keep coming back.'

At 5 p.m. Sofia pops in to finalize the deal. I flee to the kitchen on a pretext and leave Peter to talk to her. Soon I hear them apparently deep in conversation and hesitantly return.

'I met Zog once,' Peter is saying pleasantly, 'when he was in exile in Johannesburg.'

'Who?' Sofia asks.

'Zog. King Zog?'

She shrugs.

'The pretender to the Albanian throne?'

Sofia is looking uneasy now.

'Enver Hoxha, was he as bad as we all thought in the West?'

'Hmmm,' says Sofia, noncommittally. She glances at her watch. 'Oh God, I'm late for next job. I call back tomorrow,' and she rushes for the door.

We never hear from her again.

Tuesday, 13 October
Peter

One of the cures for sleep apnoea is to lose weight, so I have returned to my jogging regimen with renewed ferocity. I run beneath an arched avenue of lushly foliaged oak trees along Riverside Park, a thin green finger that stretches sixty blocks along the Hudson. To the east is Riverside Drive, lined on one side with grand apartment buildings and French Beaux Arts townhouses – it was Manhattan's poshest residential Zip code at the turn of the century. To the west, across the Hudson, is the shore of New Jersey. My northern view is framed by the gigantic iron span of the George Washington Bridge. Beyond the bridge, on the Jersey side, it is green and rustic, amazing that it is but an oar's dip from this teeming island of Manhattan.

Though it is a beautiful boulevard designed by Frederick Olmsted, the man who landscaped Central Park, Riverside Park remains a largely tourist-free zone, the crowds favouring his more famous project.

As I jog up Riverside Drive, I pass an extraordinarily cosmopolitan selection of monuments: Joan of Arc sitting astride a charger; a large limestone frieze commemorating the New York Fire Horses; a bulky medieval Japanese figure lurking under the portico of the Buddhist temple at 105th Street – Shinran Shonin, founder of the Jodo-Shinshu sect. The statue is a survivor of the Hiroshima atom bomb, and was shipped to America in 1955 to promote world peace.

At 106th Street the brooding figure of a goatee'd Franz Sigel gazes across the river as he kicks his spurs into the greened bronze flank of his steed. I have no idea who Franz Sigel is and his plaque bears nothing but his name. Samuel Tilden, Governor of New York and unsuccessful Democratic presidential candidate in 1876, stands at 107th Street.

A statue of Lajos Kossuth, Hungarian patriot, has been erected at 113th Street 'by a liberty loving race of Americans of Magyar origin'. And two streets on, at the summit of Claremont Hill – where the Battle of Harlem Heights once raged during the Revolutionary War – the tomb of

General Ulysses S. Grant, a vast, white, colonnaded mauso-leum, stands guard at the corner of the campus of Col-umbia University, itself built on the site of the Bloomingdale Insane Asylum. The august grandeur of General Grant's sepulchre is undermined somewhat by encircling Gaud-íesque benches, whose bright mosaics, depicting mermaids and sharks, camels and whales, taxi cabs and Donald Duck, were added by a Chilean artist and his 1200 local volunteers in the early 1970s.

As I turn for home, my T-shirt sticking wetly to my back now and my calves burning, I notice a small carved urn inside an enclosure on the edge of the park. It turns out to be the Monument to the Amiable Child, placed here in memory of a five-year-old boy who fell to his death from these cliffs two hundred years ago. On the urn's pedestal, its letters smoothed now by a blotchy carpet of lichen, is a reminder of our mortality from Job 14:1–2, 'Man that is born of a woman is of few days, and full of trouble. He cometh forth like a flower, and is cut down: he fleeth also as a shadow, and continueth not.'

Upon my breathless return, I look up Franz Sigel in the *Cambridge Biographical Encyclopaedia*. But the entries jump straight from 'Sièyes, Emmanuel-Joseph, Comte de – French political theorist and clergyman born 1748 . . . whose pamphlet *Qu'est-ce que le Tiers-état* stimulated great bourgeois awareness,' to the Holy Roman Emperor Sigismund, born 1368, who rebounded after a defeat by the Ottoman Turks to conquer Bosnia, Herzegovina and Serbia – a task that looks particularly impressive today.

Of Franz Sigel, there is, alas, no sign. He has not made it into world history's top 16,000, so I feel my ignorance of him is excusable.

'Have *you* heard of Franz Sigel?' I ask Joanna.

'Is he an actor?'

'No, I think he must be a German patriot of some sort, but I can't find him in my *Cambridge Biographical Encyclopaedia*.'

'Maybe he's eyeing Schwarzenegger's mantle,' she suggests, deep in a copy of *Daily Variety*.

'Schwarzenegger's Austrian. Even I know that.'

'Austrian shmostrian. Ever heard of the Anschluss?'

'Did you know that I'm related to the Earl of Wessex?' I ask, ignoring her. 'He was a Godwin. I read in the *Cambridge Biographical Encyclopaedia* that he was the chief political adviser to King Canute.'

'So your ancestor advised King Canute to stand on the shore and bid the tide not to come in. That figures.'

Tuesday, 13 October
Joanna

Today I receive my weekly update from BabyCenter.com, an online resource centre I discovered a fortnight ago while surfing the web during a sleepless night. After registering my due date, I now receive regular e-mails outlining our baby's development.

The real attraction, however, is the other subscribers' personal stories, which appear on BabyCenter's various bulletin boards. Today's story comes from the Depression Bulletin Board, where new mothers are encouraged to air their baby blues.

It is sent in by a Colleen Leslie, and her experience is not encouraging. 'I made the biggest mistake by having this baby,' she writes morosely. 'Before, my husband and I were so happy, and now our lives are completely different. My husband is stressed out, too. We both don't like being parents and wish we'd never made this mistake.

I just want to have my old life back and be able to be alone with my husband again. I've thrown away my happiness.'

Normally I forward my weekly updates to Peter to keep him abreast of what's going on. Knowing his propensity for gloom, I keep today's to myself.

Wednesday, 14 October
Peter

In addition to Columbia grad students nursing single cappuccinos while they tap away at their Macintosh PowerBooks, trying to complete their dissertations, my local Starbucks, on Broadway at 103rd Street, is populated by a flock of hands-on dads. Their babies are slung upon their chests in Baby Bjorns, a popular brand of papoose. The dads sit there, sipping their coffees and exchanging proud, goofy new-men smiles with one another. I cannot imagine that I will ever be this kind of father.

Today, at Starbucks, there is a new character who is causing a ripple of alarm through the grad students and the Bjorn-again dads. He is an amateur news impresario, a Matt Drudge of the coffee house. A huge Jabberwocky of a man, with his small head perched on the summit, he sits at a table on his own, eking out his small mug of house blend, and performing as though he is being interviewed on a chat show. His subjects are topical and he is well informed and very opinionated, plucking quotes from literature and analogies from history with a remarkable facility for both.

Actually he exudes a rather superior brand of guff than the real daytime topical talkshows, and instead of avoiding him I find myself trying to sit within earshot to hear his rant.

177

'I'm glad you asked me that, Jim,' he begins. Apparently today he is an imaginary guest on the *Jim Lehrer Show* on PBS Radio. 'Gays in the military. So what's new? Bah, there's been pansies in the armed forces for centuries, it's *full* of them. Alexander the Great, military genius, best general of all time. And a faggot.'

On the offchance, I ask him if he knows who Franz Sigel might have been.

'Another military man,' he declaims, without missing a beat. 'Civil war general, on the Union side, of course. Don't think he was gay. He *might* have been. After the end of hostilities he retired from the army to edit a German-language newspaper. Now what *was* it called?'

Wednesday, 4 October
Joanna

Though we have yet to spot our building's most famous resident, Richard Dreyfuss, this has not stopped us talking to him.

'Hello, Richard,' says Peter to an imaginary Richard Dreyfuss, as we get into the empty elevator. 'I thought you were *marvellous* in *The Valley of the Dolls*.'

'One point – everyone's seen *Valley of the Dolls*,' I scoff. According to our point system, the smaller the part, and the more obscure the film, the higher the score. We are also allowed to suggest bogus films, but if successfully challenged, forfeit six points.

'Richard, I thought you were terrific in *The Apprenticeship of Duddy Kravitz*,' I counter.

'*Apprenticeship of Duddy Kravitz*?' says Peter sceptically. 'Never heard of it. I challenge.'

'It's set in Montreal's Jewish ghetto,' I say confidently. 'Made in the seventies, I think. So that's six points you forfeit and six points to me for obscurity, plus a bonus point to me because it's Canadian.'

Thursday, 15 October
Peter

I should be working on my Zulu piece for *National Geographic*, but instead I am watching David Letterman's late-night talk show on CBS. I am watching it with the sort of fascinated horror of Europeans impaled on the satanic trident of American popular culture, affecting to despise it even as we are consumed by it. Letterman is introducing a succession of ever more bizarre guests performing novelty acts: a bald grocer tosses a toilet plunger into the air, getting it to land on his head, where it suctions onto the dome of his pate. He then takes a bow and the plunger handle describes a low arc like a unicorn's horn.

Now it's a duo who perform tricks with marshmallows. One man inserts a marshmallow up his nose and blows it out to his colleague, who tries to catch it in his mouth. He misses the first two but successfully captures the third and eats it, and the trick is repeated in instant slow-motion replay.

I have finally had enough of cranial plungers and nasal marshmallows, so I flick rapidly through the channels. A snatch of urgent Fox Newsdrive headline assails me: 'Up next – new parents, beware – there's something in your crib that could *kill* your baby!' Now they're plugging the next day's show, *New York Live*, 'Cure Cancer the Natural Way, and Real Life Encounters with Angels!' I flick channels again. 'Up next: a New Hospital for Repetitive Sexual Predators Opens in New Jersey!'

Thursday, 15 October
Joanna

Irma, our new Polish cleaner arrives. A small but determined shrimp of a woman with a Mickey Mouse headscarf that she shows no signs of removing, she grabs the vacuum and immediately repairs to the bedroom, where she remains for at least an hour. Anxious she leave sufficient time to do the laundry, I go to find her. She stares at me blankly before producing a grubby piece of paper with a number on it. 'Phone, phone!' she orders.

I dial the number, give her the receiver and she says something in Polish before handing it back.

'Hi there, this is Nicky, Irma's niece,' says a New Jersey voice on the other end. 'Irma says she doesn't understand what you need her to do. In future, rather than ask her directly can you just call me and I'll translate, OK?'

'Er, OK,' I say, my heart flagging. 'Can you ask Irma to do the laundry then?' I hand the receiver back. Irma cocks her head to one side, nods and hangs up.

Half an hour later she returns from the basement. 'Phone, phone,' she orders again. Once more she says something in Polish, then hands me the receiver. 'Hi, it's Nicky here. Irma says you should send your laundry out because the facilities in your basement are too old.'

'Oh,' I say nonplussed, handing the phone back.

'This is not going to work,' says Peter, as we retreat into his study and debate in whispers how we can resolve the situation. Ten minutes later, Irma raps on the door.

'Phone, phone,' she demands. Knowing the drill, I wait as she hands me the receiver. 'Hi, Joanna,' says Nicky. 'Irma says she can't come for the next two weeks because she's going on vacation to Orlando.'

Friday, 16 October
Peter

Joanna's brain, as has been widely predicted by her growing library of pregnancy books, is beginning to turn to mush. On the long and winding road between lobe and tongue, many words go missing – punching through the cerebral crash barriers into the gloomy mental tundra of almost recalled dreams, nearly remembered names and untethered sentence ends.

As her memory deteriorates, I am mildly panicked. She is my social seeing-eye dog. She can recognize and name people from across the room and cue me with their identities, through the side of her mouth.

Now, as she forfeits her nimble cerebral Rolodex of celebrity trivia, I am suddenly out there on my own. I am unable to tell if I recognize someone from a small role on the big screen or a big role on the small screen or because they live on our block. My failure is not really to do with lack of interest (Joanna's accusation) but rather some neurological malfunction. When I really concentrate I still tend to blurt out nomenclatural malapropisms.

Even leaving the building can present a problem. Is this doorman helping us with our luggage Ishmael, who has worked here for twenty-five years and lives in a tiny apartment on the ground floor? Or is it Igor, who lives in Queens, has his hair savagely cropped down to his scalp twice a year and had his recent holiday in Jamaica disrupted by a hurricane. Ishmael or Igor? I know I can do this.

Friday, 16 October
Joanna

Today I see my first cockroach. I know New York is riddled with the *Blatta orientalis*, to give it its full name, but I had yet to actually see one until this morning. I am going down with a bundle of laundry and when the elevator door opens at the basement there it is, sitting staring up at me as if it had called the lift and was waiting to go upstairs.

It is sticky brown, nearly three inches long, and its antennae are twitching furiously. I stare at it for several seconds and then, completely unable to walk over it or around it, I press the button and go straight back up to the apartment again.

Saturday, 17 October
Peter

On today's desultory jog I notice that successive lamp-posts bear a new poster: 'Hi!' it reads in headline type, 'I'm Otis, and I'm missing.' Underneath, Otis declares himself to be a small neutered male cat with a red flea collar and an amenable disposition. There is a full-colour picture of Otis curled up cosily in a chintzy armchair, not looking as though he's about to make a dash outdoors into the icy arms of a New York fall. Otis's owner, Steve, asks anyone who has spotted the animal to call him.

For the rest of my run I am on Otis detection duty, but no small neutered feline crosses my path.

Saturday, 17 October
Joanna

'Hello, Richard,' says Peter as we step into the empty elevator. '*Loved* you in the *The Krippendorf Tribe*.'

'Mmm, I challenge. I don't believe there's any such film.'

'Absolutely was. I saw it on the plane back from South Africa. Dreyfuss plays an eccentric professor who makes his children dress up as savages to impersonate a fictitious tribe, to cover up the fact that his research has failed.

'For what's it worth, Richard,' Peter continues, 'I thought the reviewers were quite wrong myself. I found it quite diverting.'

Monday, 19 October
Peter

The Otis poster has faded a bit now and several have been tugged off their posts by the wind. I wonder if he has been located.

'Don't you think owners of lost pets owe it to the public to do follow-ups?' I ask Joanna. 'I mean if Otis is found shouldn't Steve stand us down, rather than just leave us hanging there, in the purgatory of lost pet searching. I think I'll phone Steve and ask him if Otis has returned.'

'He'll think you're a nutter or he might even suspect you of some sophisticated con. I read about a con like that in the paper,' she says, warming to her topic. 'It was an attempted kidnap and ransom, the perp', I've noticed recently this tendency of hers to take on little bits of NYPD slang like 'perp' for perpetrator, 'demanded money before he would return the pet, which he didn't really have anyway . . .'

Her voice softens. 'Maybe Otis met the same fate as The Skipper.'

The Skipper was an expensive blue pointer kitten we acquired in London. She was so absurdly inbred and highly strung that, as well as having the definite article in her name, she disappeared on her second day, notwithstanding her diet of gourmet food and lavish attention. The reward notices I stuck on lamp-posts down Colville Road bore fruit after a couple of days – a call from the resident of the basement flat next door. 'I think I may have some news on your cat,' he said in the solemn way that the police on TV break the news of a death to the next of kin. 'You'd better come down.'

In his garden was The Skipper's delicate, over-bred, pale grey and white corpse, somewhat threadbare now, looking like the product of antique taxidermy. I nudged at her with my toe and she was stiff as a stuffed Victorian toy.

'Hmm,' said my neighbour, looking up to examine the trajectory from our top flat to his garden, 'she must have jumped.'

I said nothing, feeling embarrassed that our cat had apparently been so desperate to flee that she had hurled herself from the fourth floor.

'Don't worry, I'll bury her in the corner of my garden if you like,' he said, clasping his hands together like a concerned vicar. 'And plant a commemorative shrub on her.'

'That would be nice,' I murmured.

Monday, 19 October
Joanna

We've been informed by her New Jersey cousin that Irma will not be reappearing from her Orlando vacation. Instead a doorman recommends Maya, a Croat from Queens.

'Hi, I don't do laundry, OK,' she says, arriving for her initial visit to inspect the apartment. She is tall and rangy with gauntly attractive features, a wiry red bob and a restless manner.

'Wow, that's definitely a mini-skirt,' I gasp, as she removes her coat to reveal a crimson gymslip so short it ends before her thighs really get started.

'Yeah,' she grins, 'I may live in Queens but I dress Manhattan.'

I give her the tour and she too tut-tuts about the state of the ravaged parquet floor.

'A hundred dollars for five hours,' she says. 'And I'm serious, no laundry, OK?' I give in on both counts.

Tuesday, 20 October
Peter

On my coffee run to Starbucks this morning I discover that the Jabberwocky has a rival loon. He is a middle-aged white man, with a fierce, battered face, who clutches a video camera. Instead of declaiming to the world at large from his own table like the Jabberwocky does, this new loon is more of a roving balladeer who moves from table to table, treating each group to his *bons mots*, and apparently filming their squirming reactions.

'That fucking Clinton, it's unba-lievable what he's getting away with. What's wrong with you all? The more he lies to you, the more you like him. His approval ratings go up every time he bullshits you. The unavoidable conclusion, I'm afraid, is that you, the American People, *like* being lied to. Well? Do you?' He whips his camera lens and its attendant mike around the room, as though filming a vox pop, but though it's a good question no one will answer him.

Then, without so much as a word from our sponsors, he segues into a verbal pummelling of New York's mayor.

'Giuliani – that creep, he's a crook if ever I saw one. He's only gonna kick twenty-five per cent of tobacco taxes into health care. Where's the rest going, huh? Where?' Again no one will oblige his restless lens. 'I'll *tell* you where the rest's going. It's going to buying votes.'

I am on the verge of replying to bolster the atmosphere of general democratic debate, but a look at his crazed eyes warns me that he may well kebab me with a concealed knife or open his bulging olive anorak to reveal an AK 47. Instead I concentrate on ordering my coffee.

Tuesday, 20 October
Joanna

A notice has gone up in the lobby reminding tenants with 'roach problems' to sign up for the fumigator's quarterly visit. I sign up immediately, wondering how many roaches we need to have seen to qualify as having an official 'problem'. Since the incident in the basement I have now seen two in our apartment, both a horrible viscous brown. One was scuttling up the fridge door, the other was beetling down the wall in the tiny box room I am planning to use as my study. Both times I shuddered but backed calmly out of the room before shrieking for Peter to come and remove them.

When I complained to a neighbour, she laughed. 'I'm surprised you've only seen two. The people below you were infested,' she told me. '*Infested*.'

'The people below us were infested,' I wail to Peter, who, having grown up on the lookout for gaboon vipers and puff adders in Africa, is unmoved by a roach. I have, of course, taken suitable prophylactic measures by placing copious numbers of 'roach bombs' – black pods of poison – under the sink, behind the fridge and the loos.

The fumigator turns out to be a huge, silent, teenage girl armed with an enormous syringe. Around her midriff she wears a wide leather belt, from which dangle several cartridges of poison.

I lead her into the kitchen and she clips a cartridge into

the syringe as if arming herself for combat. With some difficulty she crawls into the cupboard under the sink, a favourite hangout for her quarry, she assures us. She emerges to refill her syringe, squinting at the tip as if she were a doctor in *ER*. It takes her five minutes to squirt her roach poison into our kitchen cabinets.

'All you need,' she nods, heaving herself back up and holstering her syringe.

'What's the highest number of roaches you've come across in this building?' I ask, as she departs.

She pauses. 'The apartment under you had about two hundred.' She taps her belt. 'They were nesting in the oven, but I sorted them out. Now remember, this stuff only lasts three months, so I'll be seeing you again in January.'

Thursday, 22 October
Peter

Dinner with Sheenah Hankin, an Irish therapist on the Upper East Side, is a strange affair. She and her husband, Richard Wessler, who is quarter Cherokee Indian and also a therapist, have rented the exterior of their brownstone, including the steps up to the front door, to a movie company, so it is bathed in bright lights and surrounded by a small crowd of curious onlookers who have come to observe Adam Sandler, the actor who played the lead in *The Wedding Singer*.

It seems that every square foot of their cavernous brownstone on 93rd Street generates a return. The basement houses their psychiatric practice and the top two floors are rented out as B&Bs.

Sheenah, Joanna and royal-watcher Richard Mineards have met on the rounds of TV chat shows – *Geraldo*, *MSNBC*, and *Larry King Live* – and are currently pitching to cable TV a daytime talk show of their own called *The Britpak*. So before dinner we pore over publicity photographs they have had taken the previous week. In the contact sheets Sheenah and Joanna wear tiaras and Richard sports a top hat and cane.

Mineards, who speaks with an aristocratic drawl, and contributes gossip to William Hickey's Diary in the *Express*, is an expert on the minutiae of minor royals around the world. He has filed a story today, a titbit he has scavenged somewhere, that Prince Andrew has come to Fergie for financial advice, a strange thing to do on the face of it, given her much-publicized three million dollar overdraft. Andrew apparently phoned her up to tell her that Princess Beatrice had lost a tooth and to enquire what the going rate was from the tooth fairy.

The day before, Mineards says, clearly on a royal roll, he filed a story that Fergie had three sets of table manners for the girls:

(a) best behaviour when eating with granny;
(b) reasonably good, to be used when eating in public, and
(c) 'spaghetti up your noses' when eating at home in Sunningdale.

Halfway through the evening there is some excitement when Professor 'Windy' Dryden arrives fresh off the flight from London. He is the author, he tells us, of no fewer than 110 books on various aspects of therapy, including the classics, *The Incredible Sulk* and *How to Overcome Procrastination*.

'How long did that take you to write, *How to Overcome Procrastination*?' I ask.

'Ooh, about six weeks.'

'How long do your books normally take you?'

'Normally? Mmm, about four.'

On hearing that Joanna now works for *The Times*, he complains that the paper was responsible for his only appearance to date in that scurrilous tabloid, the *Sunday Sport*. He had given a quote over the phone to a *Times* reporter who was writing a story about rage control.

To the question 'How would you get a male patient to control his rage?' Windy Dryden had replied, 'I try to get him to imagine his testicles are in a guillotine and if he gives in to his rage the blades will close aroundthem.' The following Sunday, he says, the *Sport* ran a piece headlined, 'PROFESSOR'S RAGE CONTROL A LOAD OF BOLLOCKS.'

Windy Dryden complains mildly that he is a compulsive obsessive and in order to prove this, he empties the contents of his bulky black nylon bum-bag onto the dinner table. As well as a dozen pens, it includes a chunky eraser in a sealed zip bag, and, in another ziploc bag, a plastic contraption called a Nozovent™. He proceeds to demonstrate how Nozovent™, a flexible, bone-shaped piece of plastic, helps him to breathe properly at night by sticking the two ends of the bone into his nostrils, causing them to flare alarmingly, and giving the benign Professor a rather fierce demeanour. With Nozovent™ in place up his nose, he exhales and inhales deeply to show his efficiently widened nasal passages.

At this point the location manager of the filmset outside comes in with a query. He takes in the Professor, who is still wheezing through Nozovent™, and clearly thinks we are all barking eccentrics, trying to have a dinner party while several thousand megawatts of krieg lighting are pouring through the windows.

Friday, 23 October
Joanna

This afternoon when I return from the Gourmet Garage with a fresh cache of Hershey's chocolate milk and more graham crackers, Vadim, the melancholy Russian doorman, is sitting at the front desk in the grand but gloomy lobby. Normally he gives a weary, 'Hello again,' which, if he's feeling chatty, will be followed by a mournful and equally weary observation about the chaos in his former Soviet homeland.

'Hello again,' he says, depressed, as I struggle in. 'When is baby due?'

'About January 22nd.'

'Then it will be Aquarius,' he says, taking my bag and walking me to the lift. 'This is good sign. Not Pisces. Pisces people too sensitive, especially with women. Like me. I am Pisces.' And he wanders back sadly to the front desk.

Friday, 23 October
Peter

Inspired by Professor Windy Dryden's Nozovent™, Joanna persuades me to purchase a set of athletes' nose wideners that are supposed to increase nostril capacity, thereby improving oxygen intake and physical performance. As an unintended side effect, or so Windy Dryden claims, these nose wideners are of great help to snorers. Though I still strongly maintain that I am not in fact a real snorer, but merely an occasional one, I agree to try them. They are stiff white adhesive strips which you stick to the outside of your nose to open your nostrils.

I apply one carefully before bed and examine the effect in the bathroom mirror. My nostrils widen substantially and I try to imagine I am a first-grade sprinter trying to squeeze that last 2 per cent out of my performance to shatter the 100-metre record. Joanna stifles a giggle as I make my entrance, and then affects indifference as she wishes to encourage me in this foolishness. In any event we both enjoy an apparently snore-free night and awake refreshed.

Saturday, 24 October
Joanna

Today's e-mail from BabyCenter.com seems particularly useful, as it attempts to answer a question we have been asking each other since May: can we really afford to have a child? Peter is doubtful and keeps making dire predictions that we will never go on holiday or eat out again. I am more optimistic, but the truth is that neither of us have any idea how much it is really going to cost to raise a child, especially if it is here in Manhattan.

I read on:

Just answer a few basic questions on your spending patterns:

1 Before you start your baby on solids, do you plan to:
   – Breastfeed exclusively?
   – Breastfeed and supplement with formula?
   – Formula feed exclusively?

2 What type of diapers do you intend to use?
   – Cloth without a diaper service?
   – Disposables?
   – Cloth with a diaper service?

3 Over the course of your child's first eighteen years, do you think you'll most likely:

– Cook your own food?

– Buy mostly prepared food (and cook some of your own)?

– Eat out a couple of times per week?

4 What type of daytime care-giver do you plan to use until your child goes to preschool?
   – Parent/relative?
   – Day-care?
   – Nanny?

5 When it comes to shopping for your child (clothes, toys, furniture, equipment, computer, etc.), do you tend to be:
   – Hand-me-down happy?
   – A bargain hunter?
   – A brand-name buyer?

6 Where do you plan to send your child to elementary school?
   – Public?
   – Parochial (church-affiliated)?
   – Private?

7 Where do you plan to send your child to junior high and high school?
   – Public?
   – Parochial (church-affiliated)?
   – Private?

8 When it comes to spending on your own entertainment (weekend babysitters) and your child's (extra-curricular enrichment activities), what kind of spender do you think you'll tend to be?

– Low (sitters once every two to three months, cost-free activities)?

– Medium (sitters once a month, city-sponsored activities)?

– High (sitters once a week, private activities)?'

I plump for a baby who will be breastfed, disposably diapered, with parents who eat out a couple of times a week, a part-time nanny, bargain kid's supplies, a parochial school and a sitter at least once a week. Then I click on the calculator icon.

'Your total expenditure will be approximately $250,548.' This staggering sum is followed by the rider, 'While this takes into account many out-of-pocket costs, such as summer camp and Saturday-night sitters, it doesn't include braces, lost wages that result from taking time off to raise children, or an additional car for your child's sweet sixteen.'

'I've been doing some research and it costs a quarter of a million dollars to raise a baby in New York,' I tell Peter as we tuck into sushi. 'And that doesn't include things like dental braces.'

'Let's hope it doesn't have buck teeth then,' he says absently, struggling with a piece of fatty tuna.

Saturday, 24 October
Peter

My reluctant enthusiasm for the nasal expander evaporates this morning when I try to remove it from my nose. It would seem that the manufacturers had not intended it for extended wear, and it has become very firmly adhered to my skin. So much so that I cannot lift even a tiny corner of it to get a grip. Eventually, using Joanna's eyebrow tweezers, I manage to achieve purchase and rip it off. It is excruciating. When I peer into the mirror through teared-up eyes, there is a nasty red raw patch etched across my nose in the shape of the nostril widener.

'What's with your nose, man?' asks Jeff when we meet for lunch at Coffee Grounds on Little West 12th Street.

'Joanna threw a shoe at me,' I say and he shrugs.

'Check this out for a surreal phenomenon,' says the young waiter. A real fly has got caught in a gooey artificial web that forms part of their Hallowe'en decorations. He pokes at the web, trying to free the trapped insect. 'Is that bizarre or what?' he asks. 'I mean like, think of the symbolism of it.'

Sunday, 25 October
Joanna

If possible, Maya's 'Manhattan-style' skirt is even shorter than the last time, it is pale blue with small red hearts and as she stoops to vacuum under the sofa with our Panasonic, which Margarita so vehemently scorned, I am presented with a flash of matching thong.

As she works she chats incessantly. 'In Croatia I trained as a pedicurist and then my father sent me to restaurant management school,' she says, vigorously mopping the kitchen floor. 'I am married but we do not have sexual relations,' she adds baldly. 'He was my childhood sweetheart, we married when we were both eighteen, then I caught him cheating on me, so pshhhtt – he was out!' She pauses to tear off a huge wodge of Brawny kitchen roll. 'Well, not totally because we still share the same house,' she sighs. 'We are separated, but I make him stay to help me with our children. I have two. My little kid is four. The other is fifteen and she is too fat, I keep telling her to lose weight, but all her friends are fat, you know? It wouldn't happen like this in Croatia.'

Maya and her errant husband came here from Croatia on a year's visa nine years ago and stayed on. 'So I'm illegal? Big deal. What do I need papers for? There's no reason to leave ever. America has everything I want.'

Sunday, 25 October
Peter

I am meeting Toby for lunch at Tea and Sympathy, a tiny café which Joanna tells me is favoured by the likes of British models Naomi Campbell, Kate Moss and Stella Tennant. It aspires to imitate a British transport café and serves tea in pots and boarding school food. Toby is late and the English waitress tells me in an Estuary accent, with Sloane peeping through, that I may not take a table until he arrives. Furthermore, due to the cramped conditions, she forbids me to wait inside.

'That's not a very sympathetic attitude,' I remonstrate feebly, pointing at the restaurant's name on the door. She indicates a handwritten notice over the counter, which reads, 'Rules of the House: the waitresses are always right.'

Toby finally turns up but without his trademark silver puffa jacket and Nikes with flashing heels. Instead he is clothed in Harris tweed and wire-rimmed glasses. 'It's part of my new strategy,' he says in his naturally amplified voice as we squeeze around a tiny table, brushing elbows with fellow diners, 'to exploit the Anglophilia currently rife in New York.'

I toy with the idea of toad-in-the-hole or Welsh rarebit, but in the end plump for shepherd's pie followed by a cuppa Tetley's.

'What happened to your nose?' Toby asks. My nasal

defacement is still evident two days after my experiment with nostril expanders. His expression suddenly brightens. 'Did someone belt you?'

'No, no. Nothing that dramatic. I caught it on the door of the bathroom cabinet.'

Toby looks unconvinced.

'Look over there,' he says, clearly audible to all twenty covers. 'It's Rupert Everett. He looks pretty depressed. I'll bet he's still smarting over not getting an Oscar nomination for *My Best Friend's Wedding.*'

Indeed it is Rupert Everett, all of three feet away from us, sitting on his own, head bent down with a woollen bobble hat pulled low over his brow, looking rather miserable.

Monday, 26 October
Joanna

In two weeks' time I will be officially land-bound, no longer able to fly safely. So, anxious to exploit our last opportunity to travel, I trawl the classified ads in the *New York Post* and book us a last-minute bargain break in the Bahamas.

I ask the agent to fax the details of where we are billeted. Eventually a groggy photocopied brochure struggles through the fax machine sufficiently smudged to make it unreadable. The only details I can make out about Elbow Cay, our destination, seem rather ominous. 'Visitors to Elbow Cay will find it one of the quieter, more informal corners of the Bahamas.' The photo of what I hope to be the palomino beach is so blotchy it appears to be strewn with seaweed or even jellyfish. I decide against showing it to Peter.

'It sounds wonderful,' I lie cheerfully. 'We can spend all

weekend reading on the white sands and have supper in a beach restaurant.' But he remains convinced I have fallen prey to a telephone rip-off and predicts that construction of the hotel will not be completed.

'Oh, who cares what it's like as long as the weather's good,' I retort.

Thursday, 29 October
Peter

Instead of the basking sun we have come here to enjoy, it is relentlessly wet on Elbow Cay. The hard, slanting rain pelts the bedraggled palms. It pimples the turquoise water and splashes against the sun-faded timber jetty. It bounces off the white veneered husks of the upended fibreglass boats, under which the mangy marina dogs have taken refuge. Only the mangrove delights, dancing to the deluge.

The island is as still as a weekday cemetery. Our fellow holiday-makers remain indoors playing solitaire, reading thrillers or week-old copies of *Time*.

On our final day the rain lessens a little and we boat over to the nearby Man o' War Cay. It is an extraordinary little island of small, gaily coloured clapboard houses and a network of narrow concrete pathways, along which the locals, most of them as big as Sumo wrestlers, ride in their electric golf buggies. In the quaint graveyard, virtually all the headstones bear the name of Albery, for Man o' War Cay is populated almost entirely by the descendants of this one family, originally from Carolina, who remained loyal to the British during the American Revolution, and were forced to flee when the Redcoats lost. For their loyalty to the crown they were promised fertile farm lands in the Bahamas, though the British knew the soil here is far too salty for crops.

We stroll around until we chance upon what is now evidently the main industry, a tiny sailcloth factory in which half a dozen large Alberys feed brightly coloured canvas into their sewing machines, fashioning it into duffel bags and holdalls, floppy hats and sponge bags. Unusually, I find myself infected with the urge to buy and I come away with an armful of these gaudy sailcloth items.

Thursday, 29 October
Joanna

In the three days we have been here we seem to have eaten nothing but conch. Conch fritters, conch stew, deep-fried conch, marinaded conch, blackened conch, conch salad, conch burger and tonight, conch *à la crème*. We are all conched out and secretly relieved to be Manhattan bound.

Friday, 30 October
Peter

In our absence a sketch of a witch, complete with pointy hat and warty chin, has appeared in the elevator, asking all residents willing to be trick or treated, to sign up. Fourteen people have already agreed and Joanna adds our names.

'I notice Richard Dreyfuss hasn't signed up,' I say.

'Shall I add his name anyway?' asked Joanna, her pen hovering.

Saturday, 31 October
Joanna

I'm rooting through our cardboard boxes frantically looking for a costume for a dinner party we are holding tonight.

'The thirty-first? Excellent,' said Mary, when I called to invite her and Bill. 'What will you be wearing?'

'Oh, the only black dress I can still squeeze into,' I said, thinking her question rather formal.

'You're not wearing a costume?' she exclaimed. 'Oh, but you must, it's Hallowe'en.'

'You can if you like, but I'm not wearing a costume,' said Peter, when I broach the subject later.

'Well, I've committed us now and everyone else will be wearing one,' I mumble. 'And I know Mary is going to go to some trouble, she told me she's going to make it herself.'

Grudgingly, Peter has purchased a rather effective wolf mask, leaving me at a disadvantage. The door bell interrupts my costume hunt. It is a small band of trick-or-treaters, including several TeleTubbies.

'Don't you have any Snickers bars?' asks Po, refusing the basket of candycorn I offer. His plastic pumpkin bucket is already half full of Milky Ways, Hershey bars and Kit-Kats.

Another group spills out of the lift and is similarly unimpressed. 'What's that,' asks a miniature Robin Hood, poking an arrow at the basket.

'Candycorn,' I reply brightly. 'I thought it was traditional at Hallowe'en.'

'We only liked wrapped sweets,' he says solemnly, already on his way to the next apartment.

'We've had to insist, I'm afraid,' his father apologizes. 'There was a case some years ago when someone used candycorn to try and poison some kids.'

'Trick or treat?' shout a new group, scampering up the stairs.

'Trick,' says Peter.

They stare back in silence. Then a small ghost steps forward. 'You're supposed to give us candy,' he says crossly.

'Or money,' a tiny wizard adds hopefully.

'Let's go do Richard Dreyfuss,' the ghost suggests and they wild off up the stairs.

I go back to my costume hunt and finally unearth an old jellaba Peter brought back once from a trip to Pakistan. It will have to do.

Saturday, 31 October
Peter

An impressive degree of high-tech imagery has been employed by our guests in their choice of Hallowe'en costumes. John is the worldwide web, Dana is Windows 98, Suzanna is 'fatal exception error'. Bill is the monster from *Mars Attacks!* and Mary, the Tin Man, handmade from foil. Walter is a mine safety inspector and Meryl is a flapper girl. Melanie is Melanie from *Gone with the Wind*, and Joanna wears her jellaba, which covers her whole body but for a lace filigree window over her eyes. I am wearing a Brazilian red wolf mask purchased at the Cathedral shop of St John the Divine. The mask is made of scarlet rubber. It has rows of impressive white rubber fangs, and a bottom jaw that toggles open by pulling a little tag. To make it more effective I have covered the exposed part of my face in scarlet face paint.

The most exciting moment of the evening comes when I open the door to an aggressive-looking character in camouflage fatigues, army boots and a face streaked with black and green cream. This is Andrew Solomon – at last – in person. In the course of the evening he banters entertainingly, gives us tantalizing glimpses of his voluminous social roster and his exotic travels. He does not appear to be at all depressed. For three-quarters of a million, I begin to suspect, I may be better qualified to write about depression.

NOVEMBER

The baby weighs nearly 5 lbs
and measures 13 inches from crown to rump.
Babies born at this time usually survive in the hospital.
Your baby is running out of room
and his head is most likely resting on the bone
in preparation for dropping into the pelvis.
BabySoon.com

Monday, 2 November
Joanna

Peter ventures out briefly, lugging a bag of dirty laundry. He returns purple faced, bearing cappuccinos and announcing it is the coldest day he can remember.

We appear to have no control over the old-fashioned cast-iron radiators in our apartment, though New York City law is myopically specific about heating. According to Section 75 of the Multiple Dwelling Act (which is pinned to our mail room noticeboard) after 1 October (known locally as Radiator Day) the heat in the apartment must be 68°F, between 6 a.m. and 10 p.m., when outside temperature falls to below 55°F. The apartment must be heated to 55°F between 10 p.m. and 6 a.m., when outside temperature falls below 40°F. Heating can be switched off again on 31 May.

The first evidence we had that our landlord took Radiator Day seriously came when we were awakened by a terrible banging and clanking coming from the radiator in our bedroom. The noise continued until 6.30 a.m. when it metamorphosed into a severe fizzing and then finally sputtered out.

Assuming that it was the system readjusting itself after six months in hibernation, we did nothing. But the next morning at the same time the chorus of banging and clanging and fizzing started again, so Peter entered the problem in the logbook kept at the front desk by leisurely Lugo, the handyman.

Just because a problem is entered in the logbook, of course, is no guarantee that Lugo will come and fix it. Sometimes I think he relies on the placebo effect that once written down the problem will go away. But after our third sleepless night and two more entries in the logbook, he appeared at 7 a.m. armed with his monkey wrench. He banged ferociously on the radiator and pronounced the problem fixed.

The next morning we woke at 4 a.m. again to even worse knocking, this time coming from the bathroom radiator.

We have slowly grown used to the individual radiators knocking and hissing on and off with no relation either to each other or to the weather outside. This morning the kitchen is freezing, though both bathroom radiators are churning out heat with a Saharan ferocity. Meanwhile, the temperature in the baby's room has plummeted so low that Peter says it's far too cold to go in and finish off the painting.

Tuesday, 3 November
Peter

'Have you heard what happened to Andrew Solomon?' gushes Suzanna down the phone. 'He was *arrested* after your party?'

'What for?'

She has no further information, so I phone him, only to be intercepted by his answer message. 'I hope the rumours of your little local difficulty with the NYPD are exaggerated,' I say, trying to make light of it. Later, however, I log on to find a round-robin e-mail from Andrew Solomon to his friends. It is written from his hospital bed.

Hallowe'en night, I attended a costume dinner party. I wore a leather camouflage outfit from John Bartlett and smeared my face with my sister-in-law's Enriching Mud Face Mask, and I looked rather convincing as a guerrilla or paratrooper – I never quite decided which. I had numerous compliments on my costume, which I was variously told was 'sexy', 'scary', 'witty', and 'chic'. At about 1.30 a.m., the party wound down. As it was a brisk, clear night, I began walking a little way by myself, enjoying the night air, replaying in my mind amusing episodes from dinner, checking out the costumes that went past on the street.

In Central Park there were giant klieg lights along the course of the New York Marathon, and TV crews busy setting up bleachers and barricades. I strolled in, thinking that I'd be able to get a cab down Fifth Avenue, and keen to see the park so lively at this implausible hour.

About two-thirds of the way across, an unmarked car going at least 60 mph spun around and drove straight at me, so that I had to jump into some shrubs to avoid being hit. It screeched to a halt and two policemen leapt out.

'OK,' said one of them, Officer Carrol, the younger and blonder and more nervous one. 'Do you have any ID?'

I quietly handed over my driver's licence.

'What's on your criminal record?' asked the other one, Officer Fox, snide and self-important.

I said that to the best of my knowledge I had no criminal record.

'Yeah, right,' said Officer Fox. 'You ever spent a night in a jail cell?'

I said that I had not.

'Well, start thinking about it because that may be where you're heading tonight.'

Utterly bewildered, I asked whether I had done something wrong. Officer Fox looked at me as though I were retarded. 'You've broken the park curfew,' he said. 'No one allowed in here from 2 to 6 a.m.'

I apologized, explained that I had never heard of such a law and noted that it was not posted at the entrances to the park. I might just as well have recited the Gettysburg Address in Inca dialect. The cops sniggered.

'We're writing you a summons,' Carrol said. 'You can tell your story to the judge.'

At that point, another car drove up, and Officer Taverna popped out. Nodding at me as though I were a dead rat, he said, 'Another one of them?' The other two guys nodded.

'Lives in the Village,' said Fox, who still had my driving licence.

'Listen,' Taverna said, sticking his face close to mine. 'We're gonna get you guys out of the parks.'

All at once, I began to understand what was going on.

'We've had enough of you guys and now we're gonna get rid of you,' he went on. I decided not to get into a confrontation. 'I'm really cold,' I said. 'Is this going to take long? Can I wait in the car?'

'It's gonna take as long as it takes,' Fox said. He took my wallet and thumbed through it. 'You've got too much money in here.'

I said I had just been to a cash machine and that I had taken out $800 to cover household expenses.

'That's a lie,' Carrol said. 'Cash machines do $400 a day – max.'

I said I had a special card, and showed him that it said 'Chase Private Bank'.

The cops had hats, while I did not. I got colder and colder and I began to shiver. 'I'm so cold,' I said meekly.

'Shove it,' said Taverna.

I stepped forward to ask Fox, who was writing my summons, whether it could be waived, and Taverna shoved me back into the bushes. 'You go sneaking up on a cop from behind like that,' he yelled at me, 'we're gonna see you locked up.'

Shaking now from the cold and from the assault, I suddenly understood how powerful Jews in Munich in 1939 had continued to think that they'd be OK. Several friends of mine had been crushed and bruised by police in the previous week's candlelight march for a murdered gay college student.

Fox began telling me about my court date.

'Can I pay a fine instead of taking off a full day to go to court?' I asked.

'You guys think you can pay us off?' said Carrol. 'Don't even think of bribing us.'

I wanted to explain that I had never bribed anyone, but I felt as though I had been frozen in my costume and nothing I had to say, nothing about my bearing or my accent or my education, could turn me into a human being in the eyes of these police.

'This is Giuliani's New York,' Taverna said. 'Guys like you are finished.'

It took the full weight of my superego not to pick up a rock and hit him over the head with it.

When they finally let me go, I raced to Fifth Avenue and caught a cab, and I sat in the back seat and sobbed and sobbed and sobbed for the humiliation, the impotence, and the lost illusions and hopes. I got home at 4.30 a.m.

I am writing this from my hospital bed, where I am recovering from emergency treatment for what could have become a fatal inner ear infection caused by my interrogation in the cold. Here I am now, dripping a steady stream of blood from the porches of my ear, sporting a messy red badge of anger and new-born activism. I have lost, utterly and profoundly, the sense of my own immunity that made my life in this town so pleasant and easy for so long.

Wednesday, 4 November
Joanna

Flicking through *People* magazine at Robert Kree, my hairdresser's on Bleecker Street, I come across an article entitled 'Miracle Babies', which features a Californian couple called Keh. Arceli Keh and her husband Isagani are pictured sitting on a taupe Dralon sofa with their laughing daughter, Cynthia, aged twenty-three months. The Kehs conceived Cynthia using IVF, not unusual, except that Mrs Keh lied to the doctors about her age. She told them she was fifty. In fact, she was sixty, and finally became pregnant just three days shy of her sixty-fourth birthday.

'There's a piece here about the oldest mother in the

world,' I say to my stylist, Diana, a cheerful woman from Long Island, who is swigging a bottle of Evian. 'She's sixty-four, but she told the doctor she was ten years younger. Imagine, when her daughter graduates she'll be ninety.'

'I wish I could knock ten years off my age and have people believe me,' says Diana. 'I did Kevin Spacey's hair the other day. He was really nice but you know what put me off? He was wearing Adidas sandals with white socks. I mean, how sad is that?'

Friday, 6 November
Peter

I have finally got around to tackling my visa status, or the lack of it, and I'm being interviewed by an immigration lawyer in his 32nd-floor penthouse office on Fifth Avenue. Scott Pullman, of Pullman and Pullman, is a serious young man who does nothing but immigration cases. I sketch out my situation and he makes notes on his legal pad.

'I think our best option,' he concludes, 'is to apply for a Green Card as "A Person of Exceptional Ability". What would you say is your area of speciality?'

I embark on a grand tour of every job I've ever done, lawyer, foreign correspondent, TV documentary maker, author, but he cuts me short.

'No, no. You don't understand. These cases are decided by people in an office in Vermont who spend an average of ten minutes on each application,' he warns. 'You don't want to confuse them. You can only present yourself as an expert in just *one* subject. What will it be?'

'Well, I suppose it would have to be Africa,' I say.

'Right. Africa. What I want you to do is go and collect every single newspaper clipping, TV documentary and book you've ever done on Africa. Any reviews, awards or commendations, over say the last fifteen years, and bring them in and I'll sift them and assemble our application. Later on I'll ask you to get letters of recommendation from any expert you can think of in the field. The more famous, the better.'

He pauses to review his notes. 'Have you ever interviewed any royalty?' he asks suddenly. 'The immigration people in Vermont are *very* impressed with royalty.'

'No,' I admit. 'I'm afraid I've never interviewed a royal. Except King Zog of Albania. But I think he was only a Pretender.'

'What, a fraud?'

'Well, he was in exile in Johannesburg at the time.'

'No,' rules Scott Pullman categorically. 'King Zog doesn't count.'

'I once covered a tour of Africa by Prince Charles,' I offer.

'Well, that might be something,' he says, perking up. 'And how was it?'

'Well, it was rather strange,' I admit. 'In Swaziland, where he attended the coronation of King Mswati III, he spent the whole time trying to avoid looking at the bare-breasted virgins at the Reed Dance, while the tabloid photographers used fish-eye lenses to try and snap a picture of "Charles Copping a Right Royal Eyeful".'

I notice that Scott Pullman appears to be writing this down. 'You're not writing this down, are you?' I ask.

'No, no.' he says. 'Then what?'

'Well, then we went to Victoria Falls.'

Scott Pullman looks blank.

'Africa's greatest waterfall? "The Smoke that Thunders" – one of the natural wonders of the world, named after Charles's great-great-great grandmother. It's a sight that has inspired poetic responses from just about everyone.

David Livingstone – the Scottish explorer – looked down at it, and said, "On sights as beautiful as this Angels in their flight must have gazed".

'Anyway, Prince Charles walks out onto the lip of the Falls, and he turns to the Zambian Minister of Tourism and asks, "Do you get many suicides over here then?"'

Here I end my royal anecdote, but there is a long pause and Scott Pullman appears puzzled, his pen still poised over his legal pad. 'What's your point?' he asks finally.

'Well, the man has no poetry in his soul,' I offer by way of moral.

Scott Pullman nods emphatically in agreement and stands to conclude our interview. He steers me past the polished yucca plants to the door, and pumps my hand. Then he cocks his head to one side. 'What *is* the answer?' he asks gnomically.

'I'm sorry?'

'*Are* there many suicides over the Victoria Falls?'

And though I am trying to pose as A Person of Exceptional Ability – Special Subject: Africa, I have to admit that I have absolutely no idea how many people have deliberately hurled themselves over the Victoria Falls.

'But I can find out,' I hear myself promising as the gold-brocaded elevator chimes my departure.

Monday, 9 November
Joanna

Suzanna, an expert business reporter, calls to say she is working on an investigative piece for *Vanity Fair* about Garth Drabinsky, the theatre impresario, producer of *Ragtime* and *Showboat*.

'Didn't you say you once sat next to him at a dinner?' she quizzes.

'Oh yes, back in May, at a Royal Shakespeare Company benefit,' I remember. 'He seemed rather depressed.'

'Well he had very good reason to be,' she says. 'You name it, Drabinsky has been accused of it. Fraud, kickbacks, breach of contract. And it was falling apart just about then.'

Well, well, no wonder he was a morose dinner companion.

Monday, 9 November
Peter

Joanna has read somewhere that wheatgerm is the answer to all health concerns and that a regular intake of it is essential. She has returned from the Nuts About Health store with a capacious glass jar of wheatgerm, which she now sprinkles over all our food without discrimination. Nothing, it seems, can cross our lips without this dusting of wheatgerm. It is like culinary dandruff – ubiquitous and disgusting.

Tuesday, 10 November
Joanna

'Time for a wake-up call!' urges today's e-mail from Baby-Center.com. 'The cost of college in eighteen years is probably more than you think. In order to start planning you need to determine the amount you're aiming for and how much time you have to get there.'

I fill in our baby's due date and the screen reconfigures. 'Based on the information you entered, your child's college costs will be $254,240.'

I stare in disbelief. This is on top of the quarter of a million it has already predicted we will spend on basic childcare – excluding braces. I try to recall how much my

ill-spent years at the University of East Anglia cost and
how much we would have to save a year to accumulate a
college fund.

But BabyCenter.com has got there before me. 'To reach
this goal of $254,240 for your child, you'll need to save
$542 per month for the next eighteen years.'

$542 per month . . . I read on. 'If the monthly amount
seems too high,' BabyCenter.com concludes cheerfully,
'don't despair! Remember, starting with a smaller monthly
investment is better than not starting at all.'

I fret throughout the day about this and resolve to start
a savings plan.

'Listen, did you read the e-mail I sent you from Baby-
Center.com today?' I ask Peter over supper of meatloaf
and onion gravy at the Metro Diner.

'No, not yet.'

'Well, they reckon that you should start saving now
if you want your kid to go to college, because in
eighteen years' time it's going to cost quarter of a million
dollars.'

'Oh, bollocks.'

'And that's in addition to the other quarter of a million.
But they say that if we manage to save $542 a month from
now on, we'll have enough to cover it.'

'Double bollocks,' says Peter and orders another cap-
puccino.

Tuesday, 10 November
Peter

I am making my first pilgrimage to Albee's on Amsterdam
Avenue. It is a haj I have been trying to delay for as long
as possible, as Albee's, New York's well-known emporium
of kiddie equipment, represents the tyranny of strollers and

other essential accessories of breeding. Albee's is even more depressing than I had anticipated, a tawdry bazaar which makes no attempt to shop dress but rather tries to give the impression of a bargain basement with prices sliced to the marrow.

Joanna tasks me to track down something called a Diaper Genie, apparently as crucial to a baby as a litter tray is to a cat. As I slouch along the winding alleys flanked by tall piles of baby merchandise, I brush against a precarious tower of tiny, gaily coloured plastic lavatory seats that are designed to fit into full-sized ones and they come tumbling down. I flee the scene in search of my designated quarry, the Diaper Genie. It is, I eventually discover, a three-foot plastic cylinder with a hinged lid, that, its advertising blurb promises, will store soiled diapers in a sanitary, odourless and convenient way. I wrestle it to the counter, carefully stepping over the scattered debris of dozens of mini loo seats.

Wednesday, 11 November
Joanna

In the last two weeks my nights have begun to follow a terrible pattern. No matter what time I go to bed I wake up at around 3.45 a.m., unable to get back to sleep.

I have always been a good sleeper, but waking in the early hours is turning me into a zombie. I feel like a car parked in a quiet street, with its ignition turned off but its engine still roaring away in neutral. A colleague, who has two children, told me cheerfully that she found this one of her most creative times and that she would usually get up and write. But I have no desire to write at 3.45 a.m. Instead I lie there sorting through the arbitrary jetsam which floats in and out on my tide of fatigue, while Peter sleeps heartily beside me, his luxurious slumber only frustrating me further.

I get up, feel my way into the kitchen without turning any lights on, make myself tea and stare out at the neighbouring block, counting the number of other insomniacs by their illuminated windows. There are seven of us tonight, not counting those others who might be huddling incognito in the dark, like me.

I sit there fretting about what sort of mother I will make and how I will cope when the baby actually comes. Then at about 5.45 a.m. I get back into bed and drift off into an unsettled sleep and dream that I have given birth to a long thin baby who never needs feeding. She looks like my sister and I stand holding her at a party and people keep coming up to me and saying, 'Hello, I hear your baby doesn't need feeding, lucky you!'

Thursday, 12 November
Peter

Joanna announces that once the baby is born she intends to chew its food before feeding it. This is a practice, she says, prevalent among French women. It is supposed to infuse the child with the mother's antibodies. She logically extends this idea and declares I will have to do the same so that the child has access to both sets of antibodies. The thought of a kid being fed a spoonful of premasticated gunk makes me want to retch.

Friday, 13 November
Joanna

No matter how long I sleep during the night, I always wake up feeling dark grey and fizzy with fatigue. This morning, trying to write a column, I find myself staring at perfectly simple sentences unable to tell if they make grammatical sense. My brain feels as if it is slowly disappearing.

Though people have warned me I will feel shattered after the birth, no one has warned me about this pre-natal fatigue. Even the books skim over the subject, suggesting a fifteen-minute nap in the middle of the day as a cure-all. Today, after sending off my article I slip back into bed, quite desperate for sleep. But even with a Virgin Airways eye mask and yellow rubber earplugs in place, it never comes. Instead I lie there worrying about not sleeping enough and about whether my worrying will harm the baby.

This must be what a degenerative brain disease feels like, a slow, lingering realization that you are losing control, coupled with a fear that you will never feel normal again.

Sunday, 15 November
Peter

I perk up this evening when I realize that Joanna has forgotten to sprinkle wheatgerm on any of our meals today. It would seem that her wheatgerm stage has drawn to a close. It has lasted a week and, naturally, has made no discernible difference to our health.

Monday, 16 November
Joanna

During another midnight surfing session I come across a rival to BabyCenter.com, the rather more urgent-sounding BabySoon.com. As well as offering competing weekly updates on foetal development, BabySoon.com also organizes daily opinion polls of new parents.

Today's question, blazoned across the home page, is, "How Has Parenthood Changed Your Sex Life?"

a) It's better than before.
b) It's the same.
c) It's not as good.

I click on the word sex to get the answer. 'Thirty-two per cent of BabySoon.com subscribers say their sex life is better than before. Twenty-six per cent say it's the same. And forty-three per cent say it's not as good.'

I decide against telling Peter.

Tuesday, 17 November
Peter

I have changed hairdressers. At Michael's suggestion I go to DopDop, a hip salon on Mercer Street, just below Houston. It is in a cavernous basement, a veritable catacomb of hair. Dozens of tiny candles have been placed on little irregular ledges that form part of a jagged, unfinished brick wall. The high priestess of DopDop is Jo, an ebullient Goth from Philadelphia, who treats me to a stream-of-consciousness riff about her 'personhood'. She notices me glancing at the faint subcutaneous candelabra on her upper arm and she stretches the skin for me to get a better view of the dime-sized insert: 'Contraception,' she explains. 'It's a two-year dispenser, the pill does bad things to my system, but necrotin is much gentler.'

Jo turns to examine my somewhat undisciplined hair, tousling it into an even wilder bush. 'Your problem is dark hair, light eyes, long face, prominent jaw. We need the cut to be boxy, sharp cornered and flatter on top. But I'm gonna give you some advice – now hear me out, OK?' She looks at my hair in the mirror and I think she is about to comment on the sprinkling of premature grey that I have managed to convince myself makes me look more distinguished. 'I would suggest that we dye your eyebrows. You'd be amazed at the difference it makes.'

'But my eyebrows are black,' I point out. 'What colour do you want to make them?'

'Well, see, though they're dark, they're not quite as dark as your hair – they need more definition.'

I raise my eyebrows quizzically, while looking at them in the mirror. Then I try to lower them one at a time. It is the first time in my life that they have enjoyed this kind of attention.

'And my advice?' continues Jo. 'Don't tell anyone, not even Joanna, that you've had it done. No woman likes to think her man is vain. She probably won't realize you've had it done – she'll think you look *great*.'

Wednesday, 18 November
Joanna

For the first time in my adult life I come back to discover I have left the apartment without my keys. I ring the bell, with the tiny autumn corn cobs still attached, but Peter has gone out. I have never done this before, I am meticulous about keys. I sit on the oxblood Chesterfield in the lobby reserved for guests, unable to do anything except gnaw on a sandwich I've been saving for later and wait for Peter.

Spotting me in the 40-watt gloom, a neighbour offers to let me wait in her apartment, but I lie and say I'm waiting for Peter, who is parking the car. We don't even have a car, but I can't face the prospect of talking to someone I hardly know.

I have also developed a cough, which I can't seem to shake. The doctor told me to take Robitussin, but when I tried to buy some the pharmacist stopped me.

'Is this for you personally?' he asked as I rummaged for my purse. I nodded.

'But ma'am, I can't help noticing you're pregnant.'

'Yes, but my doctor told me this was safe,' I explained.

'Well I can't recommend it,' he said. 'My wife had the flu when she was seven months pregnant and I looked into everything, and there was nothing she could take that was safe. I must urge you not to.'

There was something about the way he stressed the word 'urge' that made me feel I should listen. Defeated, I picked up a packet of Hall's mentholated honey and lemon cough drops. 'What about these?' I asked, feebly trying to make a joke. 'Will these do me any harm?'

'Well, personally, I would just ride it out,' he said. 'But if you're desperate, I wouldn't recommend more than two a day.' I bought them and sucked the first of my daily ration on the way home. It tasted suspiciously buttery and much too sweet to be doing me much good.

Wednesday, 18 November
Peter

Having dislodged a large chunk of tooth, I need a dentist in a hurry so I canvass friends. 'Wasserman - he's great,' recommends Ron. 'A pain-free practice. Tell him I recommended you. He's on Park and 62nd.' I call them up and the same afternoon I find myself reclining in Wasserman's chair getting a temporary filling.

Wasserman's room is equipped with all the tools of the dentist's trade. A huggy bear clings to the overhead light; on the wall facing me hangs a seaside scene from the Big

Sur, and a Dutch canal pastoral with Friesian cows grazing nonchalantly on what appears to be a dangerously precipitous bank. And on his little alcove, above a large hollow china tooth bristling with pens, is the obligatory Farside cartoon. Next to the cartoon is a home-made sign: 'Ignorance can be fixed,' it reads, 'but stupid is for ever.' A mobile of brightly coloured cancan girls dangles from the ceiling, and a nurse doll called Anna Septic stands in a bell jar by the sink.

Dr Wasserman snaps on blue rubber gloves and a mask and approaches, dazzling me with the pencil light strapped to his forehead. His eyes are huge as he squints into my mouth through the jeweller's lenses protruding from his glasses. He pokes a tiny pen camera towards my teeth and talks me through the blue movie that is my magnified mouth. The image is displayed on a TV suspended from the ceiling. It is all glistening pinks and swelling reds and pulsing whites and bubbles of translucent saliva. I feel faintly embarrassed.

'One of your wisdom teeth is impacted,' he accuses, as though I have contracted a social disease through poor oral hygiene. He and his nurse, Evelyn, laugh pityingly at the examples of pathetic English dentistry on naked display in my gob.

'Metal fillings,' says Evelyn in wonder, as though observing rare examples of the lost folk craft of coracle weaving.

Thursday, 19 November
Joanna

I had never intended to hire a yoga teacher to come to the apartment on a weekly basis, but I am unable to make the times of any local classes, so Peter gives me an early Christmas present of ten home sessions.

Today we have our fourth session and already it feels indispensable, though sometimes I have to stifle snorts at what the two of us must look like, solemnly sitting on our mats drawing quick 'Breaths of Fire', like a poor man's Sting and Trudi Styler.

Despite initial grumblings when I suggested he join in too, it's clear that Peter is beginning to enjoy our sessions, even though he goes through a ritual of protest before each one.

This morning he wakes up with a hangover. 'I'm far too ill to do yoga today,' he moans. But at 9.45 a.m., as soon as our instructor, Mary Barnes, arrives, he slopes sheepishly in, clasping his yolk-yellow camping mat and crosses his legs straight into the lotus position with no prompting.

Thursday, 19 November
Peter

When I agreed to join in Joanna's yoga classes, I didn't realize that this would entail doing sphincter exercises to tighten my pelvic floor. 'I'm fairly content with my pelvic floor just the way it is,' I tell Joanna, but this sort of attitude is thrown back at me as supercilious – further proof, she says, as if any were needed, of just how out of touch I am with my inner self. So once a week Mary Barnes, the astonishingly flexible teacher, arrives with her Peruvian nose-pipe CDs and her pimpled purple mat.

After a brief prayer we launch into our various moves, most of which have bizarre names that are supposed to be descriptive. I seem to have particular difficulty with Downward Facing Dog, which happens to be Mary's favourite. In this move we are required to kneel on all fours, extend our hands and straighten our legs 'as if hanging from a meat hook'. I always emerge red-faced and out of breath.

Annoyingly, Joanna even with her large belly performs the Downward Facing Dog with evident ease. I far prefer Angry Cat, in which all we have to do is kneel with a rounded back. The truth is I feel ludicrous doing yoga and I'm only doing it to be supportive.

Friday, 20 November
Joanna

My cough is still bad and today silver stars start shooting across my eyes while I am hacking away. Peter is unsympathetic, telling me I should have followed the doctor's advice and not listened to the pharmacist. But he shuts up when I raise the possibility that I might have contracted TB after he forced me to take the subway last week, though I had begged to take a cab.

Not having a car is usually an advantage in Manhattan. Garaging alone can cost $500 a month, and as we are saving so much money by not running a car I feel justified in taking cabs. But today I start worrying about how we will get to the hospital when I go into labour.

My greatest fear, given my due date is 22 January, is that New York will be snowbound as it was in the winter of 1996 when twenty-six inches of snow fell in twenty-four hours and people were skiing down Fifth Avenue.

What if the roads are impassable, even to ambulances?

On our maternity tour of Roosevelt Hospital, they made it pretty clear that we shouldn't arrive until I am in serious labour, otherwise we will be dismissed, to return only when the contractions are three minutes apart. The hospital is forty blocks away from our apartment, about two miles, so clearly I won't be able to walk there. But similarly I can't face the idea of squatting in the back of a grubby yellow cab, doubled up in pain, fumbling with the seat belt as the driver lurches from lane to lane. I have debated asking Michael to drive us, but I may need to go in the middle of the night. Besides, he has to give two hours' notice whenever he wants his Volvo fetched from the bowels of West 97th Street garage – by which time it may be too late. Last month it took the garage men so long to retrieve the car that Michael was convinced one of the valet parkers had borrowed it. This is apparently quite common, especially if you don't use your car very often. But a vacant parking space on a Manhattan street is as rare as an Anglophone cabbie.

Friday, 20 November
Peter

A rather embarrassing thing has happened. I have apparently started to enjoy yoga. It has somehow flanked my subversive attitude and actually seems to work. I feel a strange sense of calm when the session is over and my pulse definitely beats slower. Soon I have quite forgotten the silly names of the various moves. Oddly, the pain in my left leg that I have diagnosed as either sciatica, after a phase of fearing it might be deep-vein thrombosis (which could prove fatal if the blood clot travelled up through my artery and lodged in my heart) or gout (except that I haven't really been drinking sufficient port and brandy or eating enough Stilton to trigger it), seems to have faded, following my repeated sessions of Downward Facing Dog.

Monday, 23 November
Joanna

Today we drop into Bellini, an enchanting if pricey baby store on West 86th Street. Shocked by the eight-week lead time for furniture orders, I am promptly panicked into asking if we can buy any of the floor samples. I point out a white cupboard with a trellis of hand-painted pink roses dancing over the drawers. 'This', I say, fingering the little rose-shaped drawer-knobs, 'is perfect. I really don't mind the store wear-and-tear on it if you can deliver it soon.'

'Aren't you forgetting something?' asks Peter crossly. 'What if it's a boy? He's not going to want pink bloody roses.'

I ask the assistant to strike the order.

Monday, 23 November
Peter

My mouth is full of stainless-steel instruments when Dr Wasserman picks his moment to break the news to me. 'You need an onlay. The whole procedure will cost $1,175.00.'

I gag on the small mirror that is reflecting the offending molar.

'We have to take a cast of the tooth and send it away to the lab for them to build the onlay,' adds Dr Wasserman defensively.

Gargling with the puce mouthwash, I struggle to regain my composure. My health insurance doesn't cover dental work.

'This may feel like a small electric shock,' warns Wasserman, brandishing his syringe. After he has liberally injected me, he and Evelyn, who work on the 'hot seat' principle, depart to attend to another patient, while my anaesthetic takes effect. I sit there, assailed by the whine of his unseen drill, and turn my head to one side where a computer stands blinking my case history ominously on its screen. My onlay is already logged up there. Price: $1,175.00. I stare at the Friesian cow balancing on its steep canal bank, and then peer up at one of the cancan girls on the mobile, to see if she is wearing knickers. Finally the drill in the neighbouring room subsides and Dr Wasserman returns with Evelyn.

'Ah, is the onlay absolutely necessary?' I venture.

'Yup, 'fraid so. No way I can fill this, there's not enough tooth left to hold up,' he says.

He takes another exploratory jab with his metal spike and I jump, notwithstanding the injections.

'We could do it in gold instead of porcelain,' he offers.

Christ, for $1,750.00 I would expect a diamond stud as well, I think, but I simply shake my head and say, 'Porcelain will be fine.'

Evelyn holds a colour chart at my open mouth. It covers a spectrum from dazzling white, through various shades of yellow, to a tobacco-stained beige. 'This is the best match,' she pronounces, and Wasserman nods, making a note of their disappointingly yellowish choice.

Finished, I trudge north along a continuous row of designer stores on Madison and beat myself up. I should have known, with his Park Avenue address and the burnished plaque proclaiming his qualifications at Columbia School of Dentistry, that Wasserman was bound to be pricey.

Tuesday, 24 November
Joanna

I am beginning to find yoga so helpful that I am practising some of the easier moves on my own. There is only one thing which worries me: at the end of each session Mary thanks us and gives each of us a little bow with her hands clasped together, as if in prayer.

It is clear we are meant to return this gesture, but neither of us seems able to. I usually nod and smile in an embarrassed, English sort of way while Peter starts busily rolling up his mat. We have discussed our inability to perform this small and yet, I suspect, important detail of yoga etiquette and have put our failure down to British reserve. But today when Mary bows I catch her eye and force myself to return her gesture with a stiff little bow of my own.

I can see Peter watching me, and sensing the need to make some gesture of his own he suddenly nods and raises his left hand in a brisk, police-officer-type wave. Though certainly a start, it is not a manoeuvre I have come across before in our admittedly limited yogic repertoire.

Wednesday, 25 November
Peter

I am flattered to be offered a job today, teaching a writing course this summer at Sarah Lawrence College in Bronxville, just north of the city. It is a graduate class in something called 'Creative non-fiction'. Why is it that non-fiction is defined in the negative, forever salaaming to made-up stories? Fiction should rather be labelled non-fact. As for creative non-fiction, I'm not even sure what that means. It sounds awfully like President Clinton's definition of legal truth – something that's not demonstrably a lie.

Wednesday, 25 November
Joanna

In the lift today I see a sign asking for a twelfth man to sit shivah, the Jewish ritual of mourning. And down at the wall of mailboxes off the lobby, another sign advertising for sale the entire contents of an apartment.

'Very sorry to hear about the death of 13G,' I say to Gerard, the Toulousian super. I pause, but he knows what's coming next. 'Any idea what's happening to the apartment?' I ask lightly and immediately feel ashamed of myself. 'It's just that we have so many friends looking, you know what it's like . . .' I apologize.

'Don't worry – everyone asks – it's already gone,' he replies.

Friday, 27 November
Peter

Today there is evidence of the new tenants – a large removals van is parked outside, disgorging all the bric-à-brac of someone else's life. The side of the van is decorated with a large picture of two men pushing a trolley loaded with a giant ear. Underneath it says Van Gogh Movers: A Cut Above the Rest.

Saturday, 28 November
Joanna

This morning, leaving for the office, I enter the lift expecting as normal to be the only passenger. I'm not. Standing by the buttons is Richard Dreyfuss. I am so surprised to see him that I jump and then, trying to recover myself, blurt out, 'Hello', in what I fear may be a starstruck voice.

'Hello,' he says noncommittally.

I debate whether to mention the *Krippendorf Tribe* or *The Apprenticeship of Duddy Kravitz* or even his Oscar-winning performance in *The Goodbye Girl*, but decide against it and we descend in silence. And as we reach the front lobby he makes quickly for a scruffy white stretch limo, which lurches off down West End Avenue, a portion of its back fender hanging off.

Sunday, 29 November
Peter

Obsessively checking my Amazon.com ratings today, as others check their share prices, I am enormously cheered to see that I have rallied strongly and now stand at 9,127th instead of the high twenty thousands, where I have been languishing of late.

I boast of this fact to Michael, who is a fellow author and obsessive Amazon.com checker, but he tells me that a sudden rally such as I have just enjoyed can in fact be bad news. He has gone to the trouble of phoning Amazon.com's literary score-keeper, who explained that it's usual for books that become unavailable in bookshops (because their sales are too torpid to be worth the shelf space) to jump suddenly in their Amazon.com ratings. So this can, in fact, be a sign that a book is on the way out.

The score-keeper has also told Michael that Amazon.com uses a complex logarithmic formula, multiplying number sold with recentness of sales, to calculate a book's ranking. Apparently when you get down into the thirty thousands, the sales are so slight that a single purchase can yank you up several thousand places.

DECEMBER

Your baby's lungs and digestive tract are almost
fully developed and it can now see in utero and
distinguish light from dark.
Your baby now weighs 6 lbs.
The womb is so snug you may notice less movement.
If you are interested in breastfeeding
sign up for a class or interview lactation consultants.
BabyCenter.com

Saturday, 5 December
Joanna

Today, at ABC, the luxurious furniture store on 19th Street
and Broadway, whose interior is cunningly designed to feel
like a magical bazaar, we see a truly magnificent crib. Its
wooden panels are exquisitely hand carved with cherubs
and laurel wreaths, and its front railing cleverly drops to
convert it into a day bed. Even Peter agrees that it is an
outstanding piece of furniture. But the price is silly – we
reluctantly agree on that too. 'The kid will never appreciate
it,' he reasons. 'Let's just get a basic, safe cot, not a juvenile
throne.'

So we leave, determined to shop around.

Sunday, 6 December
Peter

I am sitting at the kitchen table on our inherited fake cowhide bar stools, trying to make notes on a book I am supposed to review, groping for a word that remains elusively on the tip of my lobe. Suddenly I feel a sharp pain in both temples simultaneously and the awful realization washes over my mind that this is it, this is what it feels like to have a brain haemorrhage. I am invaded by the prospect of myself slumped in a wheelchair, drooling and mute. Will I be loyally tended by partner, friends and family? Or will I be dumped in an underfunded institution, sentenced to inhale boiled cabbage fumes, watch daytime TV and be talked down to by jolly Caribbean caretakers for the rest of my miserable life? I give a small shriek of alarm and bring my hands gingerly up to my temples, where I encounter something cold and metallic.

'This', comes Joanna's voice from behind me, 'is what it feels like to be born by forceps delivery.' And with that she prises off the claws of the chrome pasta tongs that she has gripped onto my head.

Monday, 7 December
Joanna

Tonight it is the turn of John Guare to entertain the American Friends of the Royal Court. He has agreed to be interviewed by John Lahr, the theatre critic for the *New Yorker*, whose father played the Lion in *The Wizard of Oz*. The venue is a frightfully smart brownstone on 80th Street, within smiling distance of the Metropolitan Museum of Art – one of the chicest strips of residential real estate in the city. It is owned by someone on the board of Lazard Frères, the investment bank. As our contribution, Peter and I have been asked to invite some of our journalist friends in order to whip up media interest.

'Christ, I'll come just to see the house,' said Meredith, when I sounded her out.

It is worth the inspection, oozing expense from every interior-designed bow. As forty or so people mingle in the downstairs drawing room, they can be heard quite openly estimating the real estate value. 'Several serious Lazard bonuses,' concludes Meredith.

Guare is an hour and a half late and, anxious to make up for this spectacular rudeness, begins circulating garrulously. 'My dear,' he says, patting my belly and exhaling a generous whiff of claret, 'how *are you*, we know each other, don't we?' I smile noncommittally, knowing I have never met him before. 'Of course,' he cries, 'I recognize you from the television!'

This is not an uncommon line in New York and I have learned it is better to maintain a silent acquiescence than to deny it. So I grin back as an attractive young woman in a black leather jacket slides up to Guare and tugs his sleeve.

'Hello,' she says. 'My name's Julie and I just wanted to tell you I'm such an admirer of your work.'

Guare beams. 'My dear,' he says, taking her hand and holding onto it, petting her wrist. 'And what do you do? In the theatre perhaps?'

'I'm a screen writer,' she says proudly.

The great playwright's expression changes and he drops her hand. 'Oh, how humiliating for you,' he says. 'Ugh, how could you? You don't even own your own work and your films never get made. I fear for your mental health, my dear. An unpublished poem has more integrity than any screenplay!'

Taken aback by this onslaught, Julie attempts to defend herself. 'Well, I have many friends in the theatre who are waiting tables,' she protests. 'At least I'm earning a living.'

Guare raises his hand and, peering at her closely, declares, 'You've sold out. I see it *all* the time. It's corporate writing, my dear. I have a friend who has written sixteen screenplays, he has them beautifully bound in leather on his bookshelf, but not *one* of them has been made! Ha! Tell me, do you have any credits?'

'Yes,' says Julie quickly. 'I got a quarter credit for *Harriet the Spy*, the children's movie that came out two years ago.'

'A *quarter* credit,' laughs Guare. 'So humiliating!' And with that, he sweeps grandly off to the other end of the room.

Tuesday, 8 December
Peter

I see that drunk-driving commercial again today and, as always, it leaves me chilled and fearful. The ad starts with a sonogram of a full-term baby. In the foreground are the reassuring peaks and troughs of a normal heartbeat with its bleeping soundtrack. Suddenly there is a screech of tyres, a crash, a shattering of glass and a depressed horn. The heartbeat stops and becomes a continuous beep and the graph flatlines. Text appears over the foetal sonogram: 'Abbey Danielle – killed by a drunk driver – on the way to being born.'

Wednesday, 9 December
Joanna

This morning I suddenly hear myself announce that as soon as I have finished my decaff, I am going shopping for baby things.

'Where to?' enquires Peter.

'Oh, downtown, various places.'

'ABC?'

'I might drop by there,' I admit diffidently.

'All right, I'll come too,' announces Peter. I know he is suspicious that I am intending to order the crib we admired there. He is right to suspect me.

But it turns out to be a frustrating experience, as the assistant seems reluctant to sell us one.

'What's your due date?' she asks, eyeing my straining jacket.

'January 22nd.'

'Oh, we can't have it ready by then,' she says, sounding almost pleased.

'It's OK, the baby will spend the first eight weeks in a Moses basket,' I reply.

'Well, we need a minimum of fourteen weeks,' she says, as if this is obviously the end of the conversation.

'We'll have to hope it doesn't come early then,' I retort, suddenly determined to have the crib whatever the cost. Peter, of course, having pretended to check the safety locks while pronouncing on the quality of workmanship, has moved safely off to examine musical mobiles with bogus intensity.

'I want the green one,' I say petulantly.

'What sex is the baby?' asks the assistant.

'I don't know.'

'You don't know?'

'Not yet, no.'

'Well, what colour's the nursery?'

'Um, it's white.'

'Well, mint green is a very difficult colour to team with, it will dominate the room. Are you prepared for that?'

'The room is fairly big, I don't think it will dominate it. And the curtains will match; they're blue and green.'

'Well, what colour's your crib linen?' she persists, weirdly determined to put us off.

'White.'

'What, surely not all of it?' she challenges.

'Look,' I say firmly, reaching for my purse, 'I want the mint green crib with the engraved cherubs.'

'If it's a boy, he'll hate you for choosing the cherubs,' observes Peter, as we move towards the till.

'Honey,' says a middle-aged woman, smiling slyly as she folds her credit card slip, 'chances are he's gonna hate you anyway. They all do, you know. Eventually.'

Saturday, 12 December
Peter

Though I have an aversion to pasta, Joanna has cooked up a Medusa's head of spaghetti for dinner and splodged onto it a jar of insipid tomato topping. I am having difficulty serving the meal, for ever since they were stretched abnormally wide to effect my forceps delivery the pasta tongs refuse to clench back to their original position, and the spaghetti keeps slithering through the claws.

Monday, 14 December
Joanna

I am now going to the surgery on a weekly basis. Today, as usual, the nurse velcroes the rubber cuff round my arm and squeezes the bulb to check my blood pressure, then forces me onto the scales to confirm a total weight gain of 29 lbs.

'Good,' says the nurse. 'You can expect your baby anytime from January 1st.'

Panicked at the news it might come three weeks earlier than expected, I come home to find Peter frantically ordering Lugo, the leisurely handyman, around the baby's room, where the two of them are trying to put up curtain rails. Lugo is having difficulty because, despite our careful measurements, we appear to have ordered the wrong-sized rails.

It turns out to be my fault because I wrote the measurements down and then ordered the rails from the Pottery Barn catalogue with no apparent reference to the figures whatsoever. Even odder, I ordered more rails than we have windows. I am uncertain how this happened, but it has left Peter furious, Lugo bewildered, and me convinced that we are not sufficiently practical to be parents.

Monday, 14 December
Peter

I'm at the gym, striding away on the ski-trek machine and, through a veil of sweat, watching a CBS early evening news spot on the stress of Christmas shopping. A new study, they report, shows that for many men Christmas shopping is more stressful than being in combat. Well, I've been in combat and this test is patent nonsense. Combat is not nearly as stressful as Christmas shopping. For one thing there aren't as many choices in combat.

Tuesday, 15 December
Joanna

Despite my failure over the curtain rails, there is one achievement I do feel rather proud of. I have been slowly accumulating the layette and, according to Miriam Stoppard, I have now got everything on the list apart from six muslin 'sick-cloths'.

I do not seem able to find muslin sick-cloths anywhere in New York. Macy's, Bergdorf-Goodman, Barneys, Saks: I have tried them all. Eventually, an assistant at Albee's, the discount baby emporium, tells me that Americans do not use sick-cloths.

'But what do you use?' I ask.

'No one has ever asked me that before,' she says.

'Perhaps American babies don't vomit like English babies,' I try dryly.

'No, no, they probably vomit about the same,' she says sincerely. 'Couldn't you use a cloth diaper, maybe?'

'Aren't they a bit bulky?' I ask.

'Not if you arrange them artfully,' she says, pulling down a packet from a nearby shelf. 'You could wear them over your shoulder like this,' she demonstrates, 'as a scarf.'

I cannot imagine my grey Jil Sander suit accessorized with a cloth diaper, but I buy a packet of eight anyway.

Tuesday, 15 December
Peter

I am back in Dr Wasserman's chair, having my thousand buck onlay onlaid.

'Here it is,' says Wasserman. He reaches his big but surprisingly nimble paw into a little plastic box and, with a flourish, produces the onlay.

'Hmm,' I say, determined not to be impressed, which is not difficult – it is a tiny, rather yellow blob of resin.

He glues it into the hole in my mouth he has previously excavated, and while he waits for the adhesive to bond his nurse, Evelyn, chats to me.

'You have a nice accent,' she says. 'I think the English accent is so classy.'

'Hank yaw,' I say, my mouth still clamped open.

'D'ya think I have a Brooklyn accent?' she enquires of Wasserman in a heavy Brooklyn accent.

'Occasionally it shows through a little,' he says tactfully. He notices me checking out his framed Columbia Dental School scroll hanging on the wall. 'We were the rebel year,' he recalls proudly. 'WE thought we knew better.' I try to conjure up a class of firebrand dentists, but fail.

Wednesday, 16 December
Joanna

We have been invited back to their carolling evening by the Horatio Street Association, our old neighbourhood group. We meet at Jackson Square, a defiant triangle of grass, squeezed between Eighth Avenue and West 14th Street. Usually it is populated by weary dog owners armed with their obligatory pooper-scoopers, but tonight's assembled group is a mixed bunch of Wall Streeters, models, out-of-work actors, writers and painters, accompanied by a few precocious Manhattan children dressed against the freezing fog in puffa jackets, mufflers and bobble hats. Hymn sheets are distributed and we set off down Eighth Avenue, bathed in the festive flashing red lights of our NYPD squad car escort.

Our first stop is the steamy confines of Piccolo Angelo, where the patrons are forced to stop mid-mascarpone and listen to our unrehearsed rendition of 'Let It Snow! Let It Snow! Let It Snow!' Our song accomplished, we trek across Greenwich Street while the police officer halts the traffic, to the local supermarket, D'Agostino's, where we elbow our way past the grumbling check-out queue to the frozen food section. There we deliver a rather poor 'First Noel'.

Several more restaurants and the Village Nursing Home

later, we turn into Gansevoort Street, the transvestite promenade we used to overlook from our loft. The children are getting fractious, trying to prize open a newspaper vending machine until the officer intervenes. Adjacent to the gay club, Hell, the kids are distracted by the sight of a hefty local transvestite dressed up as Mother Christmas and perched upon a customized penny farthing tricycle, squeezing an accordion and singing. Next to her stands her companion, a small red devil complete with plastic horns, pointy tail and spandex stilettos.

'Hey, Mother Christmas, sing us a song,' the children plead. And primping her huge white wig, the transvestite breaks into a bass chorus of 'Rudolf the red nosed reindeer, had a *fucking* shiny nose . . .'

'Oh, no, no, no,' shrieks Carole, our team leader, wagging a finger. The officer thrusts his way to the front. 'Now you be nice, huh?' he threatens. 'Go ahead and sing the decent one for the kids here, or I might just lose my Christmas spirit with you, honey.'

Mother Christmas embarks sullenly on a sanitized version, singing defiantly off key.

We move on, delivering a ragged burst of 'We Three Kings of Orient Are', down the street at Florent, Peter's old lunching haunt, and fall into step with the officer.

'Do you get much trouble around here?' Peter asks him.

'Nah, I ain't seen anyone packing a gun in more than two years. No one does nothing no more,' he says, sounding disappointed.

'Why's that then?'

'It's the death penalty, ain't it?' the officer declares confidently. 'More than thirty people got the needle in Texas this year and now they've brought it back here in New York. You telling me that ain't no deterrent?' And he climbs back into his car, carolling patrol over for another year.

Friday, 18 December
Peter

We have a slight problem today at yoga because our normal exercise space is impeded by a vast Christmas tree which Joanna has finally forced me to buy from a couple of Quebecois lumberjacks operating from an old van parked on Broadway. In advance of our yoga I have plugged in the lights to make the scene more festive, but every time we do Downward Facing Dog we end up with a mouthful of conifer, which Mary Barnes, our instructor, gamely tries to ignore.

Mary ends the session by bidding us to 'Feel the energy, feel yourself taking your energy into the day with you.'

When she has gone I collapse on the floor reading *Private Eye*. Joanna starts up a mock anti-yogic mantra in which she intones, 'Feel the energy drifting out of us, feel the spite, feel the malice, feel the *Schadenfreude*, feel the envy, all flooding back into us as we realign the day according to our actual characters.'

Saturday, 19 December
Joanna

The *New York Post* reports that Tina Brown, who relinquished her editorship of the *New Yorker* in June to launch her own magazine, has finally decided on a title for her new venture. It is to be called *Talk*, with the subtitle: *The American Conversation*. The definite article makes it sound as if there is only one American conversation going on. It seems a fairly ambitious claim to the Zeitgeist.

Like most British hacks I am intrigued by the spectacularly successful Brown and her husband, Harry Evans, the former editor of the *Sunday Times*, and was rather flattered to receive an invitation last spring to dinner at their East River home.

The other guests were mostly Manhattan media A-list: Robert Hughes, the art historian; Si Newhouse, owner of Condé Nast; Julie Taymor, director of *The Lion King*; Wendy Wasserstein, the playwright; and Chip McGrath, editor of the *New York Times Book Review*.

Though the dinner was in honour of Adam Gopnik, who'd won a Polk award for his dispatches from Paris, the trophy guest was to be the actor Steve Martin, in town shooting a remake of *The Out of Towners* with Goldie Hawn.

Martin had obviously informed our hosts he was going to be late because we sat down to our lobster ravioli with his chair empty. I was on Harry Evans's table and the conversation soon turned to drugs.

'Have any of you ever done cocaine?' Evans enquired of the table. No one was forthcoming. 'I once took marijuana in the hopes of achieving an instant erection . . . It failed to materialize,' he concluded glumly.

Sitting on my right, a dark-haired, distracted man introduced himself as Elliot Goldenthal, 'a composer'.

'I'm working on the score of Neil Jordan's new movie, *The Butcher Boy*,' he said.

'I hope it's better than that awful music he used in *Interview with a Vampire*,' I replied, breaking into my bread roll.

'Actually,' said Elliot, 'that was my score too. In fact it was nominated for an Oscar.'

I was just about to slide under the table with mortification when there was a small commotion as Steve Martin finally arrived. To my astonishment, and that of the rest of my table, the silver-haired actor made a beeline straight for me, arms outstretched in hugging mode, as if we were friends of old.

In an instant I realized what had happened: he had confused me with our hostess, whose hair length and complexion I share.

'Joanna Coles,' I said loudly, leaping up and proffering my hand to fend off his faux pas.

'Oh, *how* could I have mistaken you?' he giggled, trying to mollify me as Tina approached unseen behind him. 'You're so much younger!'

The next morning I described the evening to Meredith. 'Talk about dissing your hostess,' she grinned. 'You do realize you'll never be invited back?'

Saturday, 19 December
Peter

The truth is it's just as well I'm doing yoga, or I might well have blown up by now. I think we are both more stressed by this pregnancy than either of us is prepared to admit, even to ourselves. I am now in real danger of joining those ranks of New Yorkers who walk around like loaded guns, just waiting for the smallest annoyance to trigger them.

There is a special sub-set of this category, encountered mostly on the upper reaches of Broadway, the old folk of the Upper West Side. They are pre-emptively argumentative, mithering away to themselves in low gravelly voices as they stomp along the sidewalks, elbows out defensively like tiny urban quarterbacks. Unlike their Upper East Side counterparts, they are not rich enough to be fawned over by domestic staff hoping to be dealt into wills. I imagine that if we stay here long enough we might turn into these sour denizens of the Upper West Side.

Sunday, 20 December
Joanna

I wake up at 4 a.m. this morning, as I do every morning now, unable to get back to sleep. I have never suffered sleep deprivation like this before and I think it must be the fastest route to depression.

'Come on, cheer up, it's all so exciting,' Peter says, unconvincingly. 'It's what you wanted, isn't it?' It is, but I still feel dark, dark grey.

'It'll get much worse after the baby's born, you'll never sleep at all then,' e-mails Jane cheerfully when I write to complain. I spend my waking time entirely preoccupied by how I can take a nap. Several times in the last fortnight I have woken up at 8 a.m., had breakfast and, unable to do anything else, gone straight back to bed and slept until 1.30 p.m.

It is also affecting my memory. Yesterday I wrote in my diary 'Lunch, 1 p.m., with Joanna Coles'. I still have no idea who I stood up.

'It's called pregnesia,' says Kelly helpfully, who seems to know all about it, though she has never been pregnant herself.

To break the cycle I suggest we go out to East Hampton, claiming that the change of air will do me good. By 2 p.m. we are sitting on the deserted sands of Georgica Beach, surveying the calm grey seas and the baby-blue sky, slurping tubs of steaming shrimp chowder followed by Brie sandwiches which we have purchased at Barefoot Contessa.

'There, do you feel better now?' asks Peter.

But I still feel grey.

Sunday, 20 December
Peter

Joanna is feeling insecure and unattractive. 'Bizou,' she demands in a baby voice, puckering her lips. I try to plant a perfunctory kiss, but our sunglasses clatter like the antlers of rutting stags.

She pleads to go out to the Hamptons today, though winter on the wind-swept eastern tip of Long Island is notoriously inhospitable. It is suddenly vital for her for mental rehab, she insists. I hail a cab to take us to the car hire depot, and as I load our bags into the boot I notice its bumper sticker: 'Mean people suck,' it complains.

Notwithstanding radio sexologist Dr Ruth's recorded exhortation that buckling up is the law, my seat belt refuses to uncoil from its plastic cylinder, and I narrowly miss head-butting the Perspex money window when the driver has a belated and uncharacteristic fit of caution about going through an early red light.

He takes advantage of the break to hawk up a blob of glutinous green phlegm, which he spits noisily onto a pristine white square of handkerchief. He examines the venomous hummock minutely, then folds it into his hanky with all the care of a smuggler swaddling an emerald, and thrusts it into his pocket.

Monday, 21 December
Joanna

Today I go into Second Nature, East Hampton's health food store, to buy more pre-natal vitamins. Though I am convinced they are essential, Kelly claims it is the equivalent of injecting cattle with hormones. 'That's why there are so many Caesareans in America,' she told me last week. 'The babies are getting too big to come out naturally.'

Though the prospect of squeezing out a 10lb baby worries me, I buy the vitamins anyway. 'Oh, you're having a girl,' says the man, a gentle Nigerian, smiling at me from behind the counter.

'Really?' I say.

'I can see it in your face,' he grins. 'I am never wrong. I can see it in your aura. Definitely a girl.'

Ten minutes later I walk into Top Drawer Lingerie to try on a dreaded nursing bra. I have chosen Top Drawer over the more fashionable Bonne Nuit, twenty yards away, because it has huge, individual changing rooms and I want some privacy.

The assistant hands me a selection of enormous, upholstered bras with triangular press-studded panels promising 'instant nipple access'.

'Ah ha,' she cries. 'So you're having a boy!'

'Well, I don't know yet.'

'Oh yes,' she says. 'I've had three and there's no question you're having a boy. Betsy,' she calls to the other assistant, wrenching back the cubicle curtain so the entire store can watch me struggling with my industrially wired nursing bra. 'Betsy, isn't she having a boy?'

'I should say so!' says Betsy.

'Do you think this is the right size?' I ask weakly, trying to wrestle back at least a corner of the curtain.

'Oh yes,' says the first assistant. 'Look, it's stretchy,' she hooks a thumb around the right cup and tugs at it to demonstrate. 'For the first two weeks your breasts will get very big and then they settle down, this fits you fine.'

'And then they get all shrivelled and droop,' cautions Betsy.

'And then,' adds a middle-aged customer angrily fingering a black lace teddy, 'your husband will leave you for someone half your age.'

Tuesday, 22 December
Peter

We have agreed to take Willow for a walk. She is the year-old chocolate brown American standard poodle that belongs to Ron and Betsy, our upstairs neighbours here in the Hamptons. Ron is out here working on a book about how he kicked his addiction to gambling. As he hands me the end of the leash and the bounding, enthusiastic dog, he also hands me a little bundle. It contains two polythene gloves and two small plastic bags. 'In case she poops,' he says.

And indeed, half an hour later, in front of the café veranda at Main Beach, where she can be assured of the widest possible audience, Willow decides to launch a haunch-quivering, eye-watering poop. As she uncoils herself from her ablutions, I am very tempted to mosey off. I cannot bear the thought of manhandling her effluent. But a bench of pensioners trussed in tartan rugs are glowering at me, so there is no escape. Joanna is no help either. She has walked ahead, as though she is nothing to do with us. I fit a glove onto my right hand, like a surgeon, and approach the visibly steaming coil. I hold my breath and scoop it up. It is warm and squishy through the thin skein of the customized doggy-do glove. Willow is watching me intently, head cocked to one side, as though enjoying my discomfort as I bag and tie her turd and toss it into the bin.

'You made yourself bloody scarce,' I complain to Joanna when we catch up with her. 'Thanks for the help.'

'Well, it's good training for parenthood,' she replies, and I groan at the thought.

Wednesday, 23 December
Joanna

Today, as we are poking around for baby stuff in Triangle, the one affordable furniture shop in Bridgehampton, the sales clerk pops the inevitable question. 'Is it a boy or a girl?'

'I want the surprise,' I say, somewhat wearily.

'I wanted the surprise too,' she says, 'but my doctor blurted it out by mistake. I was in his office and he suddenly said, "When your son is born . . ." I was like, "My son? You mean I'm having a *son*?" I was in total shock. I mean, it felt like I had the baby *that day*. The doctor felt so awful . . . but there was nothing we could do.'

I have been worried about this happening ever since the amnio, the first time anyone knew the sex for sure, and I now preface every doctor's visit with a jokey 'I hope you haven't forgotten I don't want to know the sex.'

It seems to me obvious that one should savour the mystery as long as possible, but our friends think that I'm being an eccentric contrarian.

'Well, how can I get anything for it, then?' Meredith moaned at me last week, as if the only choice in the world was blue or pink.

Peter accuses me of assuming it's a girl and buying accordingly – as if I was buying stuff for a miniature me. Though I protest this isn't true, I suspect he may be right.

Wednesday, 23 December
Peter

Back in a snow-laden Manhattan, I try to log onto my Amazon.com rating, which I have managed to avoid doing for several weeks now – a personal record. But I misclick and get my namesake authors instead. Peter Godwin's *Guide to HIV in East Asia* stands at number 612,344, leading Peter Godwin's *Concise Guide to Growing Pelargoniums*, which is currently out of stock. And Godwin I. Meniru's new book, *A Handbook of Interuterine Insemination* has entered the Amazon.co.uk charts at 181,548. *Mukiwa*, my African memoir, still leads the pack at 23,109. We mid-list Godwins are nothing if not diverse in our literary endeavours.

Christmas Day
Joanna

Preoccupied by pregnancy, neither of us feels remotely Christmassy. We resolve not to bother giving each other presents, though walking down Broadway on Christmas Eve, I am accosted by a man with a black plastic bin liner slung over his shoulder. It is, he says, stuffed with Furbies, the season's hottest interactive toy, which are completely sold out in toy shops.

I buy one and present it to Peter and he takes it to Christmas lunch at Dani and Michael's, where it chatters Furbish and entertains a roomful of adults while terrorizing their dog, a Yorkshire terrier of a somewhat nervous disposition. But later that evening we hit a snag. We have tickets for *The Theory of Flight*, starring Kenneth Branagh and Helena Bonham Carter, who plays a young woman crippled by motor neurone disease. At first all goes well, and we settle down with our popcorn and Movie Bites. But as soon as Helena begins using her Stephen Hawking-style electronic voice box, the Furby unaccountably breaks into a frenzy of Furbish.

'Nye-tye, nye-tye,' it chirrups frantically (which, according to the manual, means 'Tickle me' in Furbish) from the bottom of its carrier bag. The more Helena uses her synthetic voice, the more the Furby responds with its ludicrous cheeping. The whole cinema is tut-tutting and looking round for the source of the noise, but we play innocent until at last a woman sitting in the next seat rumbles us. Peter dives into the bag and, unable to remove the batteries without a screwdriver, swaddles the Furby in his scarf.

'Achoo! Hold me,' says the little falsetto voice, only slightly muffled by its cashmere gag. The surrounding tut-tuts are increasingly menacing, so Peter reaches back into the bag again. I hear a squawk and the Furby falls silent.

Back home we unwrap the little critter and examine it. Its ears are at a strange angle, and though its saucer eyes are wide open it is resolutely mute.

Tuesday, 29 December
Peter

'I had a weird dream,' declares Joanna this morning.

'You and Martin Luther King both.'

'I dreamed that I was hypnotized to stand up and sing "The Star Spangled Banner", but every time I tried to sing it, my nose began to bleed. What do you think it means? Quick! quick!' she interrupts before I have a chance to speculate. 'Feel here, the baby gave an enormous kick.' She whips up her jumper and indicates which part of her bulge has kicked, but I can feel nothing.

'You should talk to the baby, so it gets used to your voice,' she suggests.

'It hears my voice all the time.'

'No, actually address it, it can tell the difference. Talk close to my belly.'

I stoop down and gaze at the Cyclops eye of her belly-button. 'Er, hello, little one,' I say, feeling ludicrous.

'No, have a real conversation.'

'How can I? It takes two to converse.'

'All right, I'll be baby. "Hey, dad,"' she says reverting to the rasping New York accent she has given our unborn child,' "ya finished decoratin' my room, huh? I ain't comin' out till that place is all done, right?"'

'I'm sorry. I just can't do this.'

'Oh, all right then,' she says, handing me a book. 'Read to him from Dr Seuss.'

I open the book and gravely address her belly-button:

'You have brains in your head.
You have feet in your shoes.
You can steer yourself
any direction you choose.
You're on your own. And you know what you know.
And YOU are the guy who'll decide where to go.'

JANUARY

*The fingers' nails are beyond the finger tips
and almost ready for trimming.
He or she is also blinking, swallowing,
making breathing movements and passing urine.*
BabySoon.com

Saturday, 9 January
Peter

Outside it is raining and New York is still sensibly asleep. We arrive at Roosevelt Hospital for day one of our Weekend Intensive Lamaze birthing course, and make the mistake of using the Sabbath elevator. It stops at every single floor on Saturdays so that observant Jews don't have to break the Sabbath by operating machinery. After two floors I am fuming with impatience and we bale out. Soon we are on the eleventh floor in a small room with walls of swirling turquoise fingerprint patina, attending our birthing class.

Sigrid, our instructor, is a Swedish vision in a cinnamon trouser suit with a brown floral bosom, gold glasses, dyed gold hair and gold slippers. She hands out crib sheets and free maternity magazines – they come in plastic wrappings complete with some complimentary Pampers – a tiny token of things to come. In fact Pampers have a fairly high presence in today's lessons – the anatomy and physiology chart displayed on Sigrid's easel is also brought to us compliments of the nappy makers.

Sigrid soon reveals herself to be strict and irony free. Her instruction method is to reduce us to the status of small children with learning problems.

'Dancing,' she bellows, 'dancing is an excellent way to get exercise for the pregnant women. I recommend dancing for half an hour at least – every night.' She stoops over her boom box and presses the play button and on comes 'Rock Around the Clock'. 'Dance! Dance everybody!' she cries. Soon we are all doing a desultory jive in the tiny space of the room, the men are like tugs gingerly steering the great whales of pregnancy away from each other to prevent baby-inducing collisions.

The fathers are rounded up and discharged outside to write down the 'best' and 'worst' things about having a baby. We are an uneasy group with little in common but impending fatherhood – an Israeli, a Greek, two Americans and me. There is some discussion and then under 'best' we write:

— everything changes
— genetic immortality
— becoming a family
— getting to watch more cartoons

Under 'worst' we write:

— everything changes
— scatological imprisonment
— less sex
— expense
— end of aesthetics
— less attention for dad

When we go back, Sigrid is teaching the women the finer points of peeing in late pregnancy. 'You go to the bathroom and urinate, ja? Then you do like this, both hands on the belly and lift it up,' she hoists her own belly, 'and then you urinate some more – to get rid of the residual amount. OK practise!

'The vagina can stretch naturally to take a ten-pound-baby's head. So when people talk about men having a penis too big – it's a joke – pah! There is no penis big enough to even bother a vagina I tell you.' The men all look eyes downcast, as if vaguely ashamed on behalf of males everywhere who have ever claimed size mattered.

'Everyone touch your lips. Now go like this', Sigrid flubbers her lips with her index finger, 'blalalalalala – that's how the cervix feels when it's engaged. Do it, everyone, do it! Blalalala . . .'

We obediently flubber our lips in imitation of ripe cervixes. And I wonder whatever happened to pacing the waiting room with a vintage cigar in your pocket, waiting for a nurse with sensible shoes and hair clipped to a starched hat, to come in and announce, 'Congratulations, it's a . . .'

Instead I am trapped here play-acting a ripe cervix and pondering if there is any way at all I can salvage a tiny bit of dignity. Sigrid is beginning to remind me of my drill sergeant-major in the army, breaking down the recruit's personality in order to rebuild it with military instincts.

'Think of the cervix as a turtleneck of a sweater that will stretch slowly over the baby's head,' she suggests, going over the early-warning signs of labour. She wants us to read the symptoms out loud and picks on Neta, the Israeli, to begin. She keeps picking on him, and as Hebrew is his mother tongue he stumbles heroically on unfamiliar English written words. Each time he hesitates, his American wife loyally murmurs prompts in his ear.

'Mucus plug, bloody show,' reads Neta, blanching.

'In fact,' says Sigrid, 'it's stringy mucus, not like a plug at all.'

At this point I begin to feel as if I'm going to retch up my meagre breakfast and I lower my head into my hands and try to think of something else, any other image but a stringy mucus plug. 'That must be one of the most disgusting phrases I have ever heard,' I whisper to Joanna, but she is jotting diligently and frowns at me for talking in class.

'Be sure to call the doctor if blood is running down your leg,' says Sigrid. 'Write it down – CALL DOCTOR IF BLOOD RUNNING DOWN LEG.'

One of the women has asked if she can go swimming after she has 'unplugged'. 'Of course,' says Sigrid, 'your vagina doesn't stand up like a tube, you know. But you shouldn't have sex after your waters have broken.'

There are several gasps, and someone goes 'eeooouuuww'.

'Well, some have one for the road, you know,' says Sigrid.

I now find that I am trying to tune out as much of the gory detail of childbirth as possible, for fear that I might be converted to celibacy, induced by Sigrid's inadvertent sex aversion therapy. But chunks of her description penetrate my mental air defences, Scuds of disgust thudding in my consciousness: '. . . elicit your faecal ejection reflex . . . you feel like you're gonna shit a watermelon . . . old, oxidized blood . . . baby's first bowel movement . . . meconium, a greenish black sticky substance . . .'

I flip up my mental yashmak to find Sigrid picking up a plastic pelvis and a baby doll and ramming the doll's head into the pelvis, twisting it this way and that to show the various birthing positions. Then she manipulates the plastic pelvis to show how it can open to accommodate the baby's head. The pelvic jaws gape open like a fish's mouth.

'Remember, you must tap into your spiritual centre, wherever that is,' she says. 'You're not just a body having a baby. You're more than a pelvis with a passenger.'

She alights on Neta to read aloud again, and the colour rises to his cheeks as he steps reluctantly into the linguistic breach once more. I feel like screaming, 'Give him a break!' But in fact I remain head lowered, grateful that it is not my turn.

Sigrid is passionate about pain relief: she doesn't believe in it. American women, she is convinced, are far too quick in their demands to be numbed. 'They are shouting for an epidural when they're still in the parking lot,' she scorns.

The Birthing Center, the temple of natural birth to which Joanna appears now to be leaning under the influence of Sigrid's zealotry, is an epidural-free zone. The only pain relief allowed there is a shot of Demarol, a mildly numbing drug that Sigrid describes as having the same effect as a quick Martini on an empty stomach.

It is now nearly five p.m. We have been hectored for nearly eight straight hours and it is more than I can take. Thankfully she decides to show a short video of birthing experiences, which, she warns, we will be expected to critique afterwards.

On the screen a woman finally begins her contractions. To help her cope with the pain, her husband holds up a photo of their piebald cat. 'OK, honey, focus on Benson,' he says. Next he is nudging her into the shower cubicle and while she is blasted by the pellets of hot water, he sings cheerfully, 'She'll be coming round the mountain when she comes/She'll be coming round the mountain when she comes . . .'

The lights go up and Sigrid's harsh voice hauls me back to the reality of our stuffy little room. 'Remember, if you don't like a nurse you can always go and complain and get her swapped,' she is saying. 'I remember one Nurse Ratchet, who said to a husband I'd taught, "You have to leave now." He said, "No, I wanna stay." And she said, "But I have to do things to your wife – I have to do things to her *down there*." And he said, "Look, honey, I've done more things to her *down there* than you'll ever do."'

Saturday, 9 January
Joanna

'My accent is Swedish,' announces Sigrid, our birthing instructor. 'I studied in Sweden, I have a degree in nursing and a master's in midwifery. I was spirited away from Sweden by a handsome American and now we've been married forty-one years.'

She grins round at us, her pale eyes intensified by her large, gold-framed glasses. 'When I arrived here in 1958, I got the shock of my life. I was horrified to discover that most women were fully drugged during labour and woke up two days later to find that they had a baby!

'So I set off to find out why women are so scared of giving birth in this country. This', she pauses briefly, staring around at us again, 'is a class designed for people with impossible schedules and hopefully you have no plans for tonight because there will be homework.'

Another couple shuffle in late and, as they obediently stick on their name badges, have a whispered row about where to sit. 'I want to be at the back,' hisses the husband labelled Bill, as his wife tugs him towards a seat next to

Sigrid. But Bill wins the battle and soon embarks on the complicated process of trying to plug in his Walkman earpiece, undetected by Sigrid, so he can catch the latest football play-offs.

Barry, another husband sitting opposite him, mouths desperately, 'What's the score?'

At 10 a.m., the men are sent out of the room and the women ordered to sit in a circle on the floor. For one terrible moment I think Sigrid is going to make us act out the instructions on a leaflet I have spotted in our Childbirth Forum Classroom Folder. The page headed 'How to Avoid an Episiotomy' advises that women should spend the final months of pregnancy massaging the perineum. The instructions are accompanied by a crude pencil drawing of a woman sitting next to a bottle of vegetable oil and inserting two thumbs in her vagina. I am preparing to refuse vigorously when to my relief Sigrid tasks us with writing down a list of the best and worst aspects of having a baby.

This seems easy enough. 'The baby' we all chorus when asked to start with the best list. But, oddly, the worst list fills up faster:

— money worries
— being pregnant
— pain
— working pressure
— family tensions
— less freedom
— less mobility

We sit wondering what else to put under best. 'Maternity leave,' says a lawyer called Susan, due three days after me and still schlepping to her office every morning by 9 a.m.

'I've cut my court work,' she says grimly, 'but I'm still not getting home before 8 p.m. Right now, I'm more excited about taking time off work than I am about the baby.'

I know what she means. It still feels so abstract. Even as we stockpile diapers – to Peter's horror we've been warned we'll go through 600 in the first month – I can't believe we're really going to have a baby.

At snack-time I offer our chocolate raisins to my neighbour. 'Oooh, I don't think so,' she giggles, shaking her head as if I had suggested a line of cocaine. In silent reprimand, she ferrets in her bag and retrieves a chaste Tupperware box of fresh blueberries, which she savours one by one.

'I'm not sure I can stand much more of this,' says Peter, through a mouthful of chocolate raisins.

'Now write this down,' Sigrid shouts as our break ends, '"The good Lord deliver us from meddlesome obstetrics."'

Only six hours left to go. And then, of course, all day tomorrow.

Sunday, 10 January
Peter

We arrive at Room 11A29, clutching our packed lunches like schoolchildren, to find a new laminated chart propped up on the easel to welcome us. It is entitled 'Positions for Pushing'. Next to it sits a huge felt breast in a shocking shade of pink.

Sigrid bids us clear our minds and puts on a relaxation cassette of Pachelbel's Canon, under which has been recorded the sound of distant waves breaking. 'Everyone

repeat after me: take one contraction at a time!' roars
Sigrid. 'TAKE ONE CONTRACTION AT A TIME', we call out in
weary, unenthusiastic voices. It is going to be a long
day.

Sigrid tells us how important breathing and relaxation is
to a successful labour. 'Modern women have so much going
on upstairs,' she admonishes, tapping her head. 'They need
to get into a low arousal mode.' We all practise breathing
to a medley of 'London Bridge Is Falling Down', 'Rock-a-bye
Baby', 'Frère Jacques' and 'Twinkle Twinkle Little Star'. 'It's
like sex!' says Sigrid to the men. 'When a woman goes
"Oh! Oh! Oh! Oh! OH!" it's not because she's having an
orgasm, it's because she's sick of it, you've lost her rhythm
and she wants it to be over already, that's why she's faking
it.'

Nobody comments. None of our women come to our
defence. I'm beginning to feel that I'm on trial here.

'Cheer up, everybody!' she beseeches, noting our glum
faces. 'This is a happy event, not a scheduled hysterectomy!'
She decides that we will play-act a C-Section and gives
each of us a role in the operating theatre. Ten of us huddle
round the mother. I have been cast as the senior surgeon
and Joanna is the anaesthetist. 'Right, what would you
do?' Sigrid asks me as I stoop over the mother's abdomen,
imaginary scalpel in hand.

'Um, shave the pubic hair?' I ask doubtfully.

'Yes?'

'And then make the incision, a bikini incision laterally.'

Soon the repertory C-Section has got out of hand, however. 'Stand clear!' demands Joanna, holding up pretend
defibrillator paddles and preparing to shock the patient,
who is now playing dead.

'Flat lining!' warns a nurse authoritatively. For once Sigrid has lost control. She stands in the corner shaking her head at the gallows jollity.

'All right,' she claps her hands. 'Our next paper is how to avoid an episiotomy.' She pops in a video and on the screen, with only the briefest of warnings, a doctor is soon snipping at a woman's vagina. The men all groan and look away. 'Now make sure you wipe front to back,' the on-screen doctor tells his patient, and my day reaches a new low.

She presses the pause button. 'Kegels – they are most important to tone the vaginal muscles, right? And you guys, you can help. When you're having sex with your wives you can say, "OK, honey, give me five."' I try to imagine playing the role of physical trainer during sex, but I can't.

Finally our class gets round to the business of the newborn infant. Newborn babies are not always particularly attractive, warns Sigrid. Page 23 of our *Miracle of Birth* magazine lists some of the commonplace attributes of newborns. 'Cone head'; bone bruises on the head; doughnut shape on top of head; hickey on the head if born by vacuum; blue hands and feet; puffy face from pressure; whiteheads on nose; crossed eyes; 'stork bites' on forehead and nape; sucking blisters on lip; peeling skin; a general rash – flea-bite dermatitis; lanugo – downy hair everywhere even on forehead and shoulders, which is especially noticeable on dark-haired babies; a little milk leakage from the breasts of both baby boys and girls; surprisingly big balls on little boys because the testes are relaxed; oozing black meconium from the anus. And all of this is considered perfectly normal.

Sigrid is also passionate about breastfeeding. She is an apostle of the nipple. She shows us another video to help convert us all to the cult of the breast. 'Don't be depressed by the size of the breasts in this video,' she warns the mums-to-be, 'it was shot in Texas.' On the screen a new-born baby inches its way up its mother's stomach, unassisted, locates a nipple, opens its mouth as wide as it can, and with an heroic effort latches on. I look around at the rapt audience – all have open mouths pantomiming suckling.

'Remember', warns Sigrid as the film ends, 'that lactation is not a contraceptive. It depresses fertility somewhat, but six weeks after the birth you're ready to get pregnant again, and you could have Irish twins.'

She fetches the false breast and holds it aloft like some sacred chalice. Then she tweaks its nipple, screws up her face and utters a baby cry. She peels back the felt skin to reveal the milk sacs and muscle of the breast. And another icon of sexuality comes crashing down.

Tuesday, 12 January
Joanna

Today outside the Gourmet Garage I notice that a red dotted line in the shape of a little girl, just like a police scene-of-crime drawing, has appeared on the pavement close to the kerb at 97th Street and Broadway. Underneath it, also stencilled in red, is a message: 'Constance, aged two, killed by automobile 23 January 1996.' Peter takes in the scene and then says quietly, 'January 23rd? That's one day after our due date, isn't it?'

Wednesday, 13 January
Peter

I feel guilty that we haven't seen Andrew Solomon since his hospitalization. His phone has been on permanent answer service, so today I try to e-mail him and immediately receive an automatically generated reply: 'Andrew Solomon is currently abroad and will not be checking e-mail,' it reads. 'He will receive your communication after 3 February. If it is urgent that you reach him now, you may print out your message and fax it according to the following schedule.' There follows an impossibly tight itinerary. Los Angeles, Bangkok, Phnom Penh, Siem Reap, Delhi, Agra, Jaipur and finally, the Royal Tented Camp of the Maharwahl of Jaisalmer.

Thursday, 14 January
Joanna

I cannot believe I am here again. On Monday I called the hospital to confirm we'd completed our birthing course, only to be told that if we wanted the option of the Birthing Center, we would still have to complete another five-hour course. And so, as if caught in Groundhog Day, I find myself back in the stuffy room on the 11th floor of Roosevelt Hospital with a beaming Sigrid and her plastic model pelvis.

At 7.45 p.m., as we break for our dinner snack and I tuck into the huge chicken Caesar sandwich Peter has brought as compensation for my going alone, Sigrid scoots over and sits down beside me.

'I have been thinking about you since the weekend, and I have decided you're too analytical,' she says firmly.

'It's true I take a lot of notes,' I say, 'but that's because I'm writing a column.'

'No, no, it's not that,' she says, slipping her arm around my shoulders and giving me a little squeeze. I know she is trying to be kind, but two of the other couples are now looking on with interest and I feel myself shrinking from her touch.

'Joanna,' says Sigrid, fixing me with her wide, pale, Swedish eyes, 'I sense you need to get more visceral.' She hisses the word out again. 'Vissss-ceral.

'You must imagine the birth. Do you remember the birth visualization we did last Sunday?'

I nod but I am lying.

'It's still too much in your head,' she says, shaking her gold perm. 'That's what you need to do now, get into your body more.' She squeezes her knees together and puts one hand on mine. 'You must get into your vagina.'

'Oh, for God's sake, woman,' I want to shout, 'I'm British, I don't want to get into my vagina.'

Instead, I smile awkwardly and she hands me a photo-copy of her 'Birth Visualization Sheet', instructing me that I must tape myself reading it over a soundtrack of relaxing music or the sound of the sea. 'Then you must play it to yourself several times a day.'

As the couple next to me strain to see what's written on my sheet, I know I should feel pleased she has singled me out for special attention, but instead I feel cross that I am now hovering between teacher's pet and uptight Brit.

I slip it into my folder and read it discreetly on my knee. 'Breathe slowly and deeply, letting each breath take you into a deeper relaxed state,' the sheet instructs.

It tells me to imagine the baby ripening and growing until finally the birth day arrives. 'And see your baby . . . wet and warm . . . and your vagina . . . moist, soft, warm and elastic . . . massaging your baby, and you open and let your baby come . . .

'And your baby has reached the vaginal opening. You feel the skin burning, tingling, stretching and you give your body time to open . . . so you let the air out, lightly blowing, blow-ing as you feel the tissues round the baby's head . . .'

I am sure this works for many people, but I fear it will not work for me.

Thursday, 14 January
Peter

Today Joanna puts the latest issue of *Vanity Fair*, the one with Ewan McGregor and various *Star Wars* prequel robots on the cover, into the dishwasher. She slots it neatly in the plate rack, beside the dinner crockery. And when I come to empty the dishwasher I find it there, reduced to a papier-mâché glob that has spewed bits of itself all over the glasses and mugs and plates, where it has been congealed and hardened by the 'heat dry' function. When I tell Joanna what she's done, she seems unsurprised.

'Oh, I wondered where I'd left it,' she says.

Friday, 15 January
Joanna

I am beginning to suspect I may not be pregnant at all, merely fat. I hope the baby doesn't come today, I feel much too exhausted to go into labour. Despite a decent night's sleep and a long doze this afternoon, the thought of doing anything other than eat refrigerated triangles of white Toblerone fills me with panic.

Friday, 15 January
Peter

The dishwasher has now broken – unable, it seems, to digest its plump, advert-rich copy of *Vanity Fair*. When I go to open it, expecting to find rows of gleaming glasses, I am met instead by a wall of rank-smelling water which spews all over the kitchen floor.

Monday, 18 January
Joanna

At my last class Sigrid observed that a newborn baby should be allowed to spend up to an hour on the breast. The worksheet she handed out, which I am now reading for the first time, says newborns should be given between eight and twelve feeds a day. In theory, this means I could spend twelve hours a day feeding.

At Maternal Fitness they say you should start sit-ups to exercise your abdominal transverse muscles two hours after a vaginal birth, two days after a C-section. And kegels immediately – even if you are still numb. When will I have time to sleep?

'You could always express,' says Peter, when I voice these fears to him. 'Like Veronica.'

Veronica is a British friend of ours, a senior executive for a multinational pharmaceutical company, who was back to her jet-setting job a fortnight after giving birth. Adamant her child should be breastfed, however, she would express milk in her London office or on business trips abroad, and courier the milk home by motorbike or plane, sealed in a special Thermos.

Monday, 18 January
Peter

I am hugely impressed that the repairmen from Advance have turned up to fix our dishwasher on Martin Luther King Day, a public holiday. I feel vaguely guilty about it as they are both black, and I am anxious that we have kept them from celebrating the achievements of the civil rights campaigner.

'So, what happened with the machine, man?' enquires the senior repairman, like a doctor taking a case history.

'I dunno,' I lie. 'A few days ago it just stopped working.

Lugo, the handyman, looked at it and said the pump was broken.' I don't feel able to tell the truth about Joanna putting a glossy magazine in for a long-wash cycle and heat dry.

They get down, and begin to remove various panels from the dishwasher, and I leave them to work alone. Ten minutes later they call me back, the job done.

'It was all blocked up, man,' says the senior repairman, shucking on his dayglo puffa jacket. He indicates a pile of food remains; fish bones, hair, apple peel, bacon rind, pale worms of spaghetti, and a sizeable mound of grey gunk, looking remarkably like deconstructed magazine. He sifts gingerly among the gunk and retrieves a corner of intact page with a glossy photo of Ewan McGregor on it, and he snorts and rolls his eyes at the crazy things people put in their dishwashers.

I tip them ten bucks. 'And happy rest of Martin Luther King Day,' I call after them as they leave.

'Yeah. Right,' says the senior repairman and shakes his head.

Tuesday, 19 January
Joanna

I am beginning to wonder if there isn't something in Kelly's theory that taking prenatal vitamins is like force-feeding hormones to cattle. In today's paper, I read about a farmer who had to shoot his prize bull after it became too heavy for its own legs and kept toppling over.

At this afternoon's visit, the doctor remarks that the baby looks large. 'Mmnn, eight and a half pounds at least,' she says, cupping her hands round my exposed belly. 'At this stage it's difficult to know if you will be able to deliver it vaginally.

'Your pelvis doesn't look small, but you really can't tell until labour is under way. Sometimes everything's fine, sometimes big babies get stuck and you need a C-section.' It is the first time anyone has raised the real possibility of a C-section.

I have read that this is how the human race will eventually die out. That we in the First World are now incubating babies too large to be born through our pelvic cups. It's to do with our rapid progression to bipedal status. Apparently we were better designed to have babies when we swung around on all fours. I hate the idea of a C-section. I don't want to be tubed up and sliced open. I don't want to grab the first glimpse of my child through a bleary oxygen mask. I want to spend labour in a jacuzzi with the scent of lavender floating through the Birthing Center and allow the baby to crawl up my belly and latch on like they did in all those videos Sigrid showed us.

I can't bear the idea of a green linen screen being hung above my belly like an opaque tennis net, and the otherworldly feeling of a surgeon scooping my intestines aside and plunging through layers of muscle to pluck out our surprised child.

Unable to sleep for worrying about this, I eventually get up at 5 a.m., make a pot of camomile tea and call Jane in England. 'There are some advantages to Caesareans,' she says brightly. 'Vagina intacta, for one. At least you'll be able to have sex again.'

Tuesday, 19 January
Peter

After a long session with Doc Wasserman, I walk purposefully down Park Avenue to Tiffany's on a mission to buy a ring for Joanna, which I will present her with after the birth.

I have read somewhere that new mothers don't necessarily like to be defined exclusively in maternal terms and that they appreciate something which is for them alone. In the lofty main hall at Tiffany's I move among Burberried Argentinians, Brazilians, Italians and Spaniards, trying to attract a salesperson's attention. But though I am a serious buyer today, not just a diamond dilettante, I cannot get served.

I catch a glimpse of my reflection in a display case and I realize why I'm having difficulty. In my black jeans and my Nick Ashley jacket – which, despite its designer label and price, still manages to look like a Rail Track regulation issue donkey jacket – and my unkempt hair, I am not exactly the picture of a promising customer.

Then I notice a man who looks like an elegant undertaker, standing in a slightly raised booth so that he can survey the room, is paying me rather close attention. Maybe I can get him to serve me? It is only as I near his booth that I realize he is some sort of security supervisor and his scrutiny is the kind intended to make itself discreetly noticed, a visual warning shot across my potentially criminal bows. I take my hands from my pockets and he squints as though he fully expects them to emerge bearing a ski-mask and small calibre pistol.

Instead of being offended and walking out to protest their stereotyping, I become even more determined to buy something expensive. I shoulder aside a couple of indecisive Upper East Side ladies at the étoile ring counter and jab my finger at a gold band studded with diamonds, which, like all the merchandise here, is unencumbered by anything so prosaic as a price tag.

'How much is that one?' I demand brusquely, or so I intend. In fact my voice comes out slurred from the remains of Dr Wasserman's anaesthetic.

The pinch-faced man behind the counter stiffens. 'This one, sir?' he asks, deploying the 'sir' with an acid sibilance. He clearly thinks I am drunk or stoned or both.

'Yup.'

'That would be eleven hundred and fifty dollars,' he returns.

'Hmm,' I pretend to ponder.

'Plus tax, of course,' he adds, evidently hoping that this financial *coup de grâce* will send me scuttling back out into the cold, whence I have clearly come hoping for a few minutes' shelter. He looks past me to the two vacillating Upper East Side matrons, who are still peering intently at a blue baize tray on which nestle a pair of pendant earrings thickly encrusted with diamonds, glittering like quartz chips on a hot tar road.

'And is it an appropriate ring to buy for a woman who is having my child, but to whom I am not married? What is the exact etiquette in such a case?'

He looks sourly at me, choosing to ignore the irony, or perhaps not registering it at all. Or maybe he cannot decipher my dentally numbed slur. 'It goes on the ring finger, *sir*,' he says, 'like any other *ornamental* ring. Maybe you would prefer something like this.' He fishes out a rather vulgar ring with diamonds, small as spiders' eyes, set in a heart shape. 'This one is only five hundred and sixty dollars.'

On the subway home I find myself sitting opposite the '1-800-DIVORCE: When diamonds *aren't* for ever' ad, and I cheer up a little.

Wednesday, 20 January
Joanna

Today the phone rings and as I go to pick it up I have the oddest sensation that it might be the baby calling. Foolishly I mention this to Peter. 'Oh,' he says, not even looking up from the *Encyclopedia of Men's Health*. 'What did it say?'

Thursday, 21 January
Peter

Amazon.com has sent me a list of the top ten parenting books. These include *The Hip Mama Survival Guide*, which, claims the blurb, answers the vexing question, 'Is there breastfeeding after nipple piercing?' This is not a question which has overly taxed me in the past, but now I feel I must know the answer.

Friday, 22 January
Joanna

Today our revised due date comes and goes with neither bloody show nor mucus plug. Bored and restless, we visit Relax the Back and on Sigrid's advice, stock up on the essentials for a drug-free labour: a Gymnic bouncy ball with pump, and a massage stick with two spiked wooden balls fixed to one end which looks like something from a medieval torture chamber.

Relax the Back's manager leads me over to a bed, where he makes me lie down and parades a selection of bizarrely shaped cushions for me to try. They are specially designed for pregnancy and, in spite of my resistance to his sales patter, extremely comfortable. We end up ordering a hideous navy affair with arms and a neck rest, called a 'bed lounger', which he assures me is perfect for breastfeeding in bed.

'Look,' he says, slapping the sides, 'there are even sewn-in pockets for the TV remote control so you don't have to shout at your husband to fetch it.'

Friday, 22 January
Peter

Joanna lies writhing on our calico slip-covered sofa, trying to attract my attention. I ignore her and continue reading my book, and in due course she groans and gives painstaking birth to a white bolster, which she rocks maternally, breastfeeds briefly, burps and proffers to me, commanding it to, 'Say hello to daddy.'

At the moment it is not uncommon for her to perform several of these false births a day as she grows increasingly impatient with the wait.

Sunday, 24 January
Joanna

Peter has pumped up the Gymnic bouncy ball and I am now using it at my desk instead of the cheap, rustic 'Easy-folding Provence-Style' chair I bought from Pottery Barn last year.

Despite my initial scepticism, the ball is rather comfortable, even though I do feel absurd bouncing up and down at my desk. I am tempted to paint a face on the side of it and bounce off down Riverside Drive. I bet that would bring labour on.

Sunday, 24 January
Peter

Joanna is depressed. This morning BabyCenter.com, the website for the *expectanti*, has fired off an automatically generated message of congratulations, based on our due

date. 'The long wait is finally over!' it confidently pronounces. 'You've delivered your baby, brought him home,
and – now what?'

Well-meaning friends keep calling to see if we have given
birth and with each call Joanna gets more fretful. 'I feel
like this baby is never going to come out,' she moans.

Joanna deals with her mounting frustration in a New
York kind of way. She goes shopping. With every deadline-
defying day we accumulate more infantalia. Baby tschotkes
line the nursery, stuffed toys spilling off the shelves, piles
of receiving blankets, drawers stuffed full of 'onesies'.
Today's addition is a musical mobile of the solar system,
with the earth, the moon, Saturn and an arbitrary star
revolving slowly around a smiling yellow sun to the tune
of Brahms' Lullaby. I assemble it and wind up the melody
a couple of times to check it and already the tune is driving
me nuts. I find myself humming a slightly off-key, sinister
interpretation of it, like the soundtrack to some horror
movie.

Monday, 25 January
Joanna

Forget Hershey's Chocolate Milk and graham crackers. I
have now progressed to Entenmann's Pecan Danish Ring,
a wildly luxurious cake-size ring of flaky pastry studded
with brain-crinkled nuts and covered in white fondant
icing.

It is so obviously bad for me that I feel I must neutralize
it by eating a piece of fruit first. So I get up, eat a banana,
congratulate myself on a healthy start and then cut myself
a large slice of Danish Ring. I'm past caring about calories.
Today the nurse told me I had lost a pound since my last
visit. According to Miriam Stoppard, weight loss in the

final week can be a sign of impending labour. Let the revels commence.

Tuesday, 26 January
Peter

'Oh, how humiliating,' Joanna groans. She has received another e-mail, this time from a couple in our 'birthing class', Susan the lawyer and Neta, the Israeli computer programmer, proudly announcing the successful birth of their baby daughter. 'They were supposed to be three days *after* us,' she complains.

'It's not a race, you know,' I point out, but Joanna is in no place for placation. 'We should be enjoying this time,' I say. 'It'll be the last time we have alone together, the last time we have any peace.' But the truth is I am humming with impatience myself, eager to end this dragging transition, and get on with trying to make all those compromises that friends have gleefully warned us about.

My conversation with Joanna is giving me a headache as her eyeline keeps bobbing about. She is bouncing on her newly purchased Gymnic ball, a vast blue plastic inflated ball, reminiscent of those Space Hoppers of our youth, but without the stubby handles to hold on to. She has read somewhere that diligent Gymnic ball-bouncing can help to induce labour. 'A baby is not something you dislodge,' I object. 'And neither is it some foetal, dangerous sports junkie who comes flying down the birth canal like a bungee jumper, hanging on to the umbilical cord for dear life.'

Behind my bluster, however, there lurks a deep apprehension. Somehow, in the process of birthing classes, Joanna has fallen in thrall to Sigrid's proselytizing zeal for natural birth and I seem to have been manoeuvred into the role of labour coach. The whole thing strikes me as slightly scary, I feel as if we have stumbled into a cult. This is not what I wanted at all.

Wednesday, 27 January
Joanna

At 8 a.m., the phone goes. It's Meredith. 'I was just calling to ask if you're planning to breastfeed?' she asks bossily.

'Meredith, it's eight o'clock in the morning. Why are you calling so early and more to the point what are you doing up?' I mutter blearily, knowing she frequently doesn't surface until midday.

'Darling, don't ask,' she sighs dramatically. 'But listen, I've got to get you the number of this brilliant breast-milk bank.'

'A what?'

'Have you met my friend Teddy? You know he and his boyfriend adopted a bi-racial baby last year? Well, listen, they had bottles of frozen breast milk flown in once a week from California.'

'I think I'm going to feed it myself.'

'Jo-*anna*, be honest, how much do you know about breastfeeding, honey? What about engorgement? Cracked nipples? *Bleeding* nipples? This is a much better way. Just thaw and feed. The baby still gets all the anti-whatevers.'

'Antibodies.'

'Huh?'

'The baby still gets all the antibodies?'

'Sure. Whatever. Exactly. It's perfect.'

'Who does the milk come from?' I ask.

'Oh, I don't know. Mexican peasants probably, but don't worry, it's all screened for HIV. The main thing is you're not tied down, honey. You can still go out and party with me. Let me know if you want the number, OK?' And she hangs up abruptly.

Thursday, 28 January – 3.30 pm
Peter

Our entire day has been given over to medical probing. At Roosevelt a silent Chinese technician carries out a sonogram to check that the baby is still dunked in sufficient amniotic fluid. Apparently it is. Then on to an appointment with the obstetrician on Central Park West. I stand in the corner of the surgery, facing the wall, pretending to inspect a family-planning calendar while Joanna clambers up onto the examining chair. Each of the stirrups, I notice, has been thoughtfully sleeved in a striped oven glove.

'If there are still no signs of labour by early next week, we'll have to perform an intervention,' says the obstetrician. This, it seems to me, is the language of special forces, up there with surgical strikes. With phrases like operating theatres and theatres of operation, areas of infiltration and target cells, the vocabularies of medicine and war would appear to be converging.

3.30 p.m.
Joanna

'Great progress,' exclaims the doctor, peering up the paper skirt the nurse has draped over my lower body. 'You're three centimetres dilated!'

'Thank God,' I say, relieved that at last something's happening.

'Didn't you feel any contractions?' she asks. 'Your cervix is seventy per cent effaced.'

'Is that good?' asks Peter doubtfully, looking up from

the family-planning leaflet he has been studiously concentrating on throughout the internal.

'Sure it's good,' she says. 'Last week I was kinda worried because it all looked a bit tight. But something's moving. And, you know what, if we still need to do it, it will make induction easier.'

Sigrid's remedies of lavender oil and foot massage notwithstanding, I fear induction because I've heard it's a particularly painful way to start labour.

'So this is a good sign,' the doctor continues. 'But if nothing happens, how about next Wednesday for an induction?' She reaches for her diary as if we're planning supper and a movie. 'How does that sound? We could wait another coupla days until you're officially two weeks overdue, but the baby's putting on weight every day and it's already a big one . . .'

'Fine,' I nod, both apprehensive and reassured at finally having a finishing line by which this marathon will be over.

'We could bring you in at lunchtime, put you on an IV and get the Pitocin set up. By Thursday you should have a baby.'

4.00 p.m.
Peter

'Could you tell me something?' I ask the doctor as we leave. '*Is* there breastfeeding after nipple piercing?'

'I didn't notice that your nipples were pierced,' she says, reappraising Joanna.

'No, no. They're not,' Joanna says quickly. 'He's just curious.'

'Well, yes, there is breastfeeding after nipple piercing,' the doctor says, looking a little puzzled. 'Of course, you'd need to take out any, ah, mammarian jewellery.'

Joanna insists that we walk home, hoping that the exercise will help to bring on labour. So we inch along, with me towing her like a blimp behind me. So slow is our pace, in fact, that we are unable to get across Broadway within the span of one flashing green walk sign, and are marooned on the narrow traffic island. We stand there, railed at by the hobos' convocation that has gathered on the piss-stained bench, and buffeted by the slipstreams of delivery trucks and buses, until the next walk sign frees us.

4.30 p.m.
Joanna

'Good-oh,' says Peter, as we lumber slowly back from the surgery up Central Park West, its grand apartment buildings basking like ageing roués in the winter sunshine. 'Three centimetres, wow. Only seven to go.'

By the time we reach Oppenheimer's, the butcher's on 98th and Broadway, I am exhausted and have to sit down on their radiator.

A man comes in with a little girl sitting astride his shoulders. She is eating a Ben and Jerry's chocolate ice cream, which is dripping slowly on to his greying hair. 'Yup,' he says, surveying me, and reaching up to wipe off some of the chocolate with his fingers, which he then licks. 'You look like you're just about due.'

I roll my eyes and grimace. 'Don't worry, it's the best thing you'll ever do,' he beams, as his daughter absently wipes her own sticky fingers on the neck of his jacket.

We pick up lamb chops and stop next door to buy a bottle of South African red from the sour Chinese vintner at Hong Liquors.

6 p.m.
Peter

When we get home Joanna's Gymnic ball-bouncing is particularly frantic. She cannot bear the humiliation of having to be induced. To take her mind off things I offer to cook her lamb chops for dinner. But my manoeuvrings in the kitchen are even less successful than usual. I stoop to open the grill, ludicrously placed at floor level, below the oven, and as I pull at its handle to slide it out and inspect the chops, the entire front comes away in my hands and I fall back onto the greasy kitchen floor tiles, sitting heavily among a colony of black roach-bait pods.

8 p.m.
Joanna

Though I still cannot feel any contractions, I do feel odd. The smell of the lamb sizzling under the grill makes me nauseous. But Peter, normally a stranger to the oven, has gone to such trouble, laboriously spiking each chop with individual needles of rosemary, that I feel I must finish mine so as not to hurt his feelings and discourage him from these rare forays into the kitchen. I also knock back two large glasses of red wine very quickly, my first alcohol in months.

9.20 p.m.
Peter

Joanna comes into my study, pale faced. 'I think I may be having contractions.' This is not an especially noteworthy remark, however, as she says it most days.

10 p.m.
Joanna

The theme tune to *ER* has started and I know I am experiencing contractions. But they are not as I expected. They don't peak and tail off as my pregnancy manuals and Sigrid promised, but rather they peak and then sort of shift sideways into a dull, grinding backache. I spend another twenty minutes on the Gymnic bouncy ball before retreating into a hot shower. Neither remedy reduces the steadily expanding pain.

10.30 p.m.
Peter

Following Sigrid's instructions I am putting together a final selection of CDs for Joanna to give birth to. She is insisting on including Keith Jarrett's Köln Concert. But I am worried about Jarrett's unconventional keyboard antics, whereby he ventilates his piano playing with frequent and urgent porcine grunts of concentration. Might not these grunts be mistaken by the medical staff for Joanna's urgent grunts of pain?

11.45 p.m.
Joanna

We have worked through our entire repertoire of supposedly pain-relieving manoeuvres. Sigrid's 'doula houla', where I lean forward on the sofa and Peter grips my pelvis between his knees and squeezes as hard as he can, has no discernible effect. Neither does inhaling lavender oil, another of her suggestions. Nor does spritzing my face with orange water. The hot shower she espoused so vigorously makes me feel more nauseous, as does the hot-water bottle pushed against my back alternated with an ice pack, made by hurriedly stuffing ice cubes into a yellow rubber glove.

At some point, remembering my yoga, I struggle down on to all fours and launch myself into the Angry Cat, exhaling, arching my back, then inhaling and stretching out. When this fails I curl into a Child's Pose, arms forward, knees splayed, trying to 'breathe through the pain'.

Nothing helps.

The only thing which brings relief is to take off all my clothes and walk naked round and round and round the apartment, holding my belly and counting. Kitchen, study, bedroom, hall – kitchen, study, bedroom, hall. One, two, three, four, five, six, seven, eight . . . But my count bears little relation to the length or frequency of the contractions, which begin to fold into one long, swaying pain.

Forty-six, forty-seven, forty-eight, forty-nine . . . the pain remains. Fifty-one, fifty-two, fifty-three, fifty-four . . . It is still there, dark and awful, sweeping me up and making me vomit and tremble violently.

'I'm in labour, I know I'm in labour,' I groan repeatedly to Peter, who looks stricken.

We ring the doctor's answering service and leave a message.

11.50 p.m.
Peter

I know it's too late to pull out of my somewhat accidental role as labour coach, but I do wonder if the presence of men at the birth is really such a good idea. I mean there seems to be an almost universal cultural taboo against it, broken only in the last generation by Western man.

11.55 p.m.
Joanna

The doctor-on-call phones me back and I describe my symptoms.

'Try to relax, you want to spend as much of your labour at home as possible,' she says, clearly thinking I am premature in demanding pain relief. Embarrassed that I've phoned too soon, I agree to keep doing breathing exercises and hang up, unsure of what to do next.

'She says I shouldn't go to the hospital yet,' I moan.

'Why don't you have another hot shower?' asks Peter. 'What about using that lavender shower gel Sigrid suggested?'

Friday, 29 January – 12.40 a.m.
Peter

Joanna is gasping with the pain of it, pacing about and trembling uncontrollably. I try to time the contractions, but I appear to have forgotten even the most basic tenets of my Intensive Lamaze Birthing Course. Do you time from the beginning of one contraction to the end of the next? Or from the end of one to the end of the following one?

2 a.m.
Joanna

We call the doctor's answering service again.

'You're going to the Birthing Center, right?' asks the doctor groggily, when she calls back.

'God no, I need an epidural,' I gasp. The thought of natural childbirth now seems laughable.

'Why don't you set off to the hospital? They'll call me when you get there.'

I have been dreading this moment. For the last four hours I've been naked and must now, dizzy with the fug of pain, get dressed, but I can't bear the idea of anything next to my skin. Only the lure of pain relief makes me haul on leggings and a hideous, oversized T-shirt. In the hall mirror on the way out, I catch my face. It's swollen from vomiting and grey with uncertainty and fear.

Hobbling across the lobby, I realize I've never seen this night doorman before. He's young and courteous and I promptly feel guilty that we failed to leave him a Christmas tip.

2 a.m.
Peter

Joanna can bear the pain no longer and I buzz down to the doorman and ask him to hail a cab. We stand silently in the descending lift surrounded by sufficient baggage for a long-haul holiday, and I realize that we will, if all goes well, be returning with a third person. The overnight doorman is girded against the freezing damp in a uniform that would earn the envy of a Ruritanian general on a Gilbert and Sullivan stage.

'The very best of luck, sir,' he wishes. He pumps me cordially by the hand and holds open the cab door. As I duck into the cab I see that the illuminated neon wedge on its roof features a pair of cuffed wrists. '1-800-Innocent', its caption touts, 'when you're only allowed to make one call.' The taxi driver tips up the peak of his baseball cap and checks out the scene in his rearview mirror. Joanna emits a long quavering groan, and his eyes widen in alarm. 'You havin' a *baby*?' he asks incredulously, as though no one in Manhattan could be so primitive as to procreate.

'I bloody well hope so,' pants Joanna and the driver roars off, savouring the moment of drama on an otherwise sleepy weekday night. Soon we are hurtling down the deserted concrete canyon of West End Avenue, dismissing the string of late amber lights and early reds against us like so much surplus Christmas decoration.

2.10 a.m.
Joanna

At 84th Street we swing onto Broadway and, convinced I'm going to vomit again, I wind down the window. The cold air is briefly refreshing and I concentrate on the store fronts which punctuate the Upper West Side. Origins, Barnes and Noble, Banana Republic. The famous trio of delis, Zabar's, Citarella and Fairway rush by. At 70th Street, opposite Relax the Back, where we bought the Gymnic bouncing ball, another contraction takes hold and I press my lower spine against the hot-water bottle I have brought with me under my coat. The heat makes it worse. I want to do nothing but curl up and close down.

2.20 a.m.
Peter

Staggering under the weight of two kit bags and a small turquoise backpack stuffed hopefully with tiny outfits, we arrive at Roosevelt Hospital to have a baby. We take the elevator to the twelfth floor, where we are ushered into an 'observation' cubicle with a gurney bed, a sink, a bin and a chair. A nurse straps monitors to Joanna which measure her contractions and the foetal heartbeat, and then leaves us alone. The contractions are coming fast and hard and Joanna is complaining of acute back pain.

'I'm going to throw up again,' she gasps. I help her to

the sink, patting her heaving shoulders as she hugs the cold porcelain and retches violently.

'Why you throw up in the sink?' demands a nurse from the doorway.

'Where else were we supposed to do it?' I protest.

'The bin,' she scowls.

'Well, we thought that at least we could rinse out the sink,' I counter crossly.

'You should have used the bin,' she insists.

'Listen,' I say, feeling a fury bubbling up inside me, 'we have come here to have a baby, not to argue about where to vomit.'

I regret my little outburst immediately, when the nurse's shoes squeal on the lino as she wheels round and stalks out, leaving Joanna to her haze of unmoderated pain.

2:25 a.m.
Joanna

'I need an epidural,' I groan to the sulky nurse, sensing another contraction and start on a loud hissing breath which Mary Barnes, our yoga teacher, had assured me would help. 'SSSSSSSSSSSSSSSSS.'

The monitor to which I am hooked up records the contractions and spews forth a sheet of paper revealing a series of perfect U shapes. I give another hissing breath, 'SSSSSSSSSSSSSSS', and a different nurse bustles in, examines the data and promptly hurries out. 'Don't worry, we're not sending you home,' she says over her shoulder, though this thought had never occurred to me. 'I'm going to get the resident to examine you now.'

3.05 a.m.
Peter

All thoughts of using the Birthing Center and having a 'natural', drug-free labour have already been jettisoned. The stroppy nurse explains that the epidural can't be started until our own obstetrician arrives, but that in the meantime she will set up an IV drip, which is necessary in advance of the epidural, to boost the blood pressure.

Joanna looks away while she stretches a rubber tourniquet around her arm and inserts the IV needle into a bulging vein. The needle pops straight out again. The nurse tries again. And again. Each time the needle slips out with a shocking crimson blotch on the white hospital linen. I stare, appalled at each new blood patch, and find a new shape in them, like some macabre Rorschach test. They resemble continents: Africa, England, America – the tripod of our child's cultural heritage. Maybe this is a good sign, I rationalize, even in the nurse's incompetence.

'Your veins – no good,' the nurse complains.

I compose an angry riposte about her lack of skill, her transformation of Joanna's arm into a junkie's runway, but I swallow it all unspoken for fear of further punishment. She wanders off, returning shortly with a gloomy, green-smocked Russian doctor whom I overhear scolding her for using the wrong needles. He manages first time.

3.30 a.m.
Joanna

We are finally assigned a delivery room, the last one on the corridor. It has a pink floral frieze and a matching floral pelmet, whose pleats I start counting to distract me from the pain. Only now do we follow one of Sigrid's instructions and close the door, pull the curtain across the room and unpack the CD player.

'What music would you like?' asks Peter anxiously.

'SSSSSSSSSSSSS.'

I don't really care what music we have, but he is trying so hard to get it right that I pick the first one which comes into my head, *Adiemus*.

'Ah I know this track,' says yet another nurse, pulling back the curtain and fixing me up with an automatic blood-pressure cuff. 'Dammit, what is this? I know I recognize it.' She starts humming along.

'It's called *Adiemus*, *Songs of Sanctuary*, by a British guy called Karl Jenkins,' I wince, preparing for the onset of another contraction.

'I knew I recognized it,' she cries, ignoring me. 'It's the music from the Delta Airways commercial.'

Great. I'm going to give birth to an advertising jingle.

4.45 a.m.
Peter

Narcis, the splendidly named relief nurse, has come and gone, and Deborah has now taken over. She is a calming, middle-aged black woman, who, she tells me, came up to New York from the Carolinas as a child. But somehow my platitudinous small talk about how the South compares with New York has taken a potentially tricky turn into the thorny issue of American race relations.

'At least down in the South, they don't like us, they tell us to our face,' she says. 'Up here they pretend to like us, but they stab us in the back.'

'Uh huh,' I say, noncommittally. Though I realize that her 'they' probably includes me, I decline to mount a defence of the guilty white liberal over the redneck racist. This morning I have no views on anything. This morning I am in her hands. She can entertain whatever opinions she likes without fear of any contradiction from me.

5 a.m.
Joanna

My own doctor arrives and finally approves the epidural, administered by a calm Asian anaesthetist, who speaks in a low whisper and has tiny, gentle hands. In the birthing class we were warned that the epidural was complicated, didn't always work and might even puncture the dura, leaving you with a six-week migraine. Compared to what I'm feeling now, a six-week migraine would be a relief. Again, I find myself laughing at the idea of getting through this by snorting lavender oil.

'You should be fine now,' the anaesthetist smiles sympathetically as liquid Heaven courses through my legs and the back pain melts away, leaving me warm and euphoric with relief.

'Oh thank you, thank you so much,' I hear myself saying, overwhelmed with gratitude. And suddenly Sigrid's face with her large pale eyes flashes before me and I remember the brisk scorn she reserved for 'American women demanding epidurals in the parking lot'.

9 a.m.
Peter

Joanna is now rigged up to an intricate web of technological tendrils – wires to the monitors, and tubes to a drip which dispenses Pitocin – a drug to induce labour – and saline, to keep up her blood pressure. One by one we are conceding to all the things we were urged to resist in our

284

birthing class, all the gadgetry and potions of a 'medicated' birth.

The doctor decides to go in with an instrument that looks like a flattened crochet hook, 'to break the waters', she explains. Luckily Joanna cannot see it.

11.30 a.m.
Joanna

'In half an hour you can try pushing if you like,' says the doctor casually, before disappearing to change into scrubs. When the nurse returns I quiz her frantically about how long it is likely to take.

'Normally between one to two hours,' she says. 'Though I have seen some people push for three. And', she starts laughing, 'we had one woman push for five. Boy, was she determined to get that baby out!'

This is the part which scares me most. I've a secret fear I may not be able to do it and I'm terrified I'll fail this most basic test of womanhood.

'Think of the letter C,' the doctor advises, returning in a pea-green gown with worn yellow sleeves. 'You need to think of pushing as if you're a letter C, think of it going under the pubic bone.'

I have no idea what she is talking about. But I nod anyway.

'In two hours' time we'll have a baby,' I mumble to Peter, really to convince myself, because even now it seems so abstract. He smiles and squeezes my hand, busily chewing a banana and honey Balance Bar which I packed for him in advance.

Friday, 1.30 p.m.
Peter

Joanna has been pushing for an hour and a half, while I count out each push, feeding her crushed ice between times, murmuring soothing reassurances. But I seem to get things just slightly wrong. I grip her hand too hard. My lower back massage eludes the hot spot. I am devoid of all power to appease. I am a man in the delivery room.

I revert to the hunter-gatherer default and offer to go foraging for sustenance, but no one hears me.

'You're getting *so* close,' the doctor encourages Joanna. 'The baby's crowning. Can you see its head?' she asks me. Sure enough, there is the top of our baby's head, covered in a fine fuzz of oily blond hair.

'You wanna see?' Deborah offers Joanna, and brings up a mirror in front of Joanna's crotch.

Joanna lifts herself up onto her elbows. 'No!' she wails. 'I don't want to see . . .'

2 p.m.
Joanna

I have been pushing for two hours. Deborah's offer of a mirror only reflects my lack of progress. It suddenly seems absolutely clear that there's no way I will be able to squeeze out an 8.8 lb baby.

'How much longer?' I keep pleading and each time the doctor refuses to answer. 'If I say fifteen minutes and then it's longer, you'll feel discouraged,' she says, not unreasonably.

'Yes, you've got time,' she adds, as Peter enquires if he should go on a coffee run. This is definitely discouraging, it means we are not even close. I close my eyes and wonder how much longer I can keep on doing this. Maybe Sigrid was right after all and I am not sufficiently visceral for a vaginal birth. Fifteen minutes later Peter returns bearing a tray of paper cups with the green and white Starbucks logo.

'Contraction,' I croak and the three of them swoop down on me once again, the doctor and nurse holding a leg apiece and Peter grabbing my hand. Their faces loom towards me, distorted like portraits in a hubcap.

'Let's have a *baby*, Joanna,' cries the doctor.

'Come on, honey, let's get that baby *out*!' hollers the nurse.

'One, two, three, four, five,' chants Peter.

Scarcely hearing them, I take a huge breath and for the millionth time bear down with all my might. Above me their lips move soundlessly, mouthing words of encouragement and nearly suffocating me with coffee breath.

2.30 p.m.
Peter

'I think it's time for an internal baby heart monitor,' says the doctor. And from her quiver of medieval torture tools she produces an instrument shaped like a long knitting needle and declares that she intends to screw its small metal tip into the baby's head. We meekly agree. Her first attempt fails, however, and puzzled, she withdraws the applicator tube. 'They've redesigned it,' she complains, spreading out the instructions on the foot of the bed.

'Pull tab *a* and twist *b* and remove,' reads Deborah, the efficient labour nurse.

'I think the tab goes back in after you've turned, like this,' I offer, as we huddle around the applicator, as though trying to assemble Ikea furniture. Joanna groans with the

onset of another contraction, and I remember that we are
screwing a cranial spike into a baby – *our* baby.

2.45 p.m.
Joanna

As I lie here, feeling utterly drained, I remember a bizarre
birthing story on ivillage.com, a women's health website.
It came from a woman who was so exhausted that when
the baby's head eventually crowned she tried to push it
back in. Now her reaction doesn't seem so strange at all.

3.15 p.m.
Peter

Joanna's strength is beginning to wane. Between contractions she breathes now through an oxygen mask.

I lift my eyes for a moment to look out of the window.
Outside it is a busy New York Friday afternoon. Below, a
dotted line of yellow cabs, like slow-moving termites, are
jostling for position. Over on the Hudson I can see the great
grey hulk of the USS *Intrepid*, the aircraft carrier berthed
there. The panorama unfolds across the river to the New
Jersey shore, and south through a thicket of midtown high
rises to the twin towers of the World Trade Center. Across
Tenth Avenue, students with plastic messenger bags full of
case law are lounging on the steps of the John Jay College
of Criminal Justice. Helicopters throb across the view at
window height on their way to the Chelsea heliport – this
is the world into which we are trying to entice our baby to
make its reluctant debut.

When I turn back to our claustrophobic capsule, the
atmosphere has changed. I follow the doctor's anxious
eyes to the blinking monitors and the graphs they spew.
The baby's heart rate is beginning to falter between

contractions. With a magician's flourish, the doctor whips the green cloth off the trolley at her side to reveal an array of suctioning equipment. Deborah pushes a red button on the wall and suddenly the room is full of people in smocks and shower caps. An anaesthetist, theatre nurses.

The doctor has the vacuum cap leeched onto the sandy dome of the baby's head and on the next contraction she pulls, really heaves, like an old-fashioned dentist hauling at a deeply rooted molar. But unbelievably the head remains lodged. Everyone's eyes swivel back up to the monitors, where the vital signs blink wildly like Wall Street stock prices on a volatile trading day.

3.28 p.m.
Joanna

The room's alive with electronic beeping. Fast beeps, slow beeps, high beeps, low beeps and a new, urgent beeping, which has just started. People are crowding in, but I can't see them properly because Peter keeps trying to hold an oxygen mask over my face.

'Keep taking deep breaths, Jo, it's for the baby,' says Peter.

I hear the word 'episiotomy' and somewhere inside of me, away from the mayhem, I snort at the earnest advice I was given to 'massage the perineum with wheatgerm oil so it will stretch naturally, making an artificial cut unnecessary'.

Every pregnancy manual I have read suggests first-time mothers should tell their doctors they would prefer 'to tear naturally'.

But I have never been so happy to see a pair of scissors in my life.

3.30 p.m.
Peter

'Episiotomy' announces the doctor. It is a bald statement of fact, not a subject for discussion. From her crowded tray she snatches up a pair of scissors. The chromed blades scintillate in the beam of the lowered spotlight and I hastily look away. But above the beeping of the monitors and the roar of the air-conditioning, the shriek of sirens and the growl of buses down on the street, I hear two loud snips. I look back to see the doctor tossing the scissors onto the tray, and at the next contraction she takes up her grip on the handle of the vacuum, assuming a tug-of-war stance with her shoulders. I am silently appalled by the violence that's being directed towards this unborn baby; terrified that its little neck will simply snap with the force of it all.

3.32 p.m.
Joanna

'We're nearly there,' the doctor is shouting. 'Come on, guys, let's have a *baby* this afternoon!'

'Come on, big breath, honey, PUSH,' cries the nurse.

'One, two, three, four, five, six, seven, eight, nine, ten,' chants Peter, still holding the oxygen mask over my nose and mouth. Their faces loom above me again, distorted through the thick plastic of the mask. For the first time I notice they are looking tense and anxious.

'She's tired,' says the doctor.

'After three and a half hours? I don't blame her,' says the nurse. 'That's enough for anyone.'

I hear two distinct snips, but I don't feel the scissors at all and then, with the next contraction, I do feel something, a wild, burning sensation and I hold my breath and heave whatever strength I have left against the wall of this contraction.

'It's coming!' someone shouts.

'Is it here yet?' I ask, struggling to lift my head to see.

3.33 p.m.
Peter

I am about to plead for a C-section myself, when suddenly the doctor staggers back and the baby shoots out, and out – a head, arms, torso, legs – like a long bloody link of sausages, and immediately the room is filled with the instantly recognizable wail of the newborn.

'It's a boy,' says the doctor and lifts the baby, still tethered by his umbilical cord like a tiny space walker.

3.34 p.m.
Joanna

Suddenly there's a weight on my belly, warm and wet and delicious and a flash of tiny penis and chubby arms covered in watery blood and muddy green meconium.

'It's all right, it's all right, baby,' I say over and over again as I stroke his tiny arm and a long astonished cry blasts from his tiny, hunched chest.

3.35 p.m.
Peter

'Here,' says the doctor, handing me a pair of scissors. 'Cut the cord.' In a daze of delayed fatigue I take aim at the grape-blue plait between the clips and cut. The cord is surprisingly gristly and I have to take a second stroke to crunch through it.

'You gotta name for the little fella?' asks Deborah.

I look at the baby and at Joanna. 'Thomas,' I say and

Joanna nods. 'He looks like a Thomas,' she says, and Deborah carries him to a little glass tray next to the bed, to run through their tests. Another nurse reaches for my hand and fixes a tag to my wrist. It reads 'Joanna Coles No. 984787'. In the maternity ward I am a function of the mother – nothing more.

3.40 p.m.
Joanna

It is only when I see the look of profound relief on the doctor's weary face, that I realize the danger we have been in. The C-section team melts away, unneeded, thank God. Thomas looks intently at me, as though scanning me into his database, and then Deborah lifts him off me and takes him away to be cleaned up, with Peter riding shotgun, to make sure he is not inadvertently swapped.

For the first time, I hear the music from the boom box perched on the window ledge, the wonderful slow movement of Michael Torke's Saxophone Concerto, and I see the Manhattan midtown skyline. My cloud of exhaustion lifts – and I feel strangely calm and resolved. It is over and yet it is just beginning. I have a son. I am a mother. Thomas's mother. How very odd.

4.30 p.m.
Peter

The paediatric nurse pokes a tiny rubber tube down Thomas's nostrils and his mouth and he copes with this indignity with remarkably good humour. She hoists him aloft, and he flings his little wrinkled arms out in alarm.

'That's the Moro reflex,' the nurse explains, briskly examining his genitals and inserting a thermometer up his rectum. Thomas tolerates all this without major complaint.

'Go with him to the nursery,' Joanna insists, unimpressed with the security bracelets that have been fixed to the three of us. She has been riveted by a story, currently all over the papers, of two babies who were mixed up at birth. I trot along behind Thomas's trolley and when I reach the door, I look back at the room. And I see the scene as if for the first time. It looks like an abattoir. The floor around the bed-end is slick with a mixture of blood and sticky black meconium from the baby's first bowel movement, caused by fright during his struggle to escape from his incarceration in the birth canal.

At the nursery I must wash my hands and don a frayed yellow cotton gown. Only then I am allowed entry. There are two other newborn babies there, lying in their little transparent trays under heaters, like meals in a cafeteria. There is no chance of them being mistaken for Thomas. The other babies are half his size, nut brown with shocks of black hair. Thomas has straightened himself out after nine months of being curled up in the womb. The soles of his feet are black from having his footprints taken. A temperature monitor is stuck to his belly by a gold tinfoil heart. His stub of umbilical cord is dyed with a mulberry disinfectant and secured by a yellow clip. Now he lies there, breathing with a fast irregular shallow pant like a dreaming puppy. He has a crescent dimple where his chin should be, and a cone head from the suction, complete with a rosy skullcap where the cup was vacuumed on. He basks in the warm light like a pensioner on a Florida beach. I examine him closely. Though he has Joanna's colouring, he doesn't look like either of us. He looks like Sir John Gielgud, Winston Churchill, the Buddha.

A nurse approaches with a kidney dish of warm water. She wets a flannel and washes his face, and this works him up into a tiny, livid rage. She rakes a plastic comb through his sparse blond locks and then leaves us alone. Thomas regains his composure and drifts back into sleep. He has one sole cocked up on his other bandy calf, like an old farmer leaning on a rake. There he rests in a nest of warm tufted white terry cloth, looking exhausted from the ordeal of his birth. And there I remain, dizzy with fatigue, clinging to the side of his Perspex bassinet in my frayed gown, wondering who he is going to be. And then, just briefly, the melancholy of our mortality sweeps over me as I remember the words from the Book of Job, carved into the Monument to the Amiable Child up on Claremont Hill:

'Man that is born of a woman is of few days, and full of trouble. He cometh forth like a flower, and is cut down: he fleeth also as a shadow, and continueth not.'